TOMORROW, THE WORLD

TOMORROW, THE WORLD

THE BIRTH OF U.S. GLOBAL SUPREMACY

STEPHEN WERTHEIM

THE BELKNAP PRESS OF
HARVARD UNIVERSITY PRESS
CAMBRIDGE, MASSACHUSETTS
LONDON, ENGLAND | 2020

First printing

Library of Congress Cataloging-in-Publication Data

Names: Wertheim, Stephen, author.
Title: Tomorrow, the world : the birth of U.S. global supremacy /
    Stephen Wertheim.
Description: Cambridge, Massachusetts : The Belknap Press of Harvard
    University Press, 2020. | Includes bibliographical references and index. |
    Identifiers: LCCN 2020011114 | ISBN 9780674248663 (cloth)
Subjects: LCSH: Internationalism. | United States—Foreign
    relations—1933–1945. | United States—Foreign relations. |
    United States—Military relations.
Classification: LCC E744 .W5325 2020 | DDC 327.73—dc23
LC record available at https://lccn.loc.gov/2020011114

To Kristen

CONTENTS

TOMORROW, THE WORLD

INTRODUCTION
THE DECISION FOR DOMINANCE

FOR MOST OF THEIR HISTORY, Americans have claimed their nation was exceptional because it did *not* covet armed supremacy over the rest of the world. Accusing European rulers of seeking domination, Americans of all sorts—politicians, diplomats, intellectuals, and activists—generally countered that peaceful interaction would transcend the system of power politics emanating from the Old World. The circulation of goods, ideas, and people would give expression to the harmony latent among civilized nations, preventing intense disputes from arising. The mechanisms of international law, arbitration, and organization would peaceably resolve what disputes did arise. Unless and until these processes succeeded in redeeming Europe, the United States should avoid political-military entanglement there and focus instead on perfecting its own experiment in liberty and offering it as an example to the world.

In time, Americans came to identify this set of ideas with the concept of internationalism, which connoted peace, unity, and intercourse among peoples. By no means, however, did internationalist rhetoric produce pacific conduct. Internationalism helped to rationalize almost constant expansion within the imagined domain of the New World, where U.S. hegemony was supposed keep out rapacious Europeans and keep down uncivilized natives. By the early twentieth century, the United States conquered territory across North America, exercised police power throughout the Western Hemisphere, and

1

seized colonies in the Caribbean and the Pacific. Yet America's commitment to internationalism also circumscribed the expansion it licensed. To build a New World free of power politics seemed to preclude playing, let alone dominating, power politics in the Old World. Only a rupture, a qualitative break, would change this state of affairs. Until then, global supremacy would sound like the kind of great-power imperialism that Americans always condemned in others.

Several moments might seem to have produced the rupture, but they fell short. One of them came in 1898, when the United States seized the Philippines and Puerto Rico in a war with Spain and held them as colonies, dramatically breaking its pattern of conquering contiguous territories that it planned to incorporate into the union as equal states. The United States also announced itself as a great power spreading civilization alongside its European counterparts. Yet American leaders in the following decades remained absent from Europe's alliance system. Continuing to profess a posture of nonentanglement in political and military affairs, they promoted international law as an alternative to rivalry and conflict.

Nor did the rupture occur in World War I. The United States joined the fighting in 1917, but in order to defend its legal rights as a neutral state rather than reconfigure the European balance of power. Although many Americans wanted their country to enter a new world organization to keep the peace after the armistice, they expected that armed force would rarely if ever have to be used once nations joined into a collective body. A world organization would mobilize public opinion more than armed force, preventing war from breaking out rather than waging war routinely against wrongdoers. In any case, the United States steered clear. With precious little dissent, it continued to abjure commitments to use force on the landmass of Europe and Asia and did not station its military there.

By the middle of the 1940s, however, America's role in the world had fundamentally changed. "We must relentlessly preserve our superiority on land and sea and in the air," President Harry S. Truman declared in 1945.[1] Officials entered his administration determined to maintain a "preponderance of power" under the control of the United States. That objective would lead them to construe the Soviet Union as a threat and wage the Cold War in response.[2] Nor did the desire for dominance go away after the Soviet Union fell in 1991. Instead of declaring victory and bringing its troops home, the United States persisted in its pursuit of dominance and in fact resolved to seek greater supremacy than ever before.

How did the United States acquire the will to lead the world? We still do not know why, or even when, American officials and intellectuals first decided the United States ought to attain armed primacy—to become the supreme political and military power holding itself responsible for enforcing world order. Worse, analysts have not squarely posed the question. Perhaps some think that U.S. dominance is justified and thus unworthy of scrutiny that might unsettle the consensus favoring it. Others may simply fail to imagine the United States seeking any role except chief arbiter of global affairs. Either way, politicians and experts have for decades heeded the call of publishing mogul Henry Luce in the 1941 essay that hailed the arrival of the "American Century." As Luce wrote then, "We can make a truly *American* internationalism something as natural to us in our time as the airplane or the radio."[3]

Luce's hope has been achieved. Americans ever since, from experts to ordinary citizens, have considered world dominance to be their nation's natural role. And they have identified dominance with the pursuit of international engagement and cooperation, even when it has produced violence and enmity. Even presidents not known for hawkishness or idealism have affirmed the point. As he negotiated arms control agreements with the Soviet Union, for example, President Gerald Ford paid tribute to "the leadership role that has been thrust upon us by fate."[4] "Circumstances, destiny, fate, or whatever you call it," he said, "the fact is the United States of America is today the world's best and perhaps its only hope of peace with freedom."[5]

This book calls U.S. global leadership what it was: a choice. Rather than deny that American leaders made a conscious decision to seek power, it locates and explains that decision in history. Instead of asking *what took so long* to summon the willingness to lead, it poses the properly historical question of why the United States opted to install itself as the world's armed superpower at all.

The decision happened in the early years of World War II. Eighteen months before Japan's sneak attack on Pearl Harbor sent the United States into the war, it was another staggering event—the Nazi invasion and conquest of France in May and June of 1940—that caused U.S. officials and intellectuals to rethink the nature of international politics and America's place in it. As totalitarian powers led by Adolf Hitler nearly achieved mastery of Europe and tore through East Asia, American elites discarded their aspiration to one day transcend power politics. Their mission would henceforth be the opposite. Now and forever, the United States had to impose order by force or else suffer in another power's world. Even before Pearl Harbor, then, U.S. officials and intellectuals planned not only to enter the war but also to achieve global dominance long afterward. This book attempts to explain how and why.

AMERICA'S RISE TO GLOBAL POWER IS anything but a new topic. Scores of books examine each major episode of the story, especially that of World War II, the event that refounded the United States and continues to enjoy pride of place in the nation's political consciousness, seven decades into what is still called the postwar period. But the story has been consistently narrated in terms that obscure and even deny the decision for armed primacy. From the schoolhouse to the highest levels of state, Americans have imbibed a version of the same tale: the United States, once in thrall to "isolationism," cast off its antipathy to global engagement and embraced "internationalism."[6] The premise is that isolationists and internationalists squared off in a prolonged struggle, with the former winning out after one world war and the latter finally prevailing after a second.[7]

This story reads events backward. It implies that certain prominent Americans, the internationalists, favored U.S. global supremacy all along, needing only to sweep the rest out of the way. They did not. In the main, self-identified internationalists before World War II sought to make peaceful exchange supplant the reign of force in global affairs. Standing for reason and rules against force and whim, they worked to obviate the need for military supremacy by the United States or any other power. Only during the war did internationalism come to be associated with military supremacy, whose architects devised the new, pejorative term *isolationism* and redefined *internationalism* against it. For the same reason, it makes no sense to characterize a group of Americans as advocates of isolationism.[8] Essentially no one thought of him- or herself as such.[9] Nor did any group of Americans, prior to the run-up to World War II, regularly use the "i" word to describe or tar others. Isolationism—the claim that the United States ever followed it, or that influential Americans ever favored it—is a myth.[10]

Like all myths, it is produced, and reproduced, to serve a purpose. If an isolationist United States caused two world wars to break out, then the opposite posture, the deployment of U.S. power across the globe, seems necessary. More than that, armed dominance begins to look profoundly moral if it is regarded as the defining feature of internationalism. Military restraint, by contrast, becomes the antithesis of fellow-feeling and cooperation. It was precisely for this reason—in order to make global supremacy necessary and legitimate—that American political and intellectual elites determined that internationalism required armed dominance and anything else meant isolationism. Political leaders like President Franklin D. Roosevelt rallied the country in these terms; commentators like Walter Lippmann framed countless columns around them; historians like Thomas A. Bailey projected them deep into the American past. All this transpired within five years, from 1940 to 1945.

U.S. foreign policy has never been the same. America's post-1945 consensus rested on the belief that isolationism, having lost the peace after one war and brought on another, was the worst of sins. Armed leadership would be America's redemption and anchor the world's order. Some of those who originally designed U.S. supremacy had a direct hand in propagating the anti-isolationist narrative. For example, William Langer, a postwar planner in the Council on Foreign Relations (CFR), went on to coauthor influential, CFR-funded accounts of the vanquishing of isolationism in the years leading up to the attack on Pearl Harbor.[11] On the whole, though, the specter of isolationism spread not from any scheming cabal but rather from many political elites acting in good faith to come to terms with novel circumstances and to accommodate themselves, and the country, to the widespread use of force that they now believed to be warranted. To this end, *isolationism* performed a function that no other concept could. It made any limitation on force seem to imply total disengagement from the world. Peaceful interaction therefore could take place only if the United States were willing to use force on a global scale. Against isolationism, the United States could promise to dominate power politics and transcend it at the same time.

For too long, the stewards of global supremacy have been permitted to define the horizons of understanding U.S. foreign policy. Unlike other accounts, this book does not adopt the concepts of the victors as if they were neutral descriptors. Instead, it explains those concepts, documenting how they were generated as events transpired, wielded in political battle, and suffused in national consciousness.[12] The birth of primacy becomes visible by reverse engineering the vocabulary developed to mask it. We can thereby comprehend how primacy became "as natural to us in our time as the airplane or the radio," or now the Internet and the smartphone.

Americans have denied the decision for dominance in a second way as well. In place of a reluctant and belated superpower, some critics find just the opposite: a superpower in the making all along. Did not the United States, propelled to seek profits, compelled by a sense of destiny, steadily enlarge its power until realizing its supremacy across the globe? Such is the stock-in-trade of intellectuals who object to U.S. foreign policy.[13] While rejecting the canard that America was ever isolationist, however, they replace it with a narrative of untrammeled expansion that equally obscures how U.S. elites came to choose armed primacy after long declining to do so.[14] If American policy were driven by the dynamics of capitalism, or the ideology of exceptionalism, then the ideas of policymakers would scarcely matter or scarcely change. Even the United States of the 1920s and 1930s could be depicted as "feeling its way cautiously toward global dominance," in the words of one historian— never mind that Americans in those years roundly repudiated that goal.[15] The implication, perhaps an unwitting one, is that American supremacy is pervasive and inexorable and nothing within the United States militates against it.[16]

In fact, for most of its existence the United States pursued capitalist growth and fancied itself exceptional while shunning political and military entanglements in Europe and Asia. The United States possessed the largest industrialized economy in the world by the 1870s.[17] Decade after decade, its economic superiority did not persuade its ruling elites to pursue military superiority, in part because they believed Americans could generally conduct commerce without imposing the terms by force. It is possible that features inherent in the United States made each next step of expansion irresistible, but even if so, one still has to explain why the same class of people went from ruling out extrahemispheric political-military commitments before the middle of 1940 to planning them thereafter on a global scale. Why did U.S. officials and intellectuals rapidly determine that economic exchange—and not only that but liberal intercourse more broadly— required the United States to possess military supremacy and assume responsibility for ordering the world?

THIS IS A QUESTION ABOUT IDEAS, and so, in the first instance, it must be answered in the province of ideas.[18] Armed primacy (or supremacy, dominance, or leadership), as adopted by the United States, is not merely the material condition of possessing more tanks, ships, and planes than any other country.[19] Nor does it aim only to contain or defeat a particular rival and then declare its mission accomplished. Primacy is an axiom about America's role in the world, closer to the status of an identity than to that of a policy or strategy.[20] Primacy was thus expressly intended to outlive the circumstances of its origination and shape the distant, perhaps perpetual, future. While forged in the face of Europe coming under Axis rule, it addressed, from the very start, a post-Axis world as well.

Primacy holds that the superior coercive power of the United States is required to underwrite a decent world order. It assumes that in order to prevent the international realm from descending into chaos or despotism, a benign hegemon must act as the world's ordering agent. It further deems the United States to be the sole entity fit for the part. On emerging in 1940 and 1941, primacy displaced two main alternatives: that another power, namely Great Britain, should exercise predominant influence, and that no power should do so, order being supplied instead by the development of public opinion, peaceful exchange, or world organization.[21]

Though ideational in nature, primacy has concrete implications for U.S. policy across the globe. First, it directs the United States to acquire and retain military power superior to any other nation or prospective combination of nations. This objective in turn creates a U.S. interest in accessing and mobilizing the economic foundations of military power, namely the centers of industrial production and sources of vital raw materials. Second, a fortress America, armed to the hilt but guarding America alone, is not enough. Primacy requires stationing U.S. forces in regions important to the global balance of power, or at least entering into commitments to secure such regions in the event of attack. Third, primacy entails a willingness to use force routinely if preferably on a modest scale. Its adherents may aspire to achieve "peace through strength" in a general way, but they expect aggressors to arise and the United States to police them.

In order for primacy to emerge and endure, more than a single president or administration had to adopt it. On the other hand, not every American had to buy in. The protagonist of this story, the agent that made the decision for dominance, is the U.S. foreign policy elite as a group.[22] This class of people certainly included policymakers at the highest levels of state, on which most books on grand strategy center their analysis. But it also, and especially, encompassed experts in foundations, universities, think-tanks, and the media.

In the early years of World War II, such nonofficial experts possessed a singular importance. The federal government remained small, even after the dramatic expansion wrought by the New Deal. It was diminutive on matters of foreign relations.[23] In this transitional period, the tiny state bureaucracy relied on the large pool of private expertise built up over the preceding two decades—a proto–national security state whose moment had arrived.[24]

Within two weeks of the Nazi invasion of Poland, leaders in the U.S. State Department found themselves consumed by the war crisis. They turned to the CFR in New York City to study the shape of things to come. Established in 1921, the CFR assembled a formidable postwar planning outfit of nearly one hundred experts, including government officials, academics, journalists, and professionals from business, finance, and law.[25] Even after Pearl Harbor, when the State Department took postwar planning in house, it installed CFR planners atop several subcommittees, as Chapter 4 describes.[26] Arguably, the foreign policy bureaucracy would never again be so dependent on outside experts to formulate basic objectives.[27] In that sense, nonofficial planning for armed primacy turned out to be self-liquidating. Ten years hence, once the state assumed the global responsibilities that outside actors urged of it, it developed the infrastructure to generate its own strategies, and strategists.

The elites who mattered were not only those who had the ear of top officials. Beginning in 1940 and 1941 and continuing throughout the war, a host of groups sprung up to plan the future, partaking in a mania for all things postwar. Foreign policy elites saw an opportunity to shape popular discourse and official policy alike. To the public they spoke with the authority of independent experts, unsullied by political or bureaucratic interests. To government officials they stood in for the public, claiming a privileged position for divining which courses of action would command popular legitimacy. They therefore possessed a power distinct from that of direct policymakers, and in some respects greater. Appearing as the organic expression of civil society, the site of liberal freedom, they were uniquely positioned to forge an enduring political consensus.

If the distinctive influence of one or another postwar planner is impossible to specify, what is clear is the significance of the Northeast-based policy community at large. Collectively, this elite devised the project of global supremacy and turned it into the obvious-seeming response to the events of the war. *Tomorrow, the World* puts aside some differences of nuance among individual thinkers in order to elucidate the conception and evolution of a shared argument: that the United States should dominate world politics, in the name of spurning isolationism and achieving internationalism.

IN ITS FIRST HALF, this book shows how global supremacy first became imaginable and desirable as U.S. elites lost faith in ideas of internationalism. Chapter 1 begins by surveying internationalism in America from the founding era through the 1930s—a period subsequently dismissed as isolationist by advocates of U.S. supremacy. The first part of the chapter describes how U.S. diplomats, lawyers, and activists participated in projects to reform international society, especially from the late nineteenth century through the 1920s. To them internationalism meant seeking to eliminate war and power politics, often by promoting international law and organization. The League of Nations, established by forty-two states after World War I, was a product of their efforts and those of internationalists elsewhere. Even after the United States declined to join the League, self-described internationalists believed their cause was alive and well, at home and abroad, throughout the 1920s.

The chapter then charts the crisis of internationalism in the 1930s. Confronted by the rise of totalitarian states, American foreign policy elites came to doubt that greater understanding among peoples could bring about peace. They pioneered concepts like "collective security" and "world order" to convey their new sense that armed enforcement would be required in order to preserve a modicum of stability and exchange. They also began to mischaracterize as isolationists those who advocated deep neutrality toward conflicts in Europe and Asia, as though staying out of war entailed cordoning off the United States from the world in toto. Yet if conceptual underpinnings were shifting, policy implications remained elusive. The American public abhorred participation in extrahemispheric wars. Officials agreed, finding little reason for the United States to shoulder military burdens across the oceans, especially because the totalitarian powers appeared to face more capable opponents in their own regions.

The second part of Chapter 1 centers on little-known efforts in the State Department and the CFR to plan for peace during the first eight months of World War II in Europe, lasting from September 1939 through April 1940. However much the tenets of internationalism seemed to have failed, U.S. planners saw no choice but to reprise a "peace without victory," the formula of President Woodrow Wilson from the last war. With the fighting resembling a stalemate, reminiscent of the 1914–1918 experience, they sought to stay neutral and mediate a settlement. They even hoped to bring Italy, ruled by dictator Benito Mussolini, over to the side of the democracies. To explore this possibility, Roosevelt dispatched Undersecretary of State Sumner Welles to Berlin, London, Paris, and Rome. That the United States might emerge from the war as the guarantor of security in Europe and Asia was scarcely contemplated, let alone advocated. Nor were many Americans eager to revive an international organization like the League of Nations. Proponents of the League considered splitting it into several regional organizations, with the United States confined within Pan-American boundaries.

But when they steamrollered France in May 1940, the Nazis swept away the old order and with it the assumptions of American elites. Chapter 2 spans the six months that followed. It argues that the German conquest of France convinced U.S. foreign policy elites not only to enter the war, as historians have shown, but also to supplant Great Britain as the premier world power afterward. Having devoured France, Hitler stood alone as master of Europe. The Nazi war machine seemed likely to seize the British Isles and threaten Britain's empire as well. At first, in June and July, U.S. planners expected the postwar United States to inhabit no more than a "quarter sphere" extending from North America down to the area where Brazil jutted out into the Atlantic. In narrow material terms, such an outcome did not look altogether disastrous: the CFR's economists found that the largely self-contained U.S. economy would perform adequately if future trade were confined to the quarter sphere alone. By the autumn, however, American planners watched Britain withstand the Nazi onslaught and determined that the United States should defend essentially the whole world except a projected Nazi-dominated European Continent. This U.S.-led order, dubbed the Grand Area, became the basis for postwar planning through most of 1941.

Why did the fall of France trigger U.S. officials and intellectuals to recalculate America's interests and responsibilities in the world? They were not anticipating an invasion of the U.S. homeland; few believed a transoceanic attack could succeed against a well-defended Western Hemisphere, even if Germany were to defeat Britain. Instead, Hitler's victory seemed to lay bare a truth about the nature of global politics. Internationalism had it backward: rather than progressively overcoming coercion and conflict, peaceful intercourse paradoxically required armed force to back it. In the epoch to come, whichever nation possessed military supremacy would impose its concept of world order. Simultaneously, the Axis powers shattered the fundaments of British imperial power, leaving observers on both sides of the Atlantic to call on the United States to take the lead in policing the world in the postwar era. Out of the death of internationalism as contemporaries had known it, and the faltering of British hegemony, U.S. global supremacy was born.

Having glimpsed the possibility of American supremacy, foreign policy elites conceived how to achieve this objective in the pivotal year of 1941. As Chapter 3 shows, they proceeded along two tracks at once: they started to discuss postwar American supremacy publicly and, in private, to consider the institutional framework through which the United States would operate. As the U.S. Congress passed Lend-Lease legislation toward the beginning of 1941, a panoply of U.S. officials and intellectuals publicly articulated a new goal: the acquisition of global political and military supremacy by the United States, without any wider international organization. A variety of proposals were aired, their common denominator being that whatever shape the postwar world order took, the United States should be the one to define it. Well before a new world organization generated any serious discussion, the American political system rejected what it began to dub "isolationism" and embraced global supremacy.

U.S. elites scarcely wished to set up another universal political body to replace the failed League of Nations. They preferred to enter into a permanent partnership with Great Britain, including the white Dominions of the British Commonwealth. The "English-speaking peoples," bound by race and led by America, would police most of the postwar world and keep Nazi Germany confined to Europe. Chapter 3 recovers postwar planners' blueprints for building jointly run military bases and for extending near citizenship to Anglo-Saxons the world over. American interest in forming a postwar association exclusively with Britain culminated in the Atlantic Charter, issued by President Roosevelt and British prime minister Winston Churchill in August 1941. Although historians have interpreted the Atlantic Charter as favoring world organization, Roosevelt rebuffed Churchill's suggestion to endorse a new league. Reflecting the views of his postwar planners, Roosevelt maintained that only the United States and Great Britain could keep order in the postwar world.

Soon, however, planners perceived a problem. The Atlantic Charter, they observed, "fell like a dead duck" upon Congress and the public.[28] U.S. global supremacy sounded imperialistic, contrary to the country's traditional ideals.

As the United States mobilized its economy and military, en route to entering the war at the end of 1941, planners and intellectuals already fretted that postwar U.S. leadership might be thwarted from within. The American public might refuse the summons to play power politics on a global scale, especially if American firepower were put behind the morally suspect British Empire. The problem of "public opinion" preoccupied postwar-minded elites, though they projected their own anxieties onto the public as much as they took cues from the public's actual expressions. From 1942 to 1945, as the book's second half recounts, they achieved what they had conceived.

To do so, officials and intellectuals redefined armed supremacy as the epitome of internationalism and the core of international organization. Chapter 4 asks why U.S. policymakers opted to establish any general organization of nations, given that the old League of Nations looked feckless and no one thought another universal grouping could succeed in creating order. Homing in on the State Department's postwar planning committee—formed after Pearl Harbor and composed of experts outside of government, officials from the military and Treasury Department, and members of Congress—the chapter shows that world organization was revived in 1942 and 1943 as a vehicle for U.S. hegemony. The planners still wanted political power to remain with America first and Britain second, but they figured that by gaining the participation of other states they could convince the American public that U.S. leadership would be inclusive, rule bound, and worthy of support. Harnessing the resonance of prior efforts to end power politics in the name of internationalism, they fashioned the United Nations as an instrument to implement power politics by the United States.

Chapter 5 analyzes the massive campaign of public persuasion that nominally aimed to marshal support for the United States to join the United Nations. The campaign, however, was animated by a deeper objective: to turn postwar supremacy into an unanswerable position in domestic politics. In an outpouring of books, pamphlets, speeches, and film, proponents of the United Nations framed the choice as *whether* the United States should exert global leadership (internationalism) or retreat from the world altogether (isolationism). This stark binary inhibited consideration of what actually mattered: *how* the United States should participate in politics beyond its shores. In World War I, politicians and civil society groups engaged that question, debating proposals for competing forms of international organization. In World War II, no such prominent alternatives circulated, because foreign policy elites wanted it that way. Self-identified internationalists closed ranks, suppressing differences of vision lest "isolationism" capitalize. But isolationism was a phantom enemy. The moniker was hurled at those who sought simply to restrict U.S. security commitments but wished to participate internationally in every other way. In any case, such persons had vanished in number even as advocates of supremacy denounced them and expelled them from the sphere of legitimate discourse. The result was a sterile nondebate at precisely the moment when the United States ascended to world paramountcy.

When the war ended in Japan's unconditional surrender, the United States was simultaneously at the start and height of its superiority. It possessed globe-spanning military bases and an economy that produced as much industrial output as the whole rest of the world. It also set out to use its power to provide global public goods and avoid another depression and war. This was a relatively farsighted and positive-sum outlook that compares favorably with that of other superpowers in history and that of the United States since then. Not for nothing have politicians and experts in the decades that followed looked back for inspiration to the "multilateralist moment" of 1945.[29] Yet the moment was only superficially multilateralist, and idealizing it hides the contradiction at its core. At the time, American leaders hardly wished to subordinate their nation's unprecedented power to multilateral authority. They were more interested in evoking multilateral authority in order to legitimate American power. Chapter 5 ends by recovering criticisms of the postwar settlement expressed by skeptics of American dominance, who nevertheless lacked a positive program that commanded political support. Six years after U.S. global supremacy was all but inconceivable, it was now indisputable.

So it has remained. In the ensuing decades, politicians and intellectuals have taken America's armed dominance across the globe to emanate from the very identity of the nation. To be the world's "indispensable nation," they say, is just "who we are." Scholars trace exceptionalism, America's sense of destiny to lead and redeem the world, back to the settlement of the country and find it lurking behind every outward projection of U.S. power.[30] Yet exceptionalism did not make the difference in the original decision for dominance. Americans widely viewed their nation as exceptional well before World War II. Opponents of supremacy tended to be exceptionalists too, convinced that America's unique experiment in liberty mandated political separation from Old World corruption. For supremacy to take hold, the real task was to convince Americans not that their nation was superior to others but something like the opposite: that the United States would respect others rather than domineer and exploit them as previous empires had done. For this purpose, the concept of internationalism offered a resource that the concept of exceptionalism could not. In professing internationalism, Americans conveyed that they cherished the equality of others. As first among equals, the United States would follow the rules, work with partners, and serve the welfare of all. "When all is said and done," the political scientist G. John Ikenberry writes, "Americans are less interested in ruling the world than they are in a world of rules."[31]

In fact, the U.S. political class sought a simulacrum of law and equality, touting world organization as a forum for common participation while retreating from mechanisms of common control. *Tomorrow, the World* concludes with the creation of the United Nations because, despite its novelty and foreignness, the organization allowed U.S. supremacy to appear to fulfill, not traduce, venerable American principles. The original United Nations embodied the ideal template for how foreign policy elites wanted U.S. leadership to work: the United States would act together with others, but others would follow America's script. The Cold War, by contrast, was always imagined as an aberration. It was one epoch of American global leadership, which would outlast the Soviet challenge as well as the Soviet collapse.

1

INTERNATIONALISM BEFORE "ISOLATIONISM," 1776–1940

IN 1911 A YOUNG Edwin Borchard proposed a way to end war. He wanted the world's civilized states to agree to settle disputes in a court of arbitration, where "enlightened public opinion"—acting through discerning lawyers like himself—would compel governments to choose peace and, in time, disarm.[1] Two world wars later, the renowned Yale University professor of international law assailed the new United Nations (U.N.). The organization amounted, Borchard wrote, to a "thinly disguised military alliance of the three largest Powers," the United States above all. Its oxymoronic quest to "enforce peace" actually made peace impossible, authorizing the strongest powers to wage war on anyone they claimed to be an aggressor.[2] To Borchard, the emergent postwar world order harked back to the nineteenth-century Holy Alliance, whose monarchs imposed their version of international cooperation on popular revolutionaries throughout Europe.

If Borchard was an internationalist par excellence before the First World War, he possessed an equal claim to be considered an internationalist after the Second World War. His criticism of the U.N. demonstrated his consistent aspiration to tame power politics through the pacific settlement of disputes and the disarmament of nations. In addition to denouncing the U.N. Charter, Borchard proposed to rescue it by, among other measures, elevating the U.N. General Assembly, where every state got a seat, to the status of the great-power Security Council and replacing armed sanctions with peaceful conciliation. By 1945, however, the conceptual horizons of American foreign policy had changed more than Borchard had. "As force grows in importance, the law recedes," he still insisted, but most Americans who called themselves internationalists had come to the opposite conclusion: law was nothing if not backed by force, and that of the United States in particular.[3]

The new internationalists did not merely defeat Borchard's prescriptions for U.S. foreign policy and international society; they also expelled him from membership in internationalism and thus the sphere of legitimate discourse. In their eyes, Borchard now embodied "isolationism" for opposing U.S. intervention in World War II and U.S. global supremacy thereafter. Borchard had indeed been one of the most influential such opponents before the attack on Pearl Harbor sent the United States into the war. He wrote books, delivered testimony, and advised Senator Hiram Johnson to the effect that the United States should confine its political and military commitments to its own hemisphere and uphold the traditional laws of neutrality, premised on equality among nations and a sharp separation between war and peace.[4] But Borchard felt that his activities were nothing if not internationalist and that his detractors perverted the concept by redefining it in in opposition to their novel term *isolationism*. He complained two months before Pearl Harbor about "the idea that those who oppose entering the most risky of wars are 'isolationists' or malefactors of some kind." Such denigration, Borchard added, "is abhorrent and does the country no good."[5]

American policy elites might have continued to conceive Borchard as an internationalist and frame their proposals as alternatives within internationalism. Instead they claimed internationalism all for themselves now as advocates of U.S. global supremacy. This semantic shift deserves sustained scrutiny. It represented more than the rhetorical one-upmanship common to political debate. It was something of a necessity if the United States was to assume political and military leadership of world affairs. In order for U.S. global supremacy to become conceivable and appear legitimate, Americans had to erase what had hitherto been known as internationalism and invest the term with new meaning.

The task was formidable enough to give Borchard confidence that his country would slough off interventionist fantasies and steer clear of Old World entanglements. For a very long time, he was right. One world war did not convince the country to join its president's league for peace, let alone to vie for supreme power in Europe and Asia; not even ardent interventionists of the day sought the latter. The approach of a second world war hollowed out aspirations for international harmony, but throughout the 1930s and halfway into 1940, interventionists-to-be hoped for no more than to tailor U.S. neutrality to the advantage of certain parties in a conflict from which the United States would surely abstain and whose settlement it would do nothing to enforce. Once again, while American people and goods would traverse the globe, American arms would stay largely within the hemisphere. Internationalism of a traditional sort still guided U.S. foreign policy, if only by default.

Power Politics versus Public Opinion, "The Queen of the World"

Before the 1930s James Shotwell did not fear anything called isolationism. Born in Canada to American Quakers, Shotwell was a leading intellectual and networker in the burgeoning interwar realm of American semiofficialdom—a historian at Columbia University, a director of the Carnegie Endowment for International Peace and the Social Science Research Council, and the president of the League of Nations Association, a national organization dedicated to supporting U.S. membership in the League of Nations in Geneva.[6] In 1930 he assessed the condition of world politics and, despite America's refusal to join the League after World War I, saw internationalism everywhere on the ascent and mentioned isolationism not once. Judged against a decade of progress on limiting armaments, illegalizing aggressive warfare, and reviving world trade, the U.S. Senate's reluctance to pledge armed force behind the League seemed a minor matter. Besides, as Shotwell wrote, the resort to police power "declines in proportion as all the members of a community begin to be aware of the common interest."[7] A growing sense of fellow feeling would obviate the need for even the lawful use of force, superseding the controversies of 1919.

Although buoyed by recent events, Shotwell spoke the language of internationalism descended from the Enlightenment and articulated across borders in the nineteenth century. Internationalists in America, as elsewhere, did not necessarily seek to strengthen U.S. political and military power—often the opposite, in fact—and did not see isolationism as their adversary. Rather, what united them was their aspiration and expectation that nations would progressively express the harmony that was immanent in the world. Self-aggrandizement was the principle of action first of ruling princes and then of narrow nationalists; internationalists, by contrast, would bring about the broadening of interests in the service of humankind.[8] "There is no very great difference in the fundamental desires of all the civilized nations," Shotwell wrote—and so uncivilized nations should become civilized and civilized nations organized.[9] In these efforts, Americans like Shotwell and Borchard took a leading role. Far from standing aloof from internationalism before World War II, Americans ranked among its foremost advocates.

To sketch the contours of internationalism in this period requires an act of recovery, since those who came to advocate U.S. global supremacy, Shotwell included, found this history too subversive to preserve. As will be discussed in Chapter 5, they promulgated a narrative in which the United States was born isolationist and remained in thrall to isolationism until World War II. This account contains the grain of truth that U.S. diplomacy strove to avoid political and military commitments, stigmatized as "entanglements," in the system of power politics centered in Europe. Yet it is more accurate and encompassing to view nonentanglement as an aspect of internationalism, which directed the United States to stay out of power politics and seek to transform it. What follows outlines a new history of ideas of internationalism in the United States and the activities organized under its sign. In the process, it rebuts those who tell a story of untrammeled U.S. expansion culminating in the achievement of global supremacy. The United States undertook territorial aggrandizement prior to 1940 in the name of ending power politics, and this commitment imposed limits on its actions, requiring a rupture before global supremacy could be conceived.

THE UNITED STATES WAS BORN OF exceptionalist nationalism, imagining itself providentially chosen to occupy the vanguard of world history.[10] It was also born internationalist, promising and incarnating a world governed by reason and rules, not force and whim. These foundational concepts contradicted one another: exceptionalism cast the United States as a nation above others, internationalism as a nation among others. But being foundational concepts, they could not be abandoned; they had to be configured in such a way as to push the contradiction out of view. For the first century and a half of the nation's existence, successive generations achieved this feat by positioning Americanism and internationalism alike in opposition to the system of power politics centered in Europe. Abstaining from the system politically, the United States could transcend it peaceably. Without seeking global supremacy Americans could imagine themselves leading the world to better things.

Thus President George Washington famously used his farewell address to urge his successors to "steer clear of permanent alliances with any portion of the foreign world" lest American peace and prosperity become entangled in the separate and retrograde political system of Europe.[11] Even the most realpolitik-oriented of founders, Alexander Hamilton, asserted that the United States should aim to be "an ascendant in the system of American affairs" alone and proceeded to disparage Europeans for arrogantly extending their domination over the rest of mankind.[12] The founders were not content just to reject European-style power politics. They also offered positive alternatives. One was embodied by the United States itself, whose Constitution attempted to keep peace between the states through exchange and law more than compulsion by the not-quite-superior federal government.[13] America's model could be adopted by all, including European states themselves. Another approach was to act directly on the outside world. A few breaths after Washington forbade permanent alliances, he counseled Americans to engage in "liberal intercourse with all nations" and join with others to establish and spread "rules of intercourse."[14] Here was a vision of order potentially universal in scope but premised on the ability of peaceful interaction to replace clashing politics. Washington's precepts, although associated with isolationism since that term's coinage in the 1930s, better anticipated what became known as internationalism.

In the nineteenth century, internationalism, counterposed to European power politics, established itself as a framework for national policy, spurring but also limiting rapacious expansion. To strengthen its "empire of liberty," in Thomas Jefferson's phrase, the United States brutally extended its dominion across North America, seeking to populate new territories with white settlers and bring them into the federal union on equal terms with other states. For the same reason, U.S. leaders declined to pursue potential acquisitions of populous Cuba or all of Mexico, which they were unwilling to grant statehood or hold as colonies.[15] In the Monroe Doctrine of 1823, the United States designated the entire Western Hemisphere as a U.S.-protected refuge from further European colonization.[16] Yet instead of simply asserting a U.S. interest in the politics of the Americas, President James Monroe reciprocally forswore a U.S. interest in the "eminently and conspicuously different" European political system. The United States could vastly enlarge the area over which it claimed political responsibility, but that area had to be conceived as exempt from power politics, whether in the form of balance-of-power rivalry or exploitative domination. Thus the Monroe Doctrine proclaimed that the United States had a stake in the fate of the hemisphere without suggesting that the United States should enforce its writ or even challenge the British Navy for pride of place in the seas. Monroe articulated a philosophy of history in which public opinion and peaceful interaction would replace politics and war. Americans both north and south needed only to be "left to themselves" and they would reject the European system of their own accord.[17]

As the United States pursued hegemony in the New World, American activists formed a peace movement to redeem the Old World. The first self-described peace societies formed in Britain and the United States in order to contest the great-power settlement of the Napoleonic Wars.[18] They reposed faith in what they termed public opinion against its armed suppression by the great powers.[19] By midcentury these advocates of peace offered a comprehensive program for relations among states, or at least the elite club of civilized states. Through the "people-diplomacy" of free trade, open congresses, and national autonomy, states would express their true, harmonious interests and prevent disputes from arising.[20] Through disarmament and arbitration, states would resolve what disputes did arise through discussion rather than war. The term *internationalism* entered into regular usage in the 1860s and 1870s in order to describe such a program, spearheaded by the international peace movement and working men's associations.[21]

Until the end of the nineteenth century, internationalist prescriptions remained distant from diplomatic practice. Internationalists were dissenters. They glorified publics whose will was stifled in the existing order of monarchical and aristocratic states loosely organized in the post-Napoleonic Concert of Europe. In short, the concepts of public opinion and world organization were poles apart, and American internationalists chose the former. Any practicable world organization would have the European great powers at its core and small states, including the United States, at its mercy. It would be a vehicle for power politics.[22] Nevertheless, in 1840 a New Hampshire sea captain sketched how public opinion and world organization might come together. William Ladd, the first president of the American Peace Society, devised a plan for an international congress and court to which all states could voluntarily bring disputes. Ladd's proposal involved no contractual obligations, much less economic or military sanctions. He was, he wrote, "leaving the functions of the executive with public opinion, 'the queen of the world.'"[23] Ladd's plan suggested, in embryo, how world organization might amplify public opinion and thereby become an instrument against power politics.

If peace men like Ladd commanded respectability in the nineteenth century—John Quincy Adams, who formulated the Monroe Doctrine as secretary of state, expected Ladd's plan to be realized within twenty years—they faced denunciation by a new species of militant imperialist at the turn of the twentieth. One might assume that at this time the United States cast off its hostility to power politics. After all, it joined the club of the great powers by building a world-class navy and acquiring fully fledged colonies in the Caribbean basin and the South Pacific.[24] Its political and intellectual elites increasingly viewed the United States and Europe as sharing a common, industrial civilization.[25] The presidency of Theodore Roosevelt, in particular, brought to the White House a student of the balance of power and an enthusiast of the British Empire, which he held up as a model for U.S. colonial rule in the Philippines and elsewhere.[26]

On the whole, however, the turn-of-the-century United States continued to stay politically and militarily apart from the European alliance system while intensifying efforts to transform power politics globally. The United States took colonies far from the centers of European rivalry, and, to Roosevelt's chagrin, colonial empire proved unpopular with Americans.[27] In the Progressive Era, U.S. presidents preferred to discipline Latin Americans through so-called dollar diplomacy, pitched in American and internationalist terms as substituting "dollars for bullets."[28] And even as some Americans came to identify more with Europe than against it, successive administrations from the 1880s onward strengthened the hemispheric orientation of U.S. foreign policy and the internationalist credentials of U.S. hegemony in the hemisphere. They helped to build an "American international society" featuring specifically Pan-American laws and conferences. "All shall meet together on terms of absolute equality," Secretary of State James G. Blaine declared on convening the first International American Conference—naturally held in Washington, DC.[29]

More remarkable were the endeavors even of imperialists like Roosevelt to promote plans, descended from Ladd's, for ending war throughout the civilized world. As more and more states shed absolutist and dynastic rule and adopted the principle of popular sovereignty, the once revolutionary schemes of internationalists were taken up by reformist professionals in positions of power.[30] The new guild of international lawyers commanded significant influence in the United States; led by Roosevelt's secretary of state, Elihu Root, they dominated the State Department in the first two decades of the twentieth century. The United States became a foremost sponsor of transatlantic efforts to codify legal code and settle disputes between states in arbitral and judicial courtrooms.[31] At the instigation of Roosevelt and Czar Nicholas II of Russia, dozens of governments participated in two Hague conferences, which established a roster of judges known as the Permanent Court of Arbitration and endorsed the idea of forming a general pact to obligate the arbitration of disputes.[32] It was this voluntarist formula, forgoing sanctions, that attracted Borchard, who occupied the vanguard of internationalism before World War I.

As ever, national assertion and international idealism went hand in hand. Most internationalists wanted it that way, arguing not that internationalism should supplant nationalism but rather that the two should come into balance. "Sound Nationalism and Sound Internationalism" was how Roosevelt stated his creed.[33] Still, even Roosevelt's cautious brand of internationalism implied reining in nationalist excesses and broadening the horizons of moral responsibility. What nationalism had achieved for individuals, enlarging their community and outlawing war between them, internationalism would extend to nations.[34]

Internationalism therefore connoted the restraint, perhaps control, of national policy—its regulation by "the international mind," in the 1912 phrase of Nicholas Murray Butler, president of Columbia University and the Carnegie Endowment for International Peace.[35] Internationalists like Butler were not, in general, summoning Americans to wield more military power, much less to attain global military supremacy. Nor did they define their cause in opposition to "isolationism," a term yet to be coined. Before the First World War, internationalists sought to temper the nationalism of the United States and all states. Moreover, they enthroned public opinion as the underwriter of world order and world peace. Although suspicious of mass publics, and willing to claim "public opinion" favored their own preferences, internationalists at elite levels aimed to end armed conflict without authorizing states to resort to coercive sanctions and thus to wage new kinds of wars.[36] The international society they envisioned would neither require nor benefit from routine military policing by a globe-spanning United States. Nor would one great war change this judgment.

EUROPE'S DESCENT INTO violence in 1914 could not but compel U.S. officials and intellectuals to reexamine their assumptions about international society and America's role within it. After the belligerents defied international law and stifled transatlantic intercourse, driving the United States to defend its neutral rights by entering the war in 1917, many Americans turned to international organization as an answer to the newly named problem of international anarchy.[37] Parting ways with prewar pacifists and legalists, some now proposed to endow a world body with economic and even military sanctions. Once a mature power like Germany flouted its clear legal obligations, the challenge became, Root wrote, "not so much to make treaties which define rights as to prevent the treaties from being violated."[38] By putting physical sanctions behind public opinion, American internationalists took a significant step away from pacifistic formulas and toward military intervention on a global scale—or they would have done so, had two-thirds of senators voted for the United States to join the League of Nations. Instead, the Senate declined, and the United States never entered the League.

Yet even if the Senate had approved the League unanimously, the United States still would not have embarked on anything resembling the project of global supremacy that it conceived two decades later. Like internationalists before them, League advocates in World War I hewed to the premise that liberal intercourse would and should undermine the causes of war. Their innovation was to yoke the goal of transcending power politics to the instrument of world organization, thus attempting to meld what had seemed irreconcilable a century earlier. The result was a vision shot through with hesitations and contradictions. But it was *not* a vision of U.S. global supremacy, except insofar as some of its elements might have ended up undermining its intended purposes.

Most of those who supported U.S. entry into World War I did not seek to ensure that the United States would hold preeminent military power after the war; they hoped to vitiate the importance of military power instead. Like Shotwell, who helped to plan the peace in the U.S. government's wartime "Inquiry," President Woodrow Wilson assumed that the true interests of peoples were harmonious.[39] He designed the League of Nations accordingly, casting it as a means of expressing nations' genuine interests, of removing the blockages and distortions that had plagued European-dominated international society. In Wilson's words, the League would transform the balance of power into a "community of power" in which "all unite to act in the same sense and with the same purpose, all act in the common interest and are free to live their own lives under a common protection."[40] Wilson's notion of a community of power described how U.S. policymakers had long seen the Western Hemisphere. But rather than keep Europe politically separate from the Americas, Wilson now proposed to Americanize Europe. Hence his answer to accusations that he would entangle the United States in European power politics: the League was rather a "disentangling alliance."[41] By creating a universal alliance with American participation, it would forever end the capacity of European alliances to ensnare the United States. Whatever the plausibility of Wilson's ideas, doubted by the Senators he needed to convince, he argued for the United States not to counterbalance or dominate any rival but instead to render counterbalancing and domination obsolete.

So did other advocates of world organization who were quite different from Wilson. In 1915, two years before the United States became a belligerent, American diplomats, lawyers, and peace activists formed the League to Enforce Peace (LEP) and launched transatlantic discussions of a postwar settlement. Led by former president William Howard Taft, the LEP issued a four-point platform in which all states would agree to settle their legal disputes in an international court and use force collectively against any violator.[42] The LEP plan, that is, placed sanctions behind the voluntary arrangements of the prewar period and replaced informal mechanisms of arbitration with formal legal code and judicial courts. Wilson disagreed, worrying that arid legal machinery would stifle the organic growth of a common international-mindedness.[43] His League of Nations gave pride of place to politicians in the Assembly and Council, not to judges in courts. Legalists and Wilsonians thus diverged over which sort of white male of European extract, the statesman or the jurist, should take the lead in "interpreting" public opinion to resolve conflicts.

Despite clashing in their own time, legalists and Wilsonians shared more similarities than differences from the standpoint of the next generation. The diplomat George Kennan, who devised the Cold War doctrine of containment, would justifiably lump them together into a single "legalistic-moralistic approach."[44] Both legalists and moralists advocated a world organization that would produce peace more by unleashing public opinion than by mobilizing crushing armaments. Such a league promised to end war altogether, mostly by preventing violence and partly by redefining violence as either the criminal violation or the community policing of law. In this sense, as Root explicitly theorized, international society would become just like domestic society, ordering sovereign states as each state ordered individual citizens.[45] But because hardly anyone favored an overarching world government to compel compliance by states, League advocates relied on the assumption that a harmony of interest underlay the world. Ultimately, peace would be produced because states, organized through the League, would adopt an enlightened conception of their interests. As Wilson said on unveiling the League of Nations Covenant, "We are depending primarily and chiefly upon one great force, and this is the moral force of the public opinion of the world." Armed force, he acknowledged, would be in the background, but the League was "intended as a constitution of peace, not as a league of war."[46]

Envisaging the transcendence of power politics, American internationalists did not design the League to wield armed force against constant acts of aggression. They expected that after pledging to use armed force, states would rarely have to deliver on the promise.[47] Wilson went so far as to tell the Senate that Article 10 of the Covenant, the League's controversial guarantee of political independence and territorial integrity, constituted "a moral, not a legal, obligation" that was "binding in conscience only" and left Congress free to decide whether to act.[48] Likewise, while insisting on the importance of armed sanctions, LEP leaders claimed that the resort to arms "may never become necessary," as Taft assured the LEP's pacifistic members—and himself, for if military enforcement transpired too frequently, it would defeat the purpose of a league for peace.[49] Perhaps no one expressed the ambivalence better than Quincy Wright, the outstanding international lawyer and political scientist of his day. Piling qualification upon qualification, Wright wrote a colleague in 1932 that "one should make use to the utmost of moral sanctions although I believe that certain physical sanctions should be organized in a rather general way in the background."[50] By then, however, world events were exposing the contradiction in Wright's position, forcing internationalists to choose between nonintervention and collective security.

Finally, insofar as League advocates promoted a kind of global armed supremacy, the United States was not to possess it. One looks in vain for blueprints of a postwar world spanned by U.S. military bases. Although the United States emerged from World War I with a larger economy than that of the entire British Empire, and pursued naval parity with Britain, American elites recognized that Great Britain would remain the leading military power outside of the Western Hemisphere for the foreseeable future.[51] To the limited extent that the League of Nations instituted a kind of armed superiority to deter aggression, such superiority was to be possessed collectively, by League members in combination. The League lodged authority for international peace and security in the universal Assembly as well as the great-power-dominated

Council. Furthermore, the League Covenant, in Articles 10–16, specified the circumstances that would elicit sanctions so as to deter or stop aggression. At least in comparison to the drafters of the United Nations, the architects of the League attempted to govern enforcement actions through rules and collective authorization rather than leaving their deployment to the discretion of the strong.

In sum, the most interventionist of internationalists in World War I did not advocate U.S. global supremacy as later generations conceived it. Few recognized a vital U.S. interest in regulating the balance of power in Europe and Asia.[52] Fewer still sought a preponderance of military power for the United States. Despite adding coercive sanctions to nineteenth-century peace schemes, internationalists continued to rely on the moral suasion of public opinion to prevent aggressors from arising in the first place. So long as they sought to bring about the transcendence of power politics, American foreign policy elites would find U.S. global supremacy to be unnecessary at best and imperialistic at worst.

The United States, of course, declined to join the League of Nations, an outcome that historians since World War II have attributed to the strength of traditional isolationism and the unwillingness of League supporters to set aside their squabbles in the service of the anti-isolationism that they supposedly shared.[53] This interpretation, however, reveals more about the conceptual horizons of American politics in 1945 than in 1919, when the very notion of isolationism barely existed. In 1919, at the height of the League debate, the *New York Times* used the term *isolationist* one time in reference to U.S. foreign policy, and *isolationism* not at all.[54] Contemporaries, including many opponents of the League, understood and presented themselves as advancing the kind of internationalism they preferred. Advocates of the League, though they did renounce a posture of "isolation," did not understand themselves to be making common cause against isolationism. They did not deploy the *–ism* even as an epithet against their opponents. They continued to define internationalism against power politics, not isolationism.

Moreover, League advocates did not claim a monopoly on internationalism, which at the time meant both more and less than favoring world organization. For most participants in the debate, internationalism served as a discursive frame, within which alternative schemes were couched. Some of the League's harshest critics argued essentially that the League, by introducing coercive sanctions, betrayed the cause of internationalism. For Hiram Johnson, the progressive California senator, the League merely dressed up an old-fashioned alliance with the victorious great powers, and with the British Empire in particular. He castigated the League of Nations as a new "Holy Alliance," the bête noir of the nineteenth-century peace movement. Johnson had ample reason to do so: the League froze territorial borders by threatening to punish their alteration with force, and it bolstered European empires by allowing them to administer ex-German and ex-Ottoman territories.[55] Internationalism lay on both sides of the League controversy.

Perhaps it was not so much the brittleness as the self-confidence of internationalists that kept the United States out of the League of Nations. Putting forward an array of peace plans, internationalists felt little pressure to paper over their differences in order to prevent a worse outcome. *Whether* the United States should shape world affairs was a given; what politicians and intellectuals asked was *how* to do so.[56] "Internationalism has come, and we must choose what form the internationalism shall take," Gilbert Hitchcock, the Democratic leader in the Senate, declared on Wilson's return from the Paris Peace Conference in February 1919.[57] American citizens staked out nuanced positions on which provisions of the Covenant to retain and which to amend. Surveys showed that only 7 percent of Americans desired outright rejection.[58] In the end, as anti-isolationist historians later argued, the United States would have joined the League if senators had struck a compromise between full supporters and those who favored mild reservations, or if Wilson had agreed to entertain amendments to the Covenant. But at the time, the details seemed to matter: they might make the difference between ending the system of war and getting embroiled in it. Perceiving no isolationist enemy, advocates of world organization had no reason to fetishize world organization. They would rather formulate the right terms than join on any terms.

Challenged from within internationalism, Wilson and his fellow League supporters faced resistance from devotees of exceptionalism as well. Although Wilson maintained that the League of Nations would Americanize Europe, extending the Monroe Doctrine to the world, many of his contemporaries thought the League would more likely Europeanize America. Even if the United States withheld its army from Europe, Idaho senator William Borah feared the League would license European intervention in the Americas, destroying the Monroe Doctrine.[59] "We are asked to become not an integral sovereignty but a vulgar fraction of a League," complained the *North American Review*.[60] Yet this objection would resonate only so long as the United States remained a second-ranking political and military power in Europe and Asia; it would become less salient as America became more powerful. The sheer acquisition of power could therefore resolve one-half of the Wilsonian dilemma, allowing the United States to dictate to an international body and keep an international body from dictating to it. But fixing the exceptionalist problem would exacerbate the internationalist problem. If the United States were to master the game of power politics, how could it be expected simultaneously to destroy power politics?

IN THE 1920S American foreign policy elites had no need to confront this question. In eschewing formal membership in the League of Nations, the Senate had the effect of stabilizing internationalism rather than repudiating it. Unburdened from having to square the goal of peace with the methods of force, American internationalists worked more actively than ever to promote universal intercourse as a substitute for armaments, alliances, and war. They orchestrated loans from America to Germany so that private capital could underwrite the European peace.[61] They participated, unofficially, in the less politicized parts of the League system in Geneva: the Permanent Court of International Justice and the so-called technical sections, which dealt with intellectual cooperation, public heath, and economics and finance.[62] They championed disarmament, organizing the Washington Naval Conference of 1921 to fix the ratio of warship tonnage among the top five powers.[63] They also championed the pacific settlement of international disputes, getting most states to declare war to be illegal in the Kellogg-Briand Pact of 1928, originally proposed to French foreign minister Aristide Briand by James Shotwell.[64]

In all these endeavors, American diplomacy placed a renewed faith in public opinion to serve as the sanction of international law and order. On accepting the Nobel Peace Prize for his namesake pact, Secretary of State Frank Kellogg affirmed that war was heading toward abolition, not through the force of arms but rather through "the force of public opinion, which controls nations and peoples—that public opinion which shapes our destinies and guides the progress of human affairs."[65] This message attracted League nemesis Borah, who passionately supported the Kellogg-Briand Pact because it declared war to be illegal without empowering some states to enforce the rules against others.[66] In the 1920s Borah also led a bloc of anti-imperialists in criticizing U.S. military interventions in the Americas, laying the foundations of the Good Neighbor Policy of the 1930s.[67] In such a climate, ambitious young intellectuals like Raymond Leslie Buell turned critiques of European colonial empires against what he dubbed "American imperialism."[68] Buell, a lecturer at Harvard University and the research director of the new Foreign Policy Association, urged the United States to accept some form of international oversight over its interventions in Latin America. "The question," he wrote in classic internationalist terms, "is whether we are willing to submit our acts to the conscience of the world."[69]

Buell's anti-imperialism illustrates that before World War II unimpeachable internationalists had the capacity to see the United States as a potential aggressor requiring restraint. So the absence of the U.S. military from much of the globe was not a failure in internationalist terms. As late as 1930 Shotwell, the professional internationalist, could view the future with optimism. America's official abstention notwithstanding, "the League has already brought into operation a revolution in diplomacy," Shotwell wrote.[70] Internationalism seemed alive and well, not least because it did not require the United States to put its armed might at the center of a world making progress.

Internationalism from Death to Reconception

In 1938 Nicholas Murray Butler summed up one proposition on which American foreign policy elites could agree: "International law, like international morality, has disappeared in a fog."[71] Only during the late 1930s did Butler lose his "international mind." In World War I, internationalists like him ultimately affirmed their confidence in public opinion and peaceful intercourse. They slotted their German adversary into the preexisting framework of power-hungry rulers, namely Kaiser Wilhelm II and the Prussian aristocracy, who suppressed peace-loving peoples.[72] If defeated, Germany could be recast along the proper lines of national self-determination and reintegrated into international society; even if victorious, Germany would not seem to usher in a new order incompatible with existing norms and laws. The events of the 1930s, by contrast, threw the premises of internationalism into question. In the face of new "totalitarian" rivals, internationalists began to doubt that the interests of all peoples could ever come into harmony and overthrow the reign of force.

The rise of fascist and communist regimes confronted American internationalists with more than lawbreaking. These regimes embodied political, economic, and social orders that seemed so irreconcilable with liberal principles that the category of *totalitarian* emerged to characterize them despite their obvious diversity.[73] The totalitarian powers claimed to represent the "wave of the future" as liberal capitalism and parliamentary democracy reeled from the Great Depression.[74] But regardless of whether it spread any further, simply by virtue of taking root in Germany, Italy, Japan, and the Soviet Union by the mid-1930s, totalitarianism called into question the belief in "public opinion" that had allowed internationalists to imagine that the world could be ordered and war overcome without a superior power enforcing its writ.

The masses were alarmingly susceptible to state propaganda: so concluded a group of scholars convened by Wright in 1933 to assess "public opinion and world politics."[75] To American observers, totalitarian regimes either enjoyed the genuine enthusiasm of their people or controlled their people tightly enough that the difference was negligible. Totalitarians, and the Nazi regime in particular, corrupted the emancipatory potential of intercourse. They impressed all aspects of life into the service of the state and turned peacetime into a prelude to war. Facing a new political form that looked upon "war rather than peace as the normal law of life," as historian Edward Mead Earle put it, American elites struggled to see how totalitarian concepts of international law and order could be made commensurable with those of the liberal democracies.[76]

The totalitarian challenge also discredited "public opinion," understood as a sanction that could enforce international law without resort to economic or military punishment. Two crises compelled internationalists to make a decisive choice between moral and physical sanctions, the dilemma they had papered over in 1919, hoping never to have to face.[77] First, Japan conquered resource-rich Manchuria from 1931 to 1933. When the League ordered Japan to leave, Japan left the League instead. Then, in 1935, Italy invaded Ethiopia, a member state of the League. The League imposed economic sanctions that failed to blunt the Italian advance. Now, for the first time, the League of Nations was widely called an instrument for "collective security," as if it had been so intended all along.[78] The League, that is, was viewed as a vehicle for imposing material sanctions, whether economic or military, against aggressors. From Geneva, Arthur Sweetser, a well-connected American journalist serving on the League's Secretariat and Information Section, knew better. "The League has entered into a wholly new field," he reported as the Council scrambled to apply economic sanctions against Italy.[79] As the Italian Army completed its conquest, the lesson seemed undeniable. "Conciliation without force," Sweetser wrote, "is ineffective."[80]

It was a small step from there to condemn alternatives to force as dangerous conceits. In April 1940 Shotwell told CBS Radio listeners: "Reliance upon the public opinion of mankind to ensure peace serves only to entice the law breaker to go ahead with his plans in the confidence that peace-loving nations will not interfere."[81] But even after World War II broke out in Europe, it would take a larger step to specify the implications of Shotwell's principle for U.S. foreign policy. Over the past five years, among the most aggressive measures advocated by League supporters was that the United States not interfere with sanctions that the League was flailing in providing. As a concept, internationalism was changing. As a foundation for policy, however, the new internationalism offered no clear replacement for the old.

"PRACTICALLY ALL THE LEAGUERS STAND FOR [U.S.] intervention," Borchard noted in September 1939 as the Nazis invaded Poland to begin the Second World War in Europe.[82] In fact, few Americans, League advocates included, wanted the United States to become a belligerent quite yet. Over the 1930s Borchard nevertheless came to regard the logical conclusion of pro–League of Nations agitation to be a policy of universal intervention— *universal* because under the League of Nations Covenant and the Kellogg-Briand Pact every armed conflict would henceforth feature a lawbreaker, and *intervention* because military force now appeared to be the only sure method of punishment.[83] Borchard might have added that League boosters decreasingly kept faith with the League of Nations itself. In 1938 President Franklin D. Roosevelt was one of many former enthusiasts who asked whether the League should withdraw from overt politics, retaining only its sections of technical experts.[84] Shotwell and Wright now searched for some way for armed sanctions to be meted out on a regional basis while the League provided moral sanctions alone.[85] Their vision of internationalism was becoming unmoored from the aim of ending power politics through peaceful intercourse and fixed to a new anchor: the creation of "world order," ultimately by force of arms.[86]

But world order did not necessarily require the United States to enforce it. Throughout the 1930s, even those who still hoped to get the United States into the League of Nations also hoped to keep the United States out of war. The European democracies would shoulder the heaviest burdens of collective security, and the United States at best would not stand in their way. In any case, the American public wanted no part of a future war. From 1935 to 1937, the peace movement reached the height of its popularity in the United States, rallying an estimated twelve million adherents in cities, churches, and universities.[87] This time, unlike in World War I, the United States proved willing to sacrifice certain traditional neutral rights so as to avoid having to defend them by force. Starting in 1935, Congress passed a series of Neutrality Acts that automatically embargoed certain exchanges to all parties at war—even victims defending themselves from aggression. At their most restrictive, the acts banned the export of arms, extension of loans, and travel of citizens to belligerent nations. Neutrality advocates wished to avoid the kinds of officially impartial exchanges that they believed to have dragged the United States into the First World War.[88]

Advocates of collective security, Roosevelt included, countered by proposing to make the neutrality acts discriminatory, meaning that they would grant the president discretion to designate which belligerent was an aggressor and should be embargoed, while leaving the other party unaffected and thus effectively aided. In this way the United States could coordinate its diplomacy with collective sanctions without seeming to validate the fears of such critics as Kansas senator Arthur Capper, who warned against "compelling us to police the world."[89] In 1937, after an embargo applied impartially against both sides in the Spanish Civil War served to benefit the fascist rebels, the U.S. Neutrality Acts were modified to allow the president to discriminate between aggressors and victims. Still, accusations like Capper's stung. They suggested that the Wilsonian quest to end war had morphed into its opposite. In a world bereft of harmonious interests and value systems, collective security might become a recipe for perpetual conflict.

What could be less internationalist than that? As it happened, advocates of collective security formulated an answer: *isolationism*. In the mid-1930s such advocates invented this category as an antonym for *internationalism*, using it to characterize their opponents as wholly antithetical to intercourse among nations. Despite drawing on a long-standing discourse of *isolation*, the *–ism*, connoting a worldview, was new.[90] After debuting in some periodicals in the 1920s, the term *isolationism* remained sporadic in usage until the middle and late 1930s, when it ascended in earnest.[91] On April 1, 1935, Massachusetts representative Allen Treadway uttered "isolationism" for the first time on the floor of Congress—in order to complain about "the false alarm of isolationism," when in fact "there is no such thing."[92] In July 1938 *isolationism* first entered the pages of the *American Historical Review* in reference to the United States;

the historian J. Fred Rippy used the term to describe a U.S. tradition, even though fourteen years earlier he had written a book on the "American policy of isolation" that did not mention "isolationists" or "isolationism" once.[93] The –ism arrived in Walter Lippmann's regular column on March 23, 1939. By then Lippmann took it to be the nation's default foreign policy, stretching "all through American history."[94]

Isolationism, contrary to Lippmann, was just emerging, and it signaled a political realignment. In the previous decade, both supporters and opponents of coercive sanctions got behind internationalist initiatives such as the Kellogg-Briand Pact. The danger of zealous nationalism brought them together. But as the Second World War approached, supporters of sanctions came to regard opponents of them as the real problem—and such opponents, including pacifists, could hardly be understood as aggressive nationalists. Rendered as isolationists, however, advocates of peace could be conceptualized as antithetical to internationalism, the cause they had originally pioneered in the nineteenth century. The new concept, far from offering a neutral description, delegitimized noninterventionists, who immediately perceived the slight. "Isolation and isolationism, a new invention, have been used as cusswords," Borchard objected.[95] If they were cusswords, they functioned by carrying two meanings in particular, one that evoked isolation in space, the other isolation in time.

First, isolationism signified spatial enclosure and separation. It conjured a world without international interaction and a United States confined, in every respect, to its borders. Advocates of collective security affixed the isolationist label to advocates of neutrality, who renounced limited types of intercourse for the purpose of avoiding military involvement in Europe. But isolationism connoted something much more expansive than neutrality. It connoted the rejection of all intercourse everywhere. Isolationism, Secretary of State Cordell Hull warned, would "compel us to confine all activities of our people within our own frontiers."[96] Despite intending only to keep the United States out of war, isolationists stood accused of seeking to "keep us out of everything," as Roosevelt's speechwriter-playwright Robert Sherwood put it, or more precisely of favoring "a policy of walled separation from all contacts with other peoples," in the words of the Chicago Daily Tribune. For favoring peaceful intercourse without force, isolationists qualified as such, whereupon, for being isolationists, they appeared hostile to peaceful intercourse. The concept of isolationism thus destroyed peaceful intercourse as a conceptual possibility. It implied that intercourse required force to back it.

Being a pro-neutrality organ, the *Tribune* retorted that no Americans actually sought to restrict all contact with the outside world.[97] Almost all neutrality advocates—including arch-"isolationist" senators Borah and Johnson—recoiled at the prospect of cutting off all commercial activity with other states and even with belligerent states alone.[98] As a supporter of neutrality legislation, Illinois congressman Everett Dirksen admitted in 1937: "We are still attempting to eat our cake and have it, too. We say we want neutrality, but along with it we want a slice of the profitable trade of belligerent nations."[99] The concept of isolationism, however, ascended precisely because it distorted the people it named. It allowed anti-isolationists to seize the high ground and associate internationalism with the use of force.

Second, *isolationism* conveyed the regression of time in addition to the enclosure of space. The *Wall Street Journal* identified isolationism with "nothing more or less than a retrogression of civilization"; Hull projected that isolationism would "carry the whole world back to the conditions of medieval chaos."[100] Whatever the destination of isolationism's retreat was imagined to be, the concept implied being in the past and being passive. Isolationists were said to be negative, backward, reactive, aloof, blind, and emotional. In short, they sounded incapable of purposive action oriented toward the future, akin to traditional peoples imagined by ideologies of development and modernization.[101] Simply for opposing coercive sanctions, erstwhile internationalists morphed into selfish provincials. Embracing force implicitly became the condition for pursuing harmony among nations.

Isolationism was, then, more than an epithet deployed in political combat to disparage the other side. The concept also, and more importantly, brought into being a positive project: an internationalism that was first and foremost against isolationism. On the surface, the new internationalists stood for free intercourse, world peace, and the good of humankind, just like the internationalists of old. Under the surface, however, lay the novelty of their politics: the acceptance of armed sanctions as the prerequisite of world order. Force reappeared only to those who contested the very concept of isolationism. "To talk of isolation," opined the *Chicago Daily Tribune*, "is dust throwing in an attempt to give greater emphasis of sentiment to the demand for political alliance."[102] Borchard likewise insisted that "there is no such thing as 'isolation.' This is merely a denunciatory word employed by the interventionists who want to line us up with other Powers for war or hostile action."[103] While dismissing the descriptive validity of *isolationism*, the people targeted by the term acknowledged its productive power. Here was a vocabulary through which the United States could engage in the fullest power politics in the name of ending power politics.

In response, opponents of power politics sought to change language as well as laws. Denouncing the "false name—isolationism," historian Charles Beard characterized his preferred policy as "continentalism."[104] Lawyer Jerome Frank championed "integrated America" against "disintegrated Europe."[105] "What you term isolationism I term noninterventionism," Congressman George Holden Tinkham wrote to a constituent.[106] Several politicians, including Senator Arthur Vandenberg, preferred the term *insulationist,* conveying their wish only to insulate the country from war. [107] Yet by the late 1930s the "i" word was sticking, even among those who deplored the category. In a chapter titled "The Policy of Internationalism," Beard himself presented advocates of collective security as the successors of the nineteenth-century peace movement, rather than one successor among others.[108] In 1938 the *Chicago Daily Tribune*'s news writers first used internationalism and isolationism as descriptors even as the paper's editorialists lambasted every step toward war.[109]

On the eve of the Second World War in Europe, American advocates of collective security had turned isolationism into an established category of thought. They had both accepted a policy of global policing and developed a lexicon for presenting it. But they found it easier to formulate the pitch than the program. Having accepted armed force as the guarantor of world order, they could not say which entity would send in the troops. The League of Nations so dramatically failed to deliver collective security that by the time of the Munich Agreement of September 1938, permitting Germany to annex the Sudetenland, European diplomacy had reverted to great-power deal making reminiscent of the post-Napoleonic concert.[110] Abstract, almost hypothetical, anti-isolationism remained a concept in search of an agent to carry it out.

And what of America? According to polls in the final months of 1939, only 17 percent of the American public wanted the United States to enter the war at some stage. Fewer still wished to join it immediately. Strong majorities favored a policy of impartial neutrality in which the Nazis could purchase American exports.[111] Public sentiment aside, few interventionists-to-be imagined that the United States could or should emerge anytime soon as the world's supreme power, projecting its military across the globe. It is true that some elites envisaged the United States one day exercising the "controlling power in western civilization," as Lippmann foresaw in a June 1939 essay titled "The American Destiny." "What Rome was to the ancient world, what Great Britain has been to the modern world, America is to be to the world of tomorrow," he announced.[112] Yet calls to greatness were as concrete as Lippmann got; he said nothing of how, or where, the United States would exercise its "controlling power." For every person who sympathized with Lippmann, furthermore, there were more who agreed with Sumner Welles, President Roosevelt's undersecretary of state, close adviser, and future head of postwar planning. Although supporting collective security, Welles still, early in 1939, deemed the main fault of the League of Nations to be its denial of equality to the powers defeated in World War I.[113] If the next world order required stronger provisions for subduing aggressors, more important for Welles was a mechanism for "peaceful change" to satisfy have-not nations so they did not need to resort to violence.[114]

At any rate, the world already had a leader in Great Britain. Despite nursing a decades-long hope of bringing the United States to their side in the global balance of power, British officials saw their entreaties rebuffed as the war neared. At the beginning of 1939, Lord Lothian, soon to be ambassador to the United States, visited the White House to tell the president that "Anglo-Saxon civilization" needed a new guardian. As Roosevelt dismissively recounted, Lothian, an apostle of worldwide Anglophone unity, proclaimed "that the scepter of the sword or something like that had dropped from their palsied fingers—that the U.S.A. must snatch it up—that F.D.R. alone could save the world—etc., etc." Roosevelt was not in a world-saving mood. "I got mad clear through," he recalled, denouncing British despair. Unless it regained the will to lead the world, "Britain would not be worth saving anyway," he concluded. "What the British need today is a good stiff grog, inducing not only the desire to save civilization but the continued belief that they can do it."[115] The president of the United States preferred British world leadership to a Pax Americana: let them bear the brunt. What Great Britain had been to the modern world, Great Britain would remain to the world of tomorrow.

Most American foreign policy elites agreed with Roosevelt. As long as Europe and Asia stayed politically divided and Britain continued to be on top, they perceived little U.S. interest in joining the upcoming war, much less in pursuing supremacy in the postwar period. Fascists and militarists may have promised new orders for their regions, but word was not deed, especially when the superior Anglo-French alliance stood in the way. Before the Wehrmacht marched into Poland, American policy elites believed they could have universal intercourse without universal force. They continued to think so for some time after.

GREAT BRITAIN AND NAZI GERMANY had been at war for one week, but Hamilton Fish Armstrong was thinking ahead. On September 10, 1939, Armstrong, a founder of the Council on Foreign Relations (CFR) and the editor of its journal *Foreign Affairs*, telephoned a fellow council member in Washington. Armstrong told Assistant Secretary of State George Messersmith that the United States had been ill prepared for the last peace conference. Two decades before, the U.S. government had come late to planning and poorly coordinated private experts with official policymakers, as Armstrong had personally observed as Princeton University's delegate to the LEP.[116] Armstrong and CFR director Walter Mallory arrived at the State Department two days later with a proposition. The war, they predicted, would strengthen America's global standing and intensify the department's need for expertise. It might even present a "grand opportunity" for the United States to become "the premier power in the world," for which eventuality the foreign policy bureaucracy was scarcely prepared.[117] Perhaps the CFR should plan for the peace while the government dealt with the war?

Messersmith and the meeting's other attendees, Welles and economist Leo Pasvolsky, knew how to accept a good deal. They recognized the truth of Armstrong's suggestion that their short-staffed diplomatic corps could not undertake long-range planning. Day-to-day issues already absorbed the State Department, whose entire professional and clerical staff numbered nine hundred.[118] The department's leadership also feared that postwar planning, if carried out internally, might become public knowledge and raise suspicion that the Roosevelt administration was preparing for war. Better to delegate the task to the CFR men, so long as Armstrong and Mallory could ensure strict confidentiality. This they promptly agreed to do.[119]

Armstrong's proposal won same-day approval because it redressed a vulnerability of the United States. Insulation from the present war, indeed from the historical balance of power, endowed the United States with paradoxical possibilities for the postwar world. America's position between two vast oceans handed it the luxury, unique among great powers, to plan for the future while the belligerents exhausted themselves elsewhere. Yet that same geographical fortune had given Americans insufficient motivation to develop the official

capacity to seize the occasion. If it meant the United States would stay neutral throughout World War II, the United States might not receive a seat at
the peace conference. Recognizing the problem, the State Department formed
a small, short-lived advisory committee at the start of 1940 that sought to
organize the neutral powers to mediate in the war and shape the peace. More
consequential was its collaboration with the burgeoning field of American
semiofficialdom, the CFR in particular. Over the next six years of war, experts
outside the government acted as a proto-national security state, furnishing officials with knowledge and personnel.

The CFR had little trouble gathering money and talent for its postwar
planning project, titled Studies of American Interests in the War and Peace
(or War and Peace Studies for short). The project ultimately sent 682 memorandums to policymakers at a cost of $300,000, financed by the Rockefeller
Foundation.[120] On its inception it could draw on three decades of efforts to
construct a U.S. foreign policy elite, able to advise officials, educate the
public, and, not least, replicate itself.[121] The project's roster read like a cross-
section of this elite, and many of the almost one hundred participants, spread
over four groups, stood at the forefront of their professions. Heading the Economic and Financial Group were both the "American Keynes," Harvard
economist Alvin Hansen, and the leading neoclassical economist of the day,
Jacob Viner, of the University of Chicago. The Political Group was chaired
by international businessman Whitney Shepardson; the Territorial Group by
prominent geographer Isaiah Bowman, the president of Johns Hopkins University; and the Armaments Group by corporate lawyer Allen Dulles and *New
York Times* military analyst Hanson Baldwin.[122] CFR president Norman H.
Davis, a close adviser to Hull, led the entire project and along with Armstrong, the vice chair, coordinated with the State Department to make sure
the studies addressed official needs.[123] The State Department, in turn, would
make CFR planners into the backbone of the official postwar planning committee that it set up after Pearl Harbor.

The trajectory of unofficial internationalists into the corridors of power
has led some analysts to interpret this history along almost conspiratorial
lines. After the victory of popular isolationism following World War I, they
suggest, elites organized outside the state in order to hasten the day when
they could realize the interests of private capital in U.S. global leadership.[124]
Such a reading, however, credits elite institution builders with more pre-
science than they possessed. In the 1920s they created institutions as much
to forge connections abroad, in the North Atlantic and the Far East, as to

influence policy formation at home. The two largest philanthropic organizations, the Carnegie Endowment and the Rockefeller Foundation, sent millions of dollars to Geneva, funding the League of Nations' work on health, economics and finance, and intellectual cooperation.[125] Carnegie and Rockefeller money also supported the creation of the three largest foreign relations institutes in the United States: Armstrong's CFR, Buell's Foreign Policy Association, and the Institute of Pacific Relations, part of an international federation in the Far East.[126] Internationalist but not anti-isolationist, these groups aimed to foster peace by cultivating public opinion at elite and popular levels. As Butler characterized the Carnegie Endowment's guiding assumption, "The real obstacle still to be overcome is that which prevents public opinion from controlling the policy of governments. When that can be accomplished, peace will be secured."[127]

From the beginning, the CFR was the institute most oriented toward shaping official policy, and the crisis of the 1930s convinced others to follow its lead. After spending the 1920s as a critic of imperialism in the Middle East, Earle set up the nation's first "grand strategy" seminar at the Institute for Advanced Studies in Princeton. In New Haven, Connecticut, a cadre of young scholars established what they called the "power school," officially the Yale Institute for International Studies. Together the two institutes trained dozens of policy intellectuals who became influential after World War II. They reoriented American scholarship away from the fields of international law and organization and toward those of geopolitics and military conflict.[128] It would be Earle's 1943 volume *Makers of Modern Strategy* that turned Kennan into a practitioner of grand strategy.[129]

Yet members of the institutes hardly envisioned the United States attaining global military supremacy before 1940. If anything, they sought to circumscribe America's world role more sharply than before. The Yale Institute's scholars generally argued for hemispheric boundaries on U.S. political and military power. As one argued, the United States was "the safest country on the face of the earth," secure within the Western Hemisphere, and would only squander its wealth by pursuing "power politics in distant parts of the world."[130] Earle reached comparable conclusions about grand strategy. As late as 1939 he affirmed that the United States, shielded by the oceans, could abstain from military competition in Europe and Asia. "For the moment," he wrote, "a balance-of-power policy seems to be outside the realm of practical possibility, even if it were otherwise desirable." And such a policy was decidedly not desirable. Invoking the nineteenth-century British internationalist

Richard Cobden, Earle detected "something intrinsically abhorrent in the balance of power as such."[131] Even after repudiating the utopian aspirations of internationalism, the new aficionados of power politics arrived at familiar prescriptions for U.S. foreign policy.

So too during the so-called Phoney War for the first eight months of World War II: the postwar planners in the State Department and CFR found themselves following nineteenth-century formulas of commerce, mediation, and disarmament. Despite all the uncertainties of the war, the one prognostication on which planners felt they could rely was that the United States would honor its tradition of withholding political-military power from Europe and Asia. "Military and political tie-ups are taboo" was how the CFR's Political Group summarized its study of American public opinion.[132] Top State Department officials made the same assumption at the end of 1939 when they assembled the Advisory Committee on Problems of Foreign Relations, a fifteen-person group chaired by Welles until its dissolution in the summer of 1940.[133] At the first meeting, everyone agreed: "participation of the United States in a political unity such as the League of Nations is probably impossible," as Assistant Secretary of State Adolf Berle put it.[134] Even Assistant Secretary of State Breckinridge Long, the one planner who expressed disagreement with a "policy of aloofness from European political problems," rejected the possibility of U.S. membership in a postwar international organization.[135]

In part, this restriction was imposed on the planners by public opinion. But they did not disagree with it. While abhorring fascism as well as communism, they judged the U.S. stake in overseas war and peace along lines that harked back to the Napoleonic Wars: let Europe quarrel, to America's profit. Prior to May 1940 none of the State Department and CFR planners dwelled on the possibility that Germany might conquer the European Continent and threaten the British Empire. Nor did the slow-moving events of the Phoney War disprove the lesson of World War I that defense tended to trump offense. In any case, the Anglo-French alliance seemed clearly to boast military strength and political solidity superior to that of the German-Soviet team of enemies effectuated by the Molotov-Ribbentrop Pact of August 1939, when the Nazis and the Soviets agreed not to attack one another as they gobbled up Poland.[136] Italy and Japan, for their part, remained neutral toward Germany, not yet constituting the tripartite Axis.

To some planners, in fact, the danger lay in too hasty and complete a victory by Britain and France. The CFR's economists worried that the Allies could parlay wartime trading arrangements into a postwar bloc that would discriminate against the United States.[137] Berle, writing in his diary, condemned a potential Anglo-French trade bloc as "really nothing different from the German *Grossraumswirtschaft* [*sic*]."[138] Although others did not go so far, Berle's equivalence underscored the difficulty of glimpsing the faintest outlines of the postwar world and of America's interests in it. A frustrated Hugh Wilson, the vice chair of the advisory committee, admitted, "The future is so uncertain, the course of the war so problematical, and the atmosphere in which peace negotiations may take place so unknown."[139] The uncertainties did not prevent Berle from having a nightmare that the Russo-German combination would win the war and force the United States to defend the Americas for the rest of his lifetime—but the reverse scenario, of the United States triumphing with the Allies and extending its dominance across the globe, was apparently too far-fetched for Berle to dream.[140]

Expecting a drawn-out stalemate, and wary of a decisive victory by either side, the Roosevelt administration planned for peace with Hitler in the first half of 1940. It reprised the Wilsonian formula of "peace without victory," seeking a mediated settlement in Europe that would secure for the United States a maximum of peaceful intercourse at a minimum of political commitment. On January 11, the State Department planners convened and pursued Roosevelt's desire to "intervene as a kind of umpire" in the European conflict.[141] This became the committee's reason for being: to gather a conference of neutrals— including fascist Italy—that would set forth principles of a new world order and bring all belligerents to the negotiating table.[142] In February the committee sent messages to forty-five neutral nations in order to ascertain their interest in a scheme for international economic cooperation and worldwide arms reduction. (Messages were prepared for Japan and the Soviet Union but not sent.)[143] Later that month, Roosevelt dispatched Welles to Europe, where the undersecretary met with leaders in Berlin, London, Paris, and Rome.[144] Although Roosevelt publicly downplayed expectations for what he called a fact-finding mission, the *Baltimore Sun* came closer to the mark, reporting that Welles was assessing prospects for a "peace without victory."[145]

While in Europe, Welles floated the postwar proposals that his planners were developing—proposals with a pedigree in the annals of American internationalism. Welles's State Department committee wished to reestablish world trade, preferably through some kind of international economic organization, but they planned to join economic universalism with political regionalism and military disarmament.[146] The United States would not make security commitments beyond the "natural unit" of its Pan-American sphere.[147] In Europe, the planners fantasized, states would stop fighting, disarm, and join a regional organization that would keep the peace through an international air force. Even though the proposal elicited snickers in European capitals, Welles continued to host discussions on airborne police until May, perhaps because a supranational force was the only way to have collective security and national disarmament at once.[148] Those goals seemed unimpeachable, no matter how infeasible, so long as the United States was content to leave the politics of Europe to Europeans.

Most of the CFR planners also reverted to Wilsonian and pre-Wilsonian defaults in the face of geopolitical uncertainty. The military experts in Allen Dulles's Armaments Group, including General George V. Strong from the U.S. Army's War Plans Division, got to work by wringing their hands over all the conceivable outcomes the wars in Europe and Asia might bring. In their first memorandum, they paused to wonder whether the United States could expect the "mounting expansion of our military establishments, *no matter what the outcomes of the present wars may be?*"[149] Yet they decided to suppose for planning purposes that the postwar world would embark on general disarmament, despite admitting that this was only one possible outcome, no more likely than others. As the Nazis marched into Denmark and Norway in April, they proceeded to catalog proposals for disarmament spanning from the ancient Greek prohibition on poisoning wells to Winston Churchill's suggestion in 1913 of a one-year "holiday" from building new naval warships.[150]

More than pioneering fresh policies, postwar planners were reverting to pre–twentieth century patterns, in which the United States promoted universal trade, disarmament, and arbitration while Europe policed itself. Two decades into the League experiment, world organization was discredited and planners hardly considered its revival. Outside the government, the chief supporters of the League were equally unenthusiastic. After the war began, Shotwell ended his four-year tenure as president of the League of Nations Association in order to form and chair the Commission to Study the Organization of Peace (CSOP).[151] CSOP was the most prominent nongovernmental group to publicize postwar proposals, and in the spring of 1941, its dozens of mostly academic members attempted to draft blueprints for a new world order. The effort, however, only revealed the muddle in which these nominal internationalists found themselves. Having lost faith in public opinion as the basis of international order, they faced an unwelcome choice: get the League out of high politics, reducing it to social and economic activities, or espouse coercive sanctions, shorn of past illusions that force, once pledged, would not need to be used.

To some CSOP members, like the corporate lawyer and future secretary of state John Foster Dulles (the brother of Allen), a "merely consultative" League represented the most that could be achieved and the one scheme America might join.[152] In April 1940 Shotwell himself suggested CSOP might advocate a League devoted solely to economic and social work.[153] The suggestion did not satisfy Quincy Wright, who headed CSOP's internal effort to develop a program and refused to temper his ambition to transcend power politics. "We must get at the crux of the matter and deal with the problem of security," Wright wrote. He criticized "the welfare people" for repeating the mistaken assumption of the 1920s that cooperation in nonpolitical areas would trickle up.[154] Yet the problem of security had no answer, as Wright came close to admitting. "In the present state of public opinion," he wrote, effective international organization required "overwhelming force," but it was impossible to say from where the force would come, much less how the force could be regulated.[155]

Unable to compose detailed blueprints, CSOP offered vague public pronouncements through the end of 1940. A sense of failure and resignation replaced the creativity of League supporters from the interwar period. The historian William Langer, a CFR planner, reflected on the prevailing mood in early April. "I think most of us who experienced the last war," during which Langer had served in the Army, "are still rather in the position of not being able to grasp this new catastrophe." Langer placed himself and his colleagues at the shattering end of an era: "Those who hoped for the ultimate success of international organization cannot help but despair somewhat of human nature."[156]

The halfhearted Wilsonianism of the State Department, most CFR planners, and CSOP did produce one dissenter: the CFR's Economic and Financial Group. Like the others, the economic experts perceived a trend toward a "world of blocs" combining customs unions and currency areas. Unlike the others, however, they regarded this eventuality as more or less inevitable and not so bad. In contrast to artificial groupings of nations, an economic bloc, they thought, formed around a "common cohesive interest," whether "common culture, emotional ties, close economic relationship, or contiguity."[157] It provided a solid basis for order. The economists recommended that instead of associating with a disparate set of neutrals, the United States ought to orient itself economically as well as politically within the Pan-American system.

Such a hemispheric limitation on U.S. activities was not optimal, conceded Viner, the group's cochair. A world of blocs would not permit the degree of economic specialization of a unified world. But Viner thought blocs might well improve prospects for peace.[158] Calling blocs "a form of world organization," he envisioned a Pan-American bloc coexisting with an Anglo-French bloc (incorporating the empires and the sterling area) and a German-Italian bloc (including the Danube River area and possibly Scandinavia, Turkey, and even Russia).[159] This vision of blocs remained highly speculative. It ignored Asia except by way of the British and French empires. It was conceived in disregard of its palatability in U.S. domestic politics. Its exponents did, however, articulate a clear alternative to neo-Wilsonian planning: a roughly autarkic principle for military defense, political affiliation, and economic integration. For the moment, this principle suggested that all dimensions of U.S. foreign relations center on the Western Hemisphere, but its logic dictated that if America's trading area were to expand, its political-military area would have to keep pace.

On the Eve of the Invasion of France

At the beginning of May 1940, as Hitler prepared to order his forces westward, American observers were interpreting world events through a new matrix of concepts that took "isolationism" to be the gravest danger. The destruction of international law and norms, dizzyingly executed over the past five years, challenged Americans' assumption that power politics could and would be transcended. As yet, however, their apparent intellectual error had inflicted minimal costs on the United States. Judging U.S. security and prosperity to be largely unaffected by the political configuration of Europe and Asia, foreign policy elites did not translate changed assumptions into a positive program. The tenets of nineteenth-century internationalism continued to serve American interests well. The United States would pursue peaceful intercourse on the cheap while encouraging other powers to settle their differences and reduce their armaments.

As they searched for a way to rebuild world order, U.S. foreign policy elites concluded that any effective system of security required force behind its word. Yet what if one of the enforcers were Nazi Germany—or an Anglo-French bloc that cut the United States out of trade? What, anyway, was neutral America's leverage for shaping the peace? Too many circles needed squaring, one planner confessed: "I have made several attempts to get onto paper my conceptions of world order and have destroyed the results since I found they tended to be too specific."[160] The State Department's postwar committee disbanded after May 1940.

As one historian writes, the proposals of the short-lived official planning operation were "extraordinary and fantastic"—and struck its participants as such.[161] It is notable, then, that U.S. global supremacy was *not* among the extraordinary, fantastic options that planners entertained. The closest the planners came was when they suggested that if the Allies faced defeat, the United States would probably need to send its navy and air force to Europe. In this discussion, they contemplated a limited intervention in the war, but they said nothing about keeping the United States militarily committed after the fighting. Their concern was more immediate: Welles feared that "when the American people might be ready to act it might be too late to save the Allies."[162] As Welles implied, the improbable scenario of Allied calamity could unsettle the political consensus in the United States, although to what effect was difficult to say. Langer offered a similar assessment. He reported to his British colleague that Americans wholly sympathized with the Allies but equally resolved to stay out of war. "What may happen if you meet with disaster," Langer wrote, "no one can tell."[163]

At the time, well-informed participants like Welles and Langer could not tell how the United States would respond to Nazi victories. Their perception deserves to be taken seriously. No one *could* tell. Harry Elmer Barnes, however, had an idea. To Barnes, a prolific historian and public intellectual, so-called internationalists revealed their militaristic potential when they represented Barnes and his associates as isolationists. When CSOP formed, Barnes noticed that the commission excluded noninterventionist peace organizations as it undertook its supposedly objective studies. Together with his colleagues in the Keep America Out of War Congress, he wrote caustically that CSOP's members were attempting "with unlimited funds to set themselves up as the sole guardians of peace." "In the end," he projected, "the interventionist approach to peace will seem the only way."[164]

Although even Barnes did not foresee the interventionist approach leading to the global military dominance of the United States, his vision was prescient. Already in place as the Phoney War ended was a novel conceptual structure for discrediting America's traditional commitment to nonentanglement, if not yet for making global supremacy the privileged alternative. This structure grouped, under the black flag of isolationism, all opponents of the armed enforcement of world order. It made an isolationist out of critics of great-power dominance like the journalist Frank Simonds, who condemned the League of Nations as a Holy Alliance through which the strong maintained "their pleasant but precarious possession of the fruits of past conflicts."[165] It made an isolationist out of advocates of world peace like Borchard, who devised plans to eliminate the causes of war through arbitration and international control of the distribution of raw materials; like Theodore Burton, who as president of the American Peace Society, founded by Ladd, introduced the first neutrality legislation in Congress; and like Indiana representative Louis Ludlow, who proposed a constitutional amendment that in 1938 gained nearly 50 percent support in the House of Representatives and would have required a popular vote to issue a declaration of war, except in cases of armed invasion, because if other countries did the same, Ludlow believed, "wars would be brought to an end."[166] These internationalists, so considered by prewar standards, possessed the intellectual resources to believe the United States could make positive contributions to the world without dominating it by force. For a long time, the makers and shapers of American foreign policy had possessed those resources too.

2

WORLD WAR FOR WORLD ORDER, MAY–DECEMBER 1940

SIX DAYS AFTER GERMAN TANKS AND PLANES began to sweep across the Low Countries and around France's vaunted Maginot Line of defenses, Franklin D. Roosevelt lay awake confronting what he described as a "crashing truth": France was lost to Nazi Germany. Surely Britain would follow, perhaps along with its fleet. Before long "we would have nothing between us and some pretty hostile Germans except the deep Atlantic," Roosevelt mused to his assistant secretary of state, Adolf Berle. "It was interesting to see what came into your mind at a time like this."[1] Berle, no great Anglophile, nevertheless equally perceived enormous implications in the precarious position of the British Empire—implications the American people had to face. "I suppose it comes hard to realize that the foundations of the order of things as you know it may have ceased to exist," he reflected in his diary.[2]

Popular outcry was not long in coming. Five days later Berle observed a "steady wave of hysteria" developing across the country and exceeding anything he recalled from World War I.[3] By the end of June, Congress approved a multiyear military buildup of vast proportions. The U.S. Navy, currently stationed only in the Pacific, would now span two oceans and become the world's largest. More drastic still, Congress instituted the first-ever draft in peacetime. Conscription promised to swell the ranks of the U.S. Army, which then ranked nineteenth in size, smaller than the Dutch Army.[4] These measures arguably constituted the most sweeping military expansion in U.S. history outside wartime. And they "could not even have been contemplated two months before," as the British Foreign Research and Press Service, charged with monitoring U.S. opinion, reported back to the U.K. Foreign Office.[5]

In the popular memory of World War II, the fall of France in May–June 1940 pales in significance to the Japanese attack on Pearl Harbor eighteen months later. The latter readily assimilated into the national mythology as a sneak attack on Americans (more precisely, military installations in the U.S. territories of Hawaii and the Philippines) and the singular event that brought the United States into the war. Contemporaries, however, experienced at least as great a shock from the five-week implosion of the world's strongest army. Until then, Americans had regarded the defeat of Britain and France as an "abstract problem and one that probably would never actually confront us," Yale University's president, Charles Seymour, confessed in June.[6] Although the Nazis had mounted a springtime invasion of Scandinavia, it was quite another thing to see them strike at the heart of the global balance of power and goose-step down a deserted Champs-Élysées. All of a sudden, Adolf Hitler seemed to have achieved what no one since Napoleon had gone far in attempting: mastery of Europe. If Britain fell next, totalitarian powers would control Europe and Asia.

In the U.S. State Department, officials abandoned all hope of rallying neutral states to broker a negotiated peace and install a liberal international order of trade, disarmament, and regional political organization. The department disbanded its postwar planning committee at the end of May. The future was too uncertain to be planned, with one exception: the planners agreed at their final meeting that the United States possessed neither the military power nor the public opinion to commit to the "perpetual assumption of protection for spots in remote parts of the world, in other words, a replacement by the United States of the British Empire."[7] The most that could be imagined through the summer was to preserve a U.S.-led Western Hemisphere against the Nazi New Order in Europe.

While the government officials scrambled to guard the hemisphere, however, foreign policy elites largely outside the government systematically considered the president's intuition that Hitler had shattered the premises of U.S. foreign relations. The Nazi bid for *Lebensraum,* they recognized, posed an unprecedented question for the United States: What exactly was America's living space? Until now, the expansion of American influence had seemed not only imperative but forthcoming, appearing in the guise of either "manifest destiny," for territorial acquisition across North America, or the "Open Door," for economic penetration everywhere else. Americans had never before considered the prospect of a solely hemispheric existence, walled off, in every respect, from the rest of the earth.

How they would react was anything but obvious, for traditional ideas of internationalism offered contradictory guidance. On the one hand, internationalism enjoined the United States from entering into entanglements in the Eurasian system of power politics. Had not the Monroe Doctrine, in claiming the Americas for the Americans, left Europe to the Europeans and Asia to the Asians? On the other hand, internationalists had forsworn foreign entanglements in the expectation that peaceful processes—commerce, travel, discussion, and law—would operate beneath the machinations of realpolitik and progressively undermine them. But the fall of France seemed to prove, once and for all, that pacific forms of engagement, and indeed "civilization" itself, would extend only as far as military force permitted. Choices had to be made: not just whether to intervene in the present war but also what kind of peace to seek thereafter, hemispheric or global. Over the next year and a half, foreign policy elites undertook a thoroughgoing reevaluation of America's world role, ultimately concluding that the United States should underwrite international order by securing its own political and military supremacy. The attack on Pearl Harbor marked the culmination of America's decision for dominance, but it did not initiate it.

Traditional accounts of this history depict a slumbering, isolationist United States finally awakening to the Axis threat and preparing, in the run-up to Pearl Harbor, to defend itself and its eventual Allies.[8] But this version of events assumes what needs to be explained: the judgment by U.S. elites that the changed political configuration of Europe and Asia imperiled the United States and demanded action. Even revisionist interpretations, which question U.S. rationales for mobilizing for war, are unsatisfying because they ascribe narrowly economic motives to policymakers.[9] As the words and deeds of foreign policy elites indicate, they found Axis dominance to threaten neither the territorial safety nor the economic prosperity of the United States. But Axis dominance did pose a different kind of threat—it threatened to stop liberal intercourse from traversing the globe and the United States from driving world history. Such a threat proved unacceptable to U.S. elites, who had previously expected to enjoy increasing international exchange and U.S. influence without the incessant resort to force. Rather than react defensively and belatedly to an objective threat, as most narratives of this period presuppose, U.S. elites did nearly the opposite. They expanded their definition of national security, deeming the United States to possess an overriding interest in avoiding "isolation" within the Western Hemisphere. Peering far into the future, they determined that the only way for the United States to avoid such isolation would be to enforce world order as the supreme military power on earth.

Learning from Hitler, Summer 1940

"Adolf Hitler is not aiming solely nor even chiefly to win for Germany a conqueror's glory," declared a Kansas newspaperman. "He represents a new world order."[10] Better than subsequent historians did, William Allen White articulated the stakes of the fall of France as U.S. political and intellectual elites perceived them. The stakes were hardly limited to stopping Nazi Germany in the present war, even though that was the proximate purpose of the organization White headed, the Committee to Defend America by Aiding the Allies (CDA), which formed in a flash as the Nazis neared Paris. The CDA immediately declared itself to be established "for the duration of this world war and for the peace that shall follow the war."[11] As the leading interventionist group in the United States, the CDA conjoined the objective of gaining U.S. participation in the world war to that of gaining U.S. participation in the postwar world.[12] To interventionists, these causes were two sides of the same anti-isolationist coin. The CDA's infrastructure reflected its vision. The CDA got its mailing list from the former enthusiasts of the League of Nations in the Commission to Study the Organization of Peace (CSOP), which publicized postwar proposals. CSOP's scholar-networkers James Shotwell and Quincy Wright sat on the CDA's national policy board. Clark Eichelberger, the longtime director of the League of Nations Association, served in the CDA's number-two position and would later become its chairman. As Wright described the division of labor, the CDA focused on the "immediate objectives" and CSOP the "ultimate objectives."[13]

Born of the panic of the summer of 1940, the CDA became the most popular group to urge that the United States prioritize supporting the Allies, through aid if not outright co-belligerency, over keeping out of war. The CDA amassed six hundred chapters nationwide by the beginning of August, after which noninterventionists set up the America First Committee to advance their position that the United States should defend the entire Western Hemisphere from outside attack but should go no further.[14] White and his CDA were not operating in a vacuum. A range of elites—officials in the State

Department and the military, expert planners in the Council on Foreign Relations (CFR), and academics at Princeton's military strategy seminar and the Yale Institute for International Studies—reoriented their work in response to Hitler's conquests.

But why was the fall of France cause for frenetic mobilization? Americans were not reacting straightforwardly to an external threat. Hardly anyone at the time regarded an attack on North America as more than a distant prospect, even if Britain fell.[15] "We shall not be invaded," Walter Lippmann stated flatly in his column in the middle of May.[16] Although some interventionists conjured vivid but highly speculative scenarios of a German attack on the United States, often by way of economic subversion in Latin America, most conceded that Panzer tanks were not about to roll through Washington, DC.[17] The Atlantic Ocean would thwart an invading army unless it gained land bases from welcoming hosts nearby. Moreover, the advent of air power fortified the defense of coastlines more than it aided an invasion from the seas. Down to Pearl Harbor, this was a central argument of Colonel Charles Lindbergh, the aviator who gained fame for making the first nonstop transatlantic flight in 1927 and acted as a spokesperson for the America First Committee in 1940 and 1941. His interventionist opponents largely conceded the point.[18]

Confident in the safety of the continental United States, U.S. foreign policy elites experienced Hitler's conquests instead as a crisis of what they called world order. Germany, Italy, Japan, and the Soviet Union had already revised and discredited the rules established by the Treaty of Versailles after World War I, but until May 1940 the world's most powerful empires, the British and the French, remained intact. Now, in a stroke, Hitler had swept the old order away. If he seized Britain, he would hold the reins of world leadership. The Nazis were "interested in domination and in supplanting both Britain and America as [the] Number One power in the world," Raymond Leslie Buell, the former research director of the Foreign Policy Association, wrote to his colleagues in the new Post-War Committee of Henry Luce's Time Inc. publications.[19] Or as Roosevelt repeatedly underscored, Hitler sought "world domination," first in Europe and then everywhere else.[20]

It was the specter of a Nazi-led world order, a fear for the fate of international society in general rather than the security or prosperity of North America, that drove most U.S. foreign policy elites to expand their definition of U.S. interests and responsibilities. The United States, they determined, should not tolerate a world in which totalitarians possessed preeminent power. In the summer of 1940, U.S. elites expressed their reasoning in two distinct registers, which elaborated on the conceptualization of *isolationism* that they pioneered in the 1930s and now attached to the projection of an Axis-dominated Europe and Asia. One register warned against "isolation" in space: the United States should not confine peaceful, liberal exchange to its own hemisphere. The other register warned against "isolation" in time: the United States could not fulfill its mission to usher the world toward a better future if totalitarianism held the advantage. Americans might be safe and prosperous even if Britain fell, but it was objectionable enough for the United States to be "isolated," with liberal, American-style activities and friendly governments confined to one hemisphere. In this way the intellectual foundations of U.S. global supremacy were fashioned in the summer of 1940, although Germany's unstoppable war machine, and America's conspicuous military weakness, so far prevented supremacy from appearing to be a feasible solution.

Forcing Exchange to Be Free

For U.S. elites, the first problem with a world order led by Germany and the totalitarian powers was that such a world might be closed to U.S. trade and other liberal forms of intercourse. In previous generations, Americans had taken for granted their ability to send goods, money, people, and ideas far and wide without needing to take on corresponding political entanglements. In the words of Thomas Jefferson, the United States sought "peace, commerce, and honest friendship with all nations, entangling alliances with none."[21] But in a world dominated by the Nazis, would it be possible to have intercourse without entanglement? In the wake of the fall of France, foreign policy elites increasingly thought not.

If Britain were to follow France in coming under Nazi rule, the United States could no longer engage in liberal trade on a near-universal scale. Despite the domestic orientation of the U.S. economy, the potential loss of trade troubled U.S. policy elites from the president on down. Lippmann penned one of the most immediate and influential expressions of these concerns. In "The Economic Consequences of a German Victory," appearing in the July issue of *Life* magazine, he helped to convince the head of the Army, General George Marshall, to rethink the hemispheric orientation of the military's war plans.[22] If Hitler defeated Britain, Lippmann argued, totalitarian states would control all the industrial "workshops of the world" except North America— that is, Japan, Russia, and western Europe. To do business with them would resemble "naked soldiers trying to stop a charge of tanks"; individual manufacturers, farmers, and labors could not compete with "gigantic government monopolies managed by dictators and backed by enormous armed force." The result would be a paltry U.S. living space for liberal economic exchange. Lippmann wrote, "We shall be left with Canada and the small republics around the Caribbean as the only region in which we can still do business on equal terms and under something like normal conditions."

Under such circumstances, the United States could, in theory, improve its bargaining position by accepting the governmental organization of trade so as to meet the German monopoly with an American one. But Lippmann dismissed this option out of hand. If Germany held Europe, the United States would lack the bargaining power to trade fairly; and if the United States gained bargaining power by regimenting its economy or that of the hemisphere, it would compromise free-market capitalism. This concession was bad enough. Lippmann's worry, then, was not literally that Germany would completely close Europe off to American trade but rather that it would render the United States less competitive (or less capitalist). Lippmann nevertheless used imagery that opposed American openness to German closure. If the Nazis completed their conquest of Europe, he concluded, the United States would end up "isolated in a totalitarian world."[23]

Noninterventionists, who advocated hemisphere defense, were also alarmed by the fall of France, but they rebutted arguments like Lippmann's that envisioned the United States facing a unified totalitarian front and that deemed such an outcome calamitous for U.S. security. Many noninterventionists disputed the assumption that the totalitarian powers—Lippmann lumped together Nazi Germany and the Soviet Union—would become or remain united rather than fight each other.[24] Some contended that the bargaining position of postwar Germany, dependent on U.S. imports, would actually be weak. If the world divided into economic blocs, the United States, which dominated the most integrated, self-sufficient continent, ought to fare well.[25]

Nevertheless, interventionists routinely equated a prospective Nazi victory in Europe with the inauguration of a durable totalitarian world order, one that would be "closed . . . to normal intercourse."[26] Positioning themselves against closure and for openness, interventionists drew upon the long-standing internationalist aspiration that peoples of the world should engage in the widest possible exchanges across borders, the better to promote peace and harmony. Yet now peace and harmony were nowhere to be found, and interventionists cast those who prioritized avoiding military entanglements—internationalism's other fundamental commitment—as "isolationists" instead. "We are either internationalists or isolationists, and I can see nothing in the future of the United States except absolute ruin of our industrial structure if we become isolationists," wrote Thomas J. Watson, the CEO of International Business Machines, who worked with the Carnegie Endowment for International Peace to develop plans for postwar economic reconstruction.[27]

Over the next eighteen months, this depiction of a closed world would only gain in resonance as the events of the war made its realization less and less likely. Britain's defense of its home isles, Hitler's invasion of the Soviet Union, and European resistance to Nazi rule all diminished the prospect that Germany would establish long-term domination over Europe, let alone head up a cohesive totalitarian order. But the fall of France seemed to lay bare the nature of international politics; interventionists were implicitly arguing not so much that all of Eurasia *would* fall under totalitarian rule than that it *could*, now or in the future. By early 1941 the presidential candidates of both political parties from the previous autumn justified U.S. aid to Britain in terms of global economic openness and closure. Wendell Willkie, an industrialist who ran on the Republican ticket, insisted that the United States must build an "open world" in opposition to the "closed world" of the Axis. Roosevelt, who beat Willkie to secure an unprecedented third term as president, likewise declared that "freedom to trade is essential to our economic life." The United States could not tolerate a "Nazi wall to keep us in."[28] While making a variety of arguments as to why Americans would suffer economically, what Roosevelt and other interventionists emphasized above all was the need to avoid isolation as such. They thereby suggested that a world environment open to liberal intercourse, once a mere preference and expectation, was itself a U.S. vital interest, worth defending by force.

Behind closed doors, too, the fall of France compelled Roosevelt's planners to evaluate the minimum area of the world that the United States should guard for the indefinite future. Events were moving too rapidly for far-sighted planning to take place within the government; the State Department wound down its postwar planning committee in May 1940, and the army and navy prepared new war plans confined to hemispheric boundaries.[29] It fell to postwar planners in the CFR to formulate what they described as an "adequate statement of the policy and interests of the United States."[30] By the end of July, the four different CFR groups, often joined by Secretary of State Cordell Hull's adviser Hugh Wilson and several representatives of the military, hesitantly converged on a spatial concept to frame the future of U.S.

The quarter sphere, June–July 1940. In the aftermath of the Nazi conquest of France, postwar planners in the Council on Foreign Relations anticipated that for the foreseeable future the Axis powers would dominate Europe and parts of the Middle East and North Africa. They thought the United States should respond by economically integrating and militarily defending a "quarter sphere" postwar area extending into Brazil.

foreign policy. According to their idea of the "quarter sphere," the United States would economically support, and militarily defend, the area extending from Canada down to the northern portion of South America around where Brazil jutted eastward toward West Africa.[31]

Despite its limited scale, the quarter sphere concept satisfied the basic criteria of the CFR's Economic and Financial Group, namely that a U.S.-led area had to be militarily defensible and require a "minimum of trade dislocation."[32] Alvin Hansen, the Keynesian economist from Harvard University and rapporteur for the group, went so far as to praise the quarter sphere as an "excellent economic unit for the essential defense of the United States," even if Germany were to seize the Dutch East Indies, Japan, and southern South America.[33] To defend the whole hemisphere, the planners judged, would exceed the foreseeable military capacity of the United States, and it would create the problem of how to absorb the surplus goods that the southernmost states of South America typically exported to Europe.

Yet the planners, Hansen included, never regarded the quarter sphere to be desirable from an economic standpoint. They worried that the quarter sphere would likely provide "too small an area for a satisfactory American standard of life."[34] Expanding U.S. defense and trade perimeters to the whole Western Hemisphere, comprehended by the planners as "hemispherical isolation," was no better than sticking with the quarter sphere; it would still result in the loss of almost two-thirds of U.S. foreign trade.[35] In late July the economic planners therefore began to study a larger area incorporating remnants of the British Empire and the Far East. But the stumbling block to such schemes was clear and, so far, insurmountable: it was "the question of our naval power to secure this area for ourselves."[36] In a world led by totalitarian powers, liberal economic exchange would extend only as far as military force would support.

For interventionist elites, then, the fall of France gave entirely new urgency to the lesson of the 1930s that armed force was essential to the preservation of international order, lest totalitarian aggressors conquer new lands and effectively close them off to free exchange. Isaiah Bowman, America's most famous geographer and head of the CFR's Territorial Group, issued new "guiding principles" for postwar planning on May 20. "We cannot relive 1919," wrote Bowman, who had advised Wilson at Paris. "Only force will make and keep a good peace." But who could supply the needed force? Through the summer, with Great Britain struggling to survive and the United States to arm, any answer was too far-fetched to propose. One, however, could be ruled out. Hitler's conquests had driven the nail into the coffin of world organization, still associated with the search for pacific alternatives to the use of force. As Bowman declared in his guiding principles, "The League? Without force it would again become a mere debating society so far as political power is concerned."[37] The belief that public opinion could underpin world order, appearing as a false hope since the mid-1930s, now looked like a perilous delusion.

In CSOP the most ardent League of Nations advocates scarcely disagreed. They determined in June that, in order to be effective, a new world organization would require such "overwhelming force" as to render its defeat "practically impossible." But they could not devise a method that satisfied them, and they kept their blueprints private.[38] Most Americans gave the subject little mind. In June three League of Nations supporters approached Berle for funds to save the League's nonpolitical sections, which handled economics, finance, and transit, by rescuing them from Geneva and transplanting them to Princeton. The assistant secretary of state saw their bid as an attempt to stave off the end of world organization and not as the glimmer of a new dawn. The last-ditch effort marked "a sort of minor revolution," Berle reflected, recalling the triumphant formation of the League in 1919. "To see the fragments wafted our way on the wings of a storm is not the happiest picture in the world."[39] Despite Berle's chagrin, the League advocates left empty-handed, though they would eventually make their way to the Rockefeller Foundation and find the funds they needed.[40]

America's Place in a Nazi World

While U.S. foreign policy elites expressed one objection to a German-led world in the internationalist terms of economics and exchange, they articulated a second objection through an exceptionalist discourse of security and destiny. Isolated from world intercourse, they warned, Americans would also become isolated from world history if the Nazis won. The Depression had already raised the question of whether the future belonged to U.S.-style liberal democracy or totalitarian dictatorship. Now Hitler's conquests threatened to deliver a decisive answer in favor of the latter. In the United States, a chorus of politicians and commentators repeated that if Germany toppled Britain, America would be left "alone in a contemptuous world" (the *Louisville Courier-Journal*), "isolated in a world totally ruled by dictators" (Colonel Henry Breckinridge of the CDA), or "isolated in a world of furious wars and barbaric dictators" (the *Washington Post*).[41] Stuck in place, the United States would not necessarily be attacked, but it would perpetually be on the defensive. America would be on the receiving end of world history.

Stung by Benito Mussolini's decision to ally with Hitler, Roosevelt brought together the spatial and temporal registers of the specter of American "isolation" in a fiery speech he delivered in June 1940 amid France's collapse. Asking what future lay ahead for the American people, the president warned that totalitarians abroad and isolationists at home sought to turn the United States into a "a lone island in a world dominated by the philosophy of force." Such a fate, Roosevelt scoffed, "may be the dream of those still talk and vote as isolationists," but it was really "the nightmare of a people lodged in prison, handcuffed, hungry, and fed through the bars from day to day by the contemptuous, unpitying masters of other continents."[42] As Roosevelt spoke, the United States possessed the world's largest economy and remained unrivaled in its dominance of the entire Western Hemisphere. Roosevelt did not suggest that any of those circumstances would change. Even so, he rendered economic strength and hemispheric supremacy as tantamount to total enclosure, indeed imprisonment. Confined in space if the Nazis won, the United States would also be written out of the future. Like a prisoner, it would become a passive sufferer acted upon by history rather than an agent making history.

Lippmann again provided a rapid and vivid articulation of the emerging interventionist position. On the day after Germany invaded France, he warned that a British defeat would leave America "isolated in a world dominated on both sides of our oceans by the most formidable alliance of victorious conquerors that was ever formed in the whole history of man." Although the United States could "no doubt" protect its forty-eight states from direct invasion, "that is all we can be reasonably sure of doing."[43] America's exceptional identity, as a light to the world, demanded much more. In June Lippmann made explicit what was at stake: whether the United States would preserve its self-image as the font of world history. "Shaken to its very foundations," Lippmann intoned, was "the power to preserve the order of the world in which the American nations were born and have flourished." The United States might be secure if it were a normal nation-state, with an identity coterminous with its territory, but the American project was grander and U.S. security must be defined accordingly. When noninterventionists fixated on the founding fathers' admonitions against foreign entanglements, they overlooked the equally deep-rooted nature of America's mission. "Our generation does not understand the place of America in the great scheme of things," he protested. However American it might be to avoid entanglements, so too, Lippmann implied, was it American to give law and order to the world. Both aspirations expressed an internationalist opposition to power politics and an exceptionalist exemption from the norm. But whereas once avoiding entanglements and ordering the world went together, now Americans had to choose between the two.

For the moment, the course of action Lippmann counseled was to strengthen the U.S. military to enable it to defend the Western Hemisphere, a recommendation that noninterventionists shared. As Lippmann put it, the United States should establish "a citadel so strong in its defenses that by our own example the world can eventually be redeemed and pacified and made whole again." This, he concluded, was "the American destiny."[44] But even while Lippmann prioritized hemisphere defense, he embedded the objective in the globalist aspiration to make the world "whole again," echoing Undersecretary of State Sumner Welles's declaration that "the duty to hold western civilization in trust" now devolved upon the Americas.[45] Lippmann also claimed, almost in passing, that hemisphere defense required naval control of the Atlantic and the Pacific, which in turn required both sides of each ocean to be "ruled by friendly or by weak powers."[46] Tentatively in the summer of 1940, and boisterously later, Lippmann established the political order of western Europe and northeast Asia as a vital U.S. interest.

Not all interventionists in the making assumed that the Nazis or other totalitarian powers would succeed in consolidating their rule and commanding the future; some imagined a world of chaos, an outcome that also warranted global military action by the United States. While most U.S. elites feared a hostile power's domination, Buell, anticipating German-Soviet antagonism, predicted global disorder should the United States fail to act by aiding Britain, entering the war if necessary, and policing the world thereafter. If Americans held back at this moment, he foresaw the whole world descending into a directionless drift lasting one hundred years. The next century, he wrote, would witness "a turbulent sea of transitory political units floating and then sinking—a search for a new balance of power between nations or groups of nations breaking into small bits on the one hand or fusing into larger units on the other." Buell had spent the 1920s seeking to tame the imperialism of the United States and other great powers; now his preoccupation was world anarchy. In order to uphold world order, there was "no price too great for the U.S. to pay," Buell wrote to his colleagues in Luce's Post-War Committee.[47] By the end of June Buell was convinced of the inadequacy of proposals, advanced at a conference of the Institute of Pacific Relations, for U.S. leadership of an "American-Pacific Commonwealth" that would join the Western Hemisphere to all of Britain's Dominions and colonies in the Far East in case Germany conquered the British Isles. For Buell, the priority was for the United States to ally with Britain at once to destroy Nazi Germany, or, if this proved impossible, to form a bloc with Britain and its empire to counterbalance a German-dominated Europe.[48]

The CFR planners were also coming to doubt that the United States should center its defense policy on the Western Hemisphere, whether in whole or in part. Even as they contemplated a quarter sphere living space in case Germany defeated Britain, the Anglophilic planners in the CFR's Political Group upended the ideological basis of hemisphere defense. They contended that the United States enjoyed greater commonality with the British Commonwealth, and white Europeans generally, than with Americans south of the Rio Grande. "Great Britain, Canada, Australia, and even Germany have closer racial ties with the United States than does Latin America," the group reported to the State Department. It was no surprise that war "nearly always" occurred somewhere in Latin America. Anglophone countries, by contrast, were uniquely peaceful and peace-loving, the Political Group claimed, neglecting to mention those countries' many imperial wars against indigenous peoples.[49]

One of the most militant members of the Political Group was Francis P. Miller, the CFR's organizational director who also assembled the Century Group, a circle of interventionists in New York that played a critical role in brokering the agreement in September by which the United States sent destroyer ships to Britain in return for naval bases in the Western Hemisphere.[50] After taking up arms in World War I, Miller had studied international relations and theology at Oxford University on a Rhodes Scholarship.[51] His personal geography mapped his international affinities. A few weeks out from France's collapse, he dismissed the Monroe Doctrine, which had pit the warring, retrograde Old World against the pacific, progressing New World. "Technical advances," he told the planners, "had made obsolete the 'separate universe' idea of the Monroe Doctrine." But Miller emphasized race more than technology. He asked his fellow planners to put a premium on "folk-thinking, namely, a sense of kinship with Canadians, Australians, and New Zealanders."[52] For the moment, such "folk-thinking" warranted narrowing, not widening, U.S. responsibilities by excluding southern South America from the sphere of U.S. defense and trade. But such thinking would become expansionist once Britain appeared likely to survive the Nazi onslaught.

As Miller's folkish phraseology suggests, American observers sometimes expressed a sneaking admiration for Nazi Germany as it reached the apex of its military achievements in the summer of 1940. As the Nazis explained Nazism to their youth, CDA officials wrote, so "we must tell the proper story to our youth."[53] American interventionists often portrayed Germany's dictator as a master of statecraft, prescient, clever, and bold. While America and Britain slept, Hitler meticulously planned his conquests, or so Americans supposed. The seeming decisiveness and foresight of the dictatorships augmented American anxieties from the 1930s that parliamentary democracies might be less capable of acting in an emergency and solving the problems of mass society.[54] In his columns, for example, Lippmann reiterated that Hitler fixed his sights on the future while democratic publics reacted. Americans had to show that "a democracy can and will arm itself effectively while it is still at peace."[55]

The Nazis also taught a lesson about warfare that U.S. elites were keen to learn. In trouncing France, Germany had exhibited the "tremendous advantage of the offense over the defense," General George V. Strong, chief of the army's War Plans Division, told the other CFR planners.[56] The U.S. military had drawn the conclusion from the stalemates of the Great War that defensive operations ruled over offensive ones. Suddenly, military planning based on that assumption counted for nothing. "Everything preceding the 10th of May last is ancient history," Army intelligence chief General Sherman A. Miles announced. Because offense now had the upper hand in the offense-defense balance, Miles concluded that preventing aggression would require obstructing offensive power at its inception, before any aggressive act took place. Miles thus deemed "useless" the previous internationalist methods of pursuing peace by urging states to submit their disputes to bodies of inquiry and then attempting to act collectively against any party that failed to comply.[57] By the time the procedure was followed, the aggression would be accomplished. In time, the judgments of Strong and Miles would be contested by noninterventionists, who cited British resistance against a cross-channel German invasion as evidence that coastlines could still be successfully defended. But the superiority of offense would become a staple of policy elites' thinking and imply that world order required a supreme power itself able to wage offensive war in order to forestall offensive war by others.[58]

In the wake of the fall of France, U.S. elites began to piece together a new vision for foreign policy out of the tatters of traditional internationalism. They figured that if Nazi Germany succeeded in bringing down Great Britain to gain unchallenged control of Europe, the United States would remain territorially secure and economically well off but would face an intolerable situation nonetheless. Rather than unsafe or poor, America would be "isolated," confined in its activities and influence to its own hemisphere or a portion thereof. A Nazi Europe would vitiate certain international ideals—of an open world and an American world—that the United States had always held dear. Preventing this outcome, however, would require not only the accumulation of military strength but also the political will to apply it in violation of another international ideal, that of avoiding extrahemispheric power politics and the perpetual wars that came with it.

Glimpsing Global Supremacy, August–December 1940

While U.S. foreign policy elites rejected an "isolationist" future for the United States, they could not yet devise a satisfying and practicable alternative. On the surface, the historian Charles Beard seemed likely be vindicated in his prediction from early in 1940 that the United States would return to its tried-and-true hemispheric orientation.[59] How to guard the Western Hemisphere was the problem of the summer. It garnered more prominence in public debate and private planning than the issue of whether to aid Britain.[60] In newspapers and magazines, the question was just how much of the Americas the United States could salvage: North America including the Caribbean? The quarter sphere down to Brazil's bulge into the Atlantic? Or the entire hemisphere including South America?

Perceiving the same limits, the Roosevelt administration set out to create a Pan-American cartel that would purchase South American surplus commodities and sell them to a Nazi Europe. The noninterventionists Beard and Gerald Nye, the North Dakota senator who was instrumental in passing the Neutrality Acts, cheered the administration's move. By strengthening the bargaining power of Western Hemisphere countries, the cartel plan intended to make the most of so-called isolation and suggested it might not be so dire. If Germany won the war, the Americas could potentially exchange goods with Europe and, by dictating the terms of trade, still keep Germany from acquiring political influence in South America.[61] The administration's efforts to organize hemisphere defense culminated in the Havana Conference at the end of July. There Latin American states authorized the United States to seize colonies in the hemisphere threatened by a German takeover and rule them through a collectively overseen mandate.[62] Roosevelt's diplomats left Havana triumphant, having united Americans north and south against the Nazi threat. Hemisphere defense had never appeared so vital. Even Roosevelt's destroyer deal, in early September, did not clearly depart from traditional hemispheric objectives. Noninterventionists were delighted to find that the United

States had received ninety-nine-year leases on British bases in the Western Hemisphere, in exchange for sending fifty old destroyers to Britain.[63]

Then the hemisphere idea fell away. British observers scarcely believed their good fortune. "The talk was all of Anglo-American co-operation, rather than of Hemisphere defense," the British monitors of U.S. opinion marveled in October. "The remarkable fact is . . . that so little attention was paid to the Hemisphere idea, even in relation to defense."[64] This shift preceded the presidential-level milestones that historical narratives typically highlight: Roosevelt's election to a third term in November and his announcement over the new year that the United States would serve as the "arsenal of democracy" and stand for "four freedoms" throughout the world.[65] The transcendence of hemisphere defense owed less to the actions of the president than to Britain's performance in the war and its impact on foreign policy elites' projections of the future.

In May and June Nazi Germany forced British troops to evacuate the European Continent. In July it launched the Battle of Britain, unleashing the Luftwaffe to knock out British air defenses and pave the way for a cross-channel invasion. But the Royal Air Force held firm against German fighters and bombers, as did Britain's determination not to negotiate a settlement. From August onward, British resilience demonstrated that Germany might not attain dominance throughout Europe or over the British Empire. This development produced two divergent responses in the United States. One was that Europe and Asia would stay divided, invasions across seas remained ineffectual, and the United States could best ensure its safety by defending the Western Hemisphere. The America First Committee, formed in September, held such a view and advanced it for fifteen months until disbanding after Pearl Harbor.[66]

The other response, favored by most foreign policy elites, was that Britain's survival enabled the United States to act on the lesson of the fall of France: that a hemispheric existence constituted unbearable isolation but remained a possible outcome so long as the United States did not lead and enforce world order. Between August and December 1940, foreign policy elites began to take their aversion to "isolationism" to its logical conclusion. As they worked to recalculate the perimeters of U.S. security, it was principally the prospect of losing intercourse, amid cutthroat geopolitical competition with a projected Nazi Europe, that absorbed officials in government and semiofficial planners. In public articulations, meanwhile, elites stressed that America would lose its place in world history unless it made a bid for world supremacy.

From the Hemisphere to the Grand Area

As British pilots put a halt to Germany's advance, the CFR's postwar planners stopped speaking of the quarter sphere concept that had reigned in June and July. It was apparent that neither interventionists nor noninterventionists would countenance a U.S. retreat from the defense of the entire Western Hemisphere. If the United States conceded any part of South America, one planner noted, the country would decry the decision as a "Munich."[67] Yet the CFR's studies from the summer indicated that the hemisphere was undesirable as an economic unit, and inferior to the quarter sphere. The U.S. economy, if hemispherically bounded, would "suffer severely," the planners asserted more strongly than before.[68] Since the quarter sphere was not enough, and the hemisphere looked even worse, just how much of the world did the United States require?

At the request of the State Department, the CFR's Economic and Financial Group undertook a monumental study of this question from August to October.[69] A more formidable group of liberal economists would have been difficult to assemble. Hansen and his neoclassical rival, Jacob Viner, served as joint rapporteurs. They steered the group as it set out to devise a self-sufficient international space, not dependent on trade beyond its boundaries, for the United States to lead in the postwar world. If this U.S.-dominated area could be made more self-sufficient than the German-dominated area, then the United States would enjoy a strong bargaining position and prevent Germany from expanding its political influence through trade.

The economists thus aimed to achieve a basically geopolitical objective. At the same time, they took almost for granted that capitalist forms of exchange should be preserved, and on the most favorable terms for the United States. As the planners wrote, they sought to "minimize the economic costs of adjustment by the United States economy to the world in which it may function in the future."[70] To this end, they limited the use of government policy to adjust economies to the loss of imports or exports. "We wished to avoid adopting a totalitarian economy," one planner explained.[71] This restriction left only one way to increase the self-sufficiency of the non-German area: add new regions that would absorb surplus exports and supply desired imports. In effect, the price of preserving liberal economies and their maximum prosperity would be borne through "increased military expenditures and other risks," as the group phrased it.[72]

Indeed, it now seemed clear that the velvet glove of commerce required an iron fist inside. The planners at this point anticipated that the war would end in a stalemate approximating the status quo. Britain would blockade the European Continent, while Germany ran a territorial empire sweeping across Europe and into much of North Africa and the Near East. In such a divided world, armed force alone would maintain order within the U.S.-led area and hold Germany at bay. Trade would extend no farther than force allowed, but force would be committed as far as trade necessitated. Economic exchange, previously imagined as free and peaceful—as the very antidote to war—was to become the basis for America's postwar military responsibilities.

Moving commodity by commodity, the planners assembled scores of tables using figures that accounted for more than 95 percent of total world trade in 1937. They separated the postwar world into three regions: German-dominated Europe (including an expansive Mediterranean basin), the Western Hemisphere, and the British Empire and Far East. They further divided the latter into a Pacific basin area (encompassing Australasia, China, India, Japan, and Southeast Asia) and a grouping of Ireland and the United Kingdom along with South Africa.[73] Strikingly, the planners excluded the Soviet Union from their study due to the small size of its foreign trade. They would later regret the decision, but not until the German Army turned eastward in June 1941. Until then, the Soviet Union was cooperating with its ideological enemy and, to boot, technically neutral. U.S. planners did not know how to project the Soviet position in the postwar world. Nazi aims and capabilities, by contrast, seemed all too clear. It was Germany, not the Soviet Union, that provided the foil for American planning.

Distressingly, the data ascribed the greatest self-sufficiency to the German-dominated area and the lowest to the Western Hemisphere. The German area could absorb 79 percent of its exports from 1937 and 69 percent of its imports. For the Western Hemisphere, the numbers were 54 and 65 percent, respectively.[74] The Western Hemisphere sent the rest of the world nearly $3 billion in goods, especially machinery, grains, cotton, petroleum, copper, and cattle products.[75] The planners therefore ruled out postwar U.S. leadership over the hemisphere alone. Even if the United States were to assemble a cartel-like unified seller to market its surplus to the German area, the Western Hemisphere would still depend on trade with Germany more than Germany depended on trade with the Western Hemisphere. A deficient bargaining position would not do. (Not contemplated by the planners was that self-sufficiency might, by the same token, allow Germany to leave the Western Hemisphere alone.)

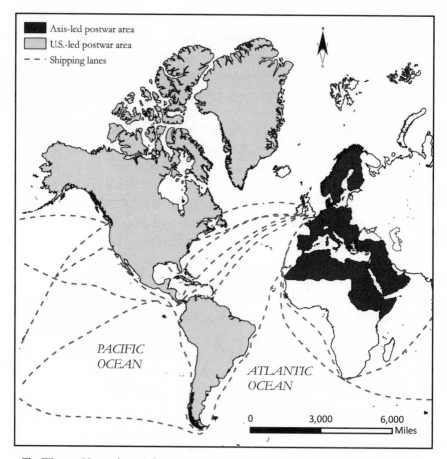

The Western Hemisphere, July–August 1940. Toward the end of the summer, the planners expanded the quarter sphere to the full Western Hemisphere but found it would be less self-sufficient than the Axis-led area.

Next the planners tried integrating the Western Hemisphere with the so-called Pacific basin, a vast grouping that represented the largest commercially significant area available to the United States should Germany successfully invade the British Isles. They included Japan in the Pacific basin; regarding the country as an afterthought in their exceedingly Eurocentric calculus, the planners assumed that Japan, despite being hostile to the United States and three years into its invasion of mainland China, could somehow be folded into the non-German area. The planners found that the U.S. economy would benefit substantially from the addition of the Pacific basin, which contained a large market for U.S. products and constituted the foremost source of such

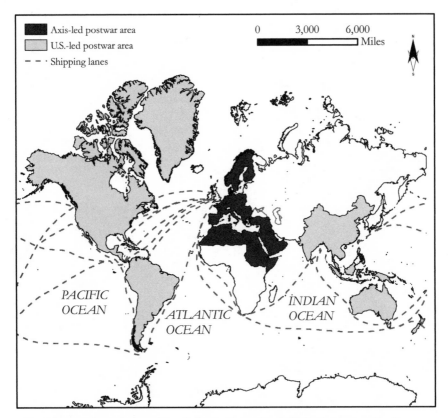

The Western Hemisphere and Pacific basin, September 1940. In September the planners breached the historic hemispheric limitation on U.S. military commitments and considered enlarging the American-led postwar area to encompass a vast section of Asia, including Japan.

crucial raw materials as rubber, jute, and tin.[76] For South America, however, the Pacific basin was more competitive than complementary. Australia, India, and New Zealand exported the same agricultural commodities as did the southern Western Hemisphere countries, especially Argentina. In the cases of meat and grain, Western Hemisphere surpluses would be "seriously aggravated."[77] As a result, the planners rejected the Western Hemisphere–Pacific basin area. Like hemisphere defense, it foundered on the twin priorities of maintaining national and international liberal capitalism (namely, maximizing prosperity while minimizing readjustments) and securing geopolitical advantage (namely, preserving a Western Hemisphere free of German influence and establishing superior bargaining power vis-à-vis Germany).

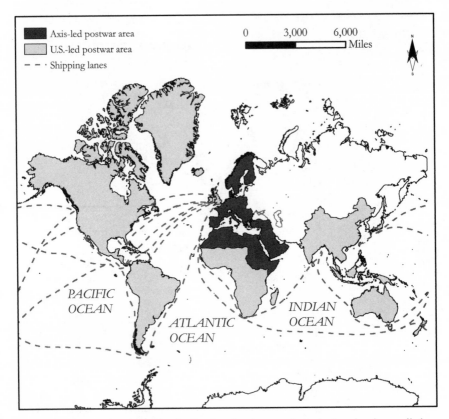

The Grand Area, October 1940. In October the planners devised what they later called the Grand Area: a blueprint for U.S. leadership of the whole world except, for the time being, a projected Axis-dominated greater Europe and a neutral Soviet sphere.

Starting in early September the CFR's Economic and Financial Group hit upon the answer it would proceed to advocate through the middle of 1941: join the Western Hemisphere to the British Empire and the Pacific basin in a "great residual area" embracing the entire non-German world except the Soviet Union. By integrating the United Kingdom, a major importer of agricultural products, the planners went far in solving the problem of surplus exports from South America. They calculated the non-German area, which they later named the Grand Area, to possess "substantially greater" self-sufficiency than German Europe, for it could consume 86 percent of its exports and supply 79 percent of its imports.[78] Finally, after months of study, the planners had discovered that if German domination of Europe endured, the United

States had to dominate almost everywhere else. In their words, "the United States should use its military power to protect the maximum possible area of the non-German world from control by Germany in order to maintain for its sphere of interest a superiority of economic power over that of the German sphere."[79]

No one expressed surprise at this expansive conclusion, perhaps because it followed all too readily from the planners' initial assumptions. They had stipulated that the U.S.-led area had to exceed the German-led area in self-sufficiency and minimize dislocations of trade: small wonder that the whole of the available world fit the bill. As Viner said, "It was clear that if the political costs were not too great the United States should aim at the largest possible bloc." Or, as economist Eugene Staley explained, because self-contained areas created economic problems, there was a "tendency to expand the area to its optimum economic limits in spite of contractions which might be advisable for political or military reasons."[80]

The outcome of the Economic and Financial Group's analysis was a novel proposition in the history of U.S. foreign relations: the United States had to hold "unquestioned power" in the world. Such was the group's recommendation to the State Department, delivered in an October 19 memorandum entitled "Needs of Future United States Foreign Policy."[81] The planners endorsed the Grand Area because it exceeded the projected German area in both productive capacity and bargaining power. Within the Grand Area, moreover, the United States would be supreme, the war having decimated France and destroyed Britain's ability to maintain its positions in Asia and the Mediterranean simultaneously.[82] What the Roosevelt administration needed, in short, was an "integrated policy to achieve military and economic supremacy for the United States within the non-German world."[83]

At the end of their recommendations, the planners briefly turned from establishing the need for U.S. global preeminence to suggesting ways to implement it—the issue that would orient postwar planning in the coming years. One set of recommendations concerned military preparedness and intervention. Foremost in importance was the rapid fulfillment of ongoing U.S. armament drive.[84] The United States also had to render "every assistance, except by expeditionary force," to the British Empire in order to rescue its control of the world's sea lanes and thereby preserve the possibility of building the Grand Area.[85] The planners recognized that the administration was already moving in this direction, but they boldly advised policymakers to incorporate Japan into the Grand Area "through peaceable means if possible, or through force."[86] The latter method looked increasingly necessary after Japan concluded the Tripartite Pact, a defensive alliance with Germany and Italy, at the end of September. By November the planners devoted several meetings to the question of how to convince or compel Japan to join the Grand Area.[87]

The other set of recommendations seemed on the surface to revive the highest ambition of Wilsonian internationalism: a league of all nations rather than an alliance pitting some against others. "Political arrangements should be developed for the kind of 'world organization' that the United States formerly has wished for all of the world—not only for a part of it," one planner summarized.[88] The idea of a truly worldwide organization thus resurfaced in CFR planning, albeit embryonically, for the first time since Hitler's conquests had wrecked its appeal. But now world organization was the hope of a distant future. Organizing the Grand Area came first. Its purpose was to achieve not perpetual peace but rather the economic and military supremacy of the United States, or as the planners wrote, "the greatest measure of economic bargain-power to maintain economic superiority which, in turn, can lead to decisive military superiority." Having attained this superiority, America might one day make the divided world whole again, presumably because the Nazi Reich would collapse or be toppled. The planners ended their memorandum by speculating that "perhaps ultimately such a non-German world organization can become a complete world organization."[89]

The Economic and Financial Group took evident pride in its plentifully underlined blueprint for U.S. supremacy. The Grand Area, it emphasized, was "*the basis of which United States foreign policy may be framed.*"[90] But when the group presented its study at an October 16 meeting of the other CFR planners—also attended by Leo Pasvolsky, a Brookings Institution economist whom Secretary of State Hull brought into the State Department to head up research on postwar foreign policy—members of the Political Group were intrigued but not convinced. One balked at the economists' desire to draft a constitution for "this statistical, economic utopia."[91] It was not the objective of U.S. global supremacy per se that elicited the Political Group's skepticism. All, Pasvolsky included, regarded the hemisphere as a grossly inadequate basis for U.S. foreign policy. The political planners pointed out, however, that the Grand Area presupposed a postwar peace that actually represented a cold war between Germany and the Anglo-American powers. "Better to fight at once," the group felt, "than to face the prospect of such a prolonged and feverish armed truce." A divided world would necessitate "increasing our economic and military might ad infinitum, lest the German area succeed in closing the war-potential gap." The upshot would be another world war, or at best a peace with warlike characteristics.[92]

Would the American people sacrifice blood and treasure to bring so wretched a world into existence? Henry Wriston, the president of Brown University and a member of the Political Group, doubted it, asking whether "American men would be willing to fight and die for such a scheme."[93] Other CFR members worried that the U.S. public still opposed extrahemispheric military commitments. The public might recoil particularly at the proposal to integrate Japan by force into the Grand Area. That proposition smacked of the "crassest kind of imperialistic methods . . . at radical variance with our traditional stand that peaceable international relations must rest on a moral basis."[94] Globalism was a tough enough sell as it was. A nakedly imperialistic globalism might be impossible. In November the Political Group suggested splitting the Grand Area into two "Anglo-Saxon-dominated areas," allowing the United States to limit its political obligations to the Western Hemisphere and reap the benefits of trade with the eastern area, led politically and militarily by Britain.[95] The CFR's Political Group, then, accepted the need for a globe-spanning non-German living space but questioned the American public's will to lead it.

The dissent of the Political Group revealed that a presentational problem stood in the way of realizing U.S. global supremacy. Prepared though they were to play power politics on a global scale, foreign policy elites believed the American public was not. How could the projection of U.S. political and military power beyond the Western Hemisphere be made to look different from the imperialism of European and Asian powers, against which the United States defined itself? The planners did not yet answer this question frontally, so novel was their argument for U.S. supremacy. Yet the CFR's economists discerned the challenge. "To be acceptable to those who favor isolation, a policy of world leadership must be framed in such a way that its positive gains are shown to be unmistakably greater than the apparent comfort and security of isolation," they wrote. "This obviously is not easy to do."[96]

A New Order for the Ages

Nothing as extravagant or concrete as the CFR's blueprint for global supremacy appeared in public discourse in the autumn of 1940. The election campaign dampened expansive expressions of U.S. military responsibilities;

both Roosevelt and Willkie, despite favoring all aid to Britain short of war, highlighted their intention to avoid full-scale belligerency. Interventionist elites nonetheless argued that in order for the United States to continue to imagine itself as a world-historical entity, it would need to acquire world supremacy.

The most urgent task was to build support for aiding Britain and its empire, in effect initiating the global alliance of the non-German world envisioned by the CFR planners. In May and June 1940, Gallup polls had recorded that 64 percent of Americans preferred to stay out of the war than to aid Britain at the risk of war. September was the first month when the majority switched sides. By January 1941 the reversal was complete: 68 percent of Americans prioritized helping Britain win over avoiding war. Roughly that level was maintained throughout the year.[97] A new consensus identified the vital interest of the United States with the survival of Britain and therefore with a favorable preponderance of power globally. When the noninterventionist America First Committee—tarred as the epitome of isolationism—formed in early September 1940, its leaders argued not that Britain's survival was irrelevant to the United States but rather that Britain would endure without U.S. aid, permitting the United States to concentrate its resources on defending its entire hemisphere.[98]

Interventionists, for their part, did not abandon hemisphere defense but steadily expanded its requirements as to include substantial participation in European politics. Where noninterventionists touted the defense of hemispheric territory, interventionists accentuated the importance of controlling the seas as well. "When we speak of defending this Western Hemisphere," President Roosevelt declared in October, "we are speaking not only of the territory of North, Central, and South America and the immediately adjacent islands; we include the right to the peaceful use of the Atlantic and Pacific Oceans."[99] Thereupon Lippmann, the preacher of Anglo-American naval power, added that securing the oceans required "the unquestioned friendship of free peoples living on the other shores of the seas."[100] Now the defense of the New World led into the heart of the Old World. The hazy frontiers of future U.S. responsibilities extended all the way to Africa when State Department officials and CFR planners contemplated taking positions in West Africa lest Germany establish naval or air bases there. Increasingly the whole of the British Empire, from Africa to the Far East, looked imperative to defend.[101] "We have been saying that the English Channel is our first line of defense," read an internal CDA memorandum in September. "What will people say when we urge tanks for the campaign in Egypt?"[102]

In theory, the expansion of U.S. interests remained tethered to hemisphere defense. Another line of argument, however, threatened to sever the cord: that it was not the Axis but the United States that had to realize a new world order. After Germany, Italy, and Japan concluded the Tripartite Pact at the end of September, Japanese prime minister Fumimaro Konoe proposed to recognize U.S. leadership in the Americas provided the United States did the same for Germany and Italy in Europe and Japan in East Asia. Together the four powers could cooperate "in the construction of a new world order," Konoe suggested.[103] Neither the Roosevelt administration nor commentators in the American press seriously considered accepting the offer. To the contrary, the pact provoked U.S. elites to declare aims that transcended the defense of the hemisphere. Already on the day after the announcement of the Tripartite Pact, Welles delivered a speech that, despite its Pan-American theme, linked U.S. national security with conditions worldwide. The United States, he said, must "aid in the construction of that kind of a world peace based on justice and on law through which alone can our security be fully guaranteed."[104]

But why not accept a world peace compatible with the Axis vision of Europe for the Europeans and Asia for the Asians? In responding to the Tripartite Pact, U.S. elites foregrounded American exceptionalism: Axis supremacy in Asia and Europe would deny the destiny of the United States to define the direction of world history. "Ours is the new order," Lippmann wrote in reply to Konoe's offer. "It was to found this order and to develop it that our forefathers came here. In this order we exist. Only in this order can we live."[105] In a remarkable address six days after his election to a third term, Roosevelt echoed Lippmann in asserting America's inherent right to set the terms of world order. "In almost every century since the day that recorded history began, people have thought, quite naturally, that they were creating or establishing some kind of 'new order of the ages,'" he began, belittling the pretensions of the Axis. In fact, "civilization" had witnessed few genuinely new orders. These Roosevelt traced from ancient Greece and Rome, the birthplaces of democracy and orderly government, to the British Isles and finally the United States. Britain and America—joined together, in Roosevelt's telling—had "led the world in spreading the gospel of democracy among peoples, great and small." But it was the United States that "truly and fundamentally . . . was a new order." For Roosevelt and Lippmann, the Axis bid to lead the world to a new order was undertaken by the wrong party.

Hence the problem with the Tripartite Pact: a German-dominated Europe and Japanese-dominated Asia would reverse the realization of America's role

in human events. It would negate the United States as a political project—
"that new order for the ages founded by the Fathers of America," as Roosevelt put it, blurring the distinction between the United States proper and its
world environment.[106] Roosevelt said precious little, at this juncture, about
the means by which America's sense of destiny would be maintained after the
United States denied leadership to the Triple Axis. Even so, he delivered a
public statement of American objectives that surpassed the defense of any
particular territorial space and framed the stakes of the war in terms of who
would lead the world in the epoch to come.

Nothing was unusual, in U.S. politics, about vindicating a consensual
American order against Old World force and domination. Lippmann spoke as
a good nationalist and internationalist in averring that "our order is founded
on the free consent of men and of peoples," completely unlike the "fire and
sword" wielded by the Axis. More innovative was that the proclamations of a
new world order went only that deep. Lippmann and Roosevelt said next to
nothing about the problems of international society itself. They put forth no
proposal for replacing a system of power politics with a scheme to prevent
war, as did the legalist internationalists of the League to Enforce Peace in the
years before the United States entered World War I. They conveyed no sense
that the need to use force would one day disappear. A new world order was
becoming a mere idea, detached from concrete programs. Its only tangible
content was the mobilization of U.S. power, first to defeat the Axis and then,
presumably, to preserve an American-style world order. "What our neighbors
fear among us," Lippmann wrote, "is not our power but the insufficiency of
our power and the hesitations and divisions which paralyze our power."[107]
Prefiguring Roosevelt's "arsenal of democracy" concept by three months,
Lippmann argued that America must become the "workshop and arsenal of
the free nations" and outbuild Germany, Italy, and Japan combined.[108]

Lippmann did make an effort to reconcile his nominal aspiration for a
consensual world order with his arguments for U.S. military superiority. Inheriting centuries-old justifications of the British Empire based on its maritime methods, he suggested that sea power, distinct from the power of land
armies, nurtured freedom.[109] As he sensed, the contradiction between a free
world and an armed superpower, between internationalism and imperialism,
had somehow to be papered over. Achieve this and the presentational
problem on which the CFR planning foundered might be solved. Against
appeals to America's nonentanglement tradition, interventionists could reply
that the higher objective was always to redeem the world. It was better to

preserve free intercourse and the American destiny, at the price of entanglement, than to hold fast to nonentanglement, at the price of isolation.

"We Could Win Everywhere"

Admiral Harold Stark did not need explicit orders from his commander in chief in order to tell which way the wind was blowing. Stark, the navy's top official, and his army counterpart, General Marshall, were responsible for approving war plans in case the United States became a belligerent. Military leaders had spent the summer obsessed with hemisphere defense and wary of civilian enthusiasms for aiding Britain; the United States appeared to present a classic, lamentable case of political objectives outstripping military capabilities. But hemisphere-centered war plans did not survive the summer. As Stark, Marshall, and their planning staffs saw—General Strong, chief of the War Plans Division, attended numerous CFR planning meetings—neither their civilian leaders nor the U.S. political class as a whole would accept the strictures of hemisphere defense. At the end of October, with Roosevelt closing in on his third term, Stark drew up a comprehensive statement of U.S. objectives, finalized on the day after the president's "new world order" speech and then approved by Marshall.

Historians have recognized the resulting Plan Dog memorandum, so named for its endorsement of the course of action in paragraph D, as "perhaps the most important single document in the development of World War II strategy," for it devised the Europe-first war strategy of concentrating U.S. forces in the Atlantic while holding a defensive posture in the Pacific.[110] Stark's memorandum was also seminal in another way. It was the first U.S. war plan to condition the security of the United States on the global balance of power and hence the survival of the British Empire.[111] "A very strong pillar of the defense structure of the Americas has, for many years, been the balance of power existing in Europe," Stark wrote. "The collapse of Great Britain or the destruction or surrender of the British Fleet will destroy this balance and will free European military power for possible encroachment in this hemisphere."[112]

Stark's rationales for seeking to aid Britain showed their debt to the anti-isolationist arguments that had been articulated since May. One held that a world open to liberal economic intercourse had to be enforced by preponderant military power. Stark claimed that the United States required a "profitable foreign trade" in order to produce heavy armaments, and it might lose that trade if Britain lost its fleet. Trade—"particularly with Europe,"

Stark added, surpassing the CFR's ambitions for the Grand Area so far—depended on the "continued integrity of the British Empire." Stark's second rationale combined discourses of security and sociability. If Germany won, "we would find ourselves acting alone, and at war with the world," he wrote. "To repeat, we would be thrown back on our haunches." Stark found no need to argue that the continental United States would be in danger of invasion if American haunches had to be activated, although he surmised that the Axis might, after "some years," turn on Latin America. It sufficed to cite the lack of initiative, the loss of sociable relationships in the world, that the United States would suffer—and the gains that a British victory would enable. If Britain lost, Stark wrote, "while we might not *lose everywhere,* we might, possibly, not *win anywhere.*" On the other hand, "if Britain wins decisively against Germany we could win everywhere."[113]

Over the coming year, Roosevelt and his cabinet acted on Plan Dog's prescription to defend Britain in the Atlantic while neglecting to adopt the strictly defensive posture in the Far East preferred by the navy and especially the army. After Plan Dog, as before it, civilian officials led the military toward more expansive commitments in the world, not the other way around. That Plan Dog constituted relative *restraint* testified to the transformation that had taken place since the summer. Within six months, the world role imagined for the United States changed as dramatically as it had in the previous half century.

At first Nazi Germany, having flattened France, seemed destined to seize Britain, forcing the United States to retreat to a position of dominance over little more than North and Central America—a hegemonic space closer to that of 1890 than 1939. British resistance provided the most immediate reason why the United States avoided such a fate and then began to envision a preeminent world role for itself. And the strength of the American economy, despite its halting recovery from the Depression, made plausible a policy of U.S. world leadership as it became evident that Britain, unable to defend its positions in the Far East and the greater Mediterranean at once, would end up severely weakened however it survived. Berle seemed to have these factors in mind when he recorded in his diary in September, "I have been saying to myself and other people that the only possible effect of this war would be that the United States would emerge with an imperial power greater than the world had ever seen; but I thought of it as something that would happen more or less in the future. It has happened off the bat, and there isn't much that anyone can do about it."[114]

Still, important though they were, geopolitical and economic circumstances cannot fully explain why U.S. policy elites embarked on a veritable reconceptualization of their nation's world role. After all, they might have agreed with noninterventionists that Britain's survival would allow the United States to return to normalcy, leaving the pursuit of global dominance to foreign powers or none at all. Most members of the U.S. political and intellectual class reacted differently because they interpreted events through the prism of ideas of internationalism descended from previous generations. From the founding of the republic up to the summer of 1940, the United States had two universalist aspirations—the promotion of liberal intercourse and the realization of America's world-historical destiny—that might have caused its leaders to seek global hegemony were it not for the work performed by internationalist ideology. According to this ideology, the processes of liberal intercourse operated freely and organically, independent of politics and antithetical to war. Those processes, led by the United States, would progressively replace armed rivalry with peace. When Hitler conquered France, he seemed to disprove the very premise of internationalism, which the rise of "totalitarianism" had already called into question. In a Nazi-led world—in any case, in a world in which the Nazis could come *close* to leadership—no harmony was immanent. There could be no free exchange without force. Americans could no longer imagine themselves as ushering in a new and better order unless they acquired political and military power to make it so.

In Plan Dog, Stark defined "our major national objectives in the near future as . . . the territorial, economic, and ideological integrity of the United States, plus that of the remainder of the Western Hemisphere." Stark's three-part schema usefully frames the interests that convinced foreign policy elites to pursue political and military preeminence. First, concerns for territorial and economic integrity jointly rendered worldwide intercourse more imperative than nonentanglement. Over the summer, the Roosevelt administration and its postwar planners had come to agree that the United States was committed, at minimum, to the defense of the entire Western Hemisphere; domestic politics would accept no less. When this hemispheric territorial imperative combined with liberal-capitalist economic imperatives— of maximizing trade and of minimizing disruptions to the status quo—the CFR planners concluded that the United States had to dominate the entire non-European world if Germany held continental Europe. Finally, the prospect of Nazi preeminence appeared to contradict America's ideological integrity as a world-historical nation. Regardless of whether it would eventually attack or impoverish North America, Germany would enfeeble the United States by defining the terms on which nations would live and relate.

AFTER A GRIM SUMMER, U.S. elites eyed leadership of a new world order—of some sort. Basic questions remained to be asked, let alone answered. How would the American political system, hitherto averse to European war and power politics, be convinced to go along? How would Great Britain and the United States cement their partnership and apportion their responsibilities? Could the United States accept an Anglo-German armed truce that left the Nazis in charge of continental Europe? How would the Far East, the Soviet Union, and colonial areas figure in an American new order? And what would become of world organization, the great hope after the First World War?

It was easy to bash "isolationism," but salvaging internationalism would be harder. From Geneva, a group of League of Nations supporters, including Americans in CSOP, issued a despairing report assessing why the League had failed. "There is at present no possibility to appeal to values which are held in common by the various nations and political systems," the group wrote in October. Case in point was the belligerents' avowed desire to annihilate their opponents. Even eighteenth-century practices compared favorably. In present circumstances, international law was "practically meaningless," and international organization scarcely better. Both depended on a common ethos, and "it is precisely that international ethos that has lost its binding force."[115] No inner harmony lay waiting to be unleashed while the world remained spiritually and ideologically divided.

League supporters could have kept faith that the internationalist project would resume once some new political unity was forged, yet they indicated deeper doubts about the possibility of universal peace and cooperation. Until now, they wrote, they had presumed "that the human mind has not yet been given its real opportunity and that if all reactionary and obscurantist influences which still play upon men can be removed and if true education can be universalized, men will recognize each other as men, forget their sterile conflicts, and proceed to build a better and brighter world." Alas, the devotees of Geneva-style internationalism had demonstrated a "facile optimism concerning the nature of men and the power of human reason."[116]

Those who spoke assuredly of the future subscribed to a concept of internationalism that was different from the old one. For these Americans, internationalism now meant anti-isolationism and therefore less the realization of world harmony than the projection of world power by the United States. In the same month of the desperate postmortem from Geneva, Berle marveled at his country's fortunes. In the previous war, the United States had become "virtually an adjunct to the British war machine," Berle noted. But "this time it seems to me that the thing should be the other way around. We have the ultimate strength. We also have the ultimate consistency of principle; we are the inevitable economic center of the regime which will emerge—unless, of course, we all go under."[117]

Anti-isolationism was acquiring the program it lacked before the fall of France. The world leadership of the United States was in the offing. "For twenty years we have been longing for a job—longing for a task worthy of our heritage and our faith," declared Miller, fresh off the destroyers deal, to the Daughters of the American Revolution. "We became unhappy and distraught because we did not know what to do next. Now we have found our job."[118] When Miller went to rent a Manhattan office for his fellow interventionists, he got number 2940 of the Albee Building on West Forty-Second Street. That was the year until which Hitler vowed his thousand-year Reich would rule. The room number delighted Miller and his compatriots; it was a "good omen for free men." Their cause, they believed, was the one that would last a millennium.[119]

3

THE AMERICO-BRITISH NEW ORDER OF 1941

THE "AMERICAN CENTURY" COMMENCED BY means of folksy prose. As publishing mogul Henry Luce summed up in his instantly famous essay with that title, "The big, important point to be made here is simply that the complete opportunity of leadership is ours."[1] That Luce could write these words, as he did on February 17, 1941, reflected yet another spectacular reversal. Six months earlier, reeling from the implosion of France, Americans had steeled themselves for a hemispheric future within an Axis-led world order. But by the new year, the fortunes of the war, and thus the imagined peace, had reversed so dramatically that Luce and other American observers now judged it was Nazi Germany that would end up confined to its own continent, perhaps rolled back within it. Why, then, were U.S. foreign policy elites not content to aid Britain and let it do the fighting in the war and the postwar world? Why seek to seize the "complete opportunity of leadership" if the actual danger was lessening and could be opposed by less costly methods?

The reason was that American politicians and intellectuals were rethinking the very nature of international society. Peaceful forms of exchange no longer appeared capable of transcending power politics and war, as previous generations had hoped. To the contrary, intercourse seemed to require the backing of force in order to exist at all. For the first time, policy elites believed the United States could enjoy liberal trade and common norms of conduct no further than its military force would permit. Even if Nazi Germany were defeated, power politics would not be. The world would remain prone to war, ordered only by an armed superior imposing its own "philosophy of life."[2] To the extent that American interests spanned the globe, so must American political and military power. It was to impart this lesson that Luce took to the pages of *Life,* which, less than five years after Luce had founded it, ranked as the nation's most popular magazine.[3]

Immediately after the fall of France, Luce had channeled his alarm into helping to organize and fund the militant Century Group. Its few dozen men, operating out of a private club in New York, gave President Franklin D. Roosevelt the idea to send fifty destroyers to Britain in return for ninety-nine-year, rent-free leases on British military bases in the Caribbean and Newfoundland.[4] After the consummation of the destroyers deal in September 1940, however, the group could no longer contain Luce's ambitions. He left it in November, judging the country to be "pretty generally agreed" on the merits of arming itself and backing Britain.[5] The urgent task, he thought, was not to persuade the president about the war; it was rather to exhort the public about the postwar.

To this end, Luce threw himself into political advocacy as he had never done before. Crisscrossing the country, he delivered the speeches that became the basis for his American Century essay. The results justified Luce's confidence in his capacity to mold middle-class opinion. *Life* received an extraordinary 4,541 letters, overwhelmingly favorable, in reply to the essay. In 1941 alone, the essay was reprinted in the *Washington Post* and *Reader's Digest* and as the centerpiece of a short book. It was assigned in high schools and universities.[6] Not merely in retrospect, it mattered in its own moment as an argument that one fawning *Life* editor dubbed a "modern Federalist Papers for this world A.D. 1941."[7]

The foundational principle of the post-1941 world was simple and sweeping: "America is responsible, to herself as well as to history, for the world environment in which she lives." Although Luce disclaimed U.S. responsibility for the "good behavior of the entire world," any place that seemed to bear on the overall "world environment" warranted American action. Luce did not shrink from appropriating the language of the Third Reich to articulate the scale he envisioned. "Tyrannies may require a large amount of living space," he wrote. "But Freedom requires and will require far greater living space than Tyranny."[8] No less world-historical than Adolf Hitler's vision of a thousand-year Reich were the ambitions of American elites like Luce—the latter ultimately proving more successful.

In 1941, however, success was hardly foreordained. True, the rest of the world had, Luce believed, served up a golden opportunity for American leadership. But Luce wrote "The American Century" because he feared his compatriots would decline the invitation. Until Pearl Harbor, according to surveys, 75 to 80 percent of the public opposed an immediate declaration of war on Germany even though the public supported aid to Britain in equal numbers.[9] America's will to power would not flow automatically from its material capability, as Luce saw at the start of 1941. The nation's leaders could not simply mobilize the economy and build up the military and expect to lead the world for a century to come. They would also have to convert the American people to a new way of thinking, contrary to the old.

Luce's anxiety derived from more than reading the latest polls. After all, that he could write "The American Century," to the plaudits of readers, indicated the direction of popular sentiment; global supremacy, only glimpsed by elite planners at the end of 1940, was now a matter of vigorous public discussion. Luce remained uneasy, however, because he thought popular isolationism might keep the century from being American. He thus framed his essay around a contest between "those old, old battered labels—the issue of Isolationism versus Internationalism." Luce was demonstrably wrong: hardly anyone before the 1930s had heard of isolationism, much less considered internationalism to be its opposite. Yet Luce read this dichotomy back through decades of history, blaming the world's ills on a stubbornly isolationist U.S. public and its equally isolationist political representatives. "The fundamental trouble with America," Luce wrote, "has been, and is, that whereas their nation became in the 20th Century the most powerful and the most vital nation in the world, nevertheless Americans were unable to accommodate themselves spiritually and practically to that fact."[10] Americans had chosen to be passive. Despite acquiring millions of colonial subjects, practicing gunboat diplomacy across the greater Caribbean, and sending an expeditionary force to Europe, the United States, in Luce's telling, did not trust itself to wield power.

Thankfully, Luce thought he possessed the antidote to "this virus of isolationist sterility" infecting (or sterilizing) much of the country. Luce wanted his fellow interventionists to turn world leadership, political and military supremacy, into the only thinkable mode of American engagement in the world. "We can make isolationism as dead an issue as slavery," he envisaged, "and we can make a truly *American* internationalism something as natural to us in our time as the airplane or the radio."[11] With this, Luce set forth the objective of the campaign that American political elites embarked on in 1941 and completed by the close of World War II. Amid the battles across Europe and Asia, they would keep one eye fixed at home. They would refashion armed supremacy from a strange-sounding proposition to the obvious consummation of America's destiny. They would create the will to lead the world.

LUCE WAS HARDLY ALONE. The idea of an American century became a mainstream proposition in 1941. Countless officials and intellectuals decided that the United States must attain political and military supremacy across the globe and sustain it in the era to come. America's future world leadership seemed so likely indeed that postwar planners began to work out the institutional form it should take, even before the United States joined the war in December.

On March 7, less than three weeks after Luce's essay appeared, this effort began in the Council on Foreign Relations (CFR). For the past year, the council had used Rockefeller Foundation funds to conduct postwar planning for the short-staffed State Department. Now the department asked the group to focus its work on a new question: "What are the alternative methods open to the United States for maintaining the peace of the world after the current conflict?"[12] The request presupposed the planners' conclusion from the autumn that "this country must squarely face the issue of political responsibility for world peace," in the words of Henry Wriston, the president of Brown University.[13] The planners knew then that they were making recommendations that might be impossible for the United States to fulfill, but by the spring of 1941 it seemed the country might actually be willing to follow through. Germany's advance had been halted, and the American public, as the State Department noted, was showing interest in what would follow the war. U.S. elites thus set out to devise a framework for postwar world politics.

One year later their discussions produced the basic structure for international relations after 1945: American supremacy operating through a world organization with universal membership but profound great-power privilege. Yet the path there was anything but linear. Throughout most of 1941, postwar planners wanted U.S. world leadership without world organization. They preferred America to police the world through an exclusive alliance with Great Britain and its white Dominions. Drawing up extensive blueprints, postwar planners called for building joint military bases and extending a form of citizenship to Anglo-Saxons the world over.

The most vocal advocate of American-British partnership was the prominent military affairs commentator George Fielding Eliot, who had lived Anglophone unity as a Brooklyn-born Australian infantry lieutenant turned Canadian Mountie and then U.S. Army major.[14] An advocate of hemisphere defense before the fall of France, Eliot now reasoned that America and Britain should police the world as the only powers possessing the requisite moral solidarity and military might to do so. No general grouping of states, with divergent interests and ways of life, could hope to accomplish the same. In his words, "The chief lesson of the post-war years is that peace cannot be assured without force."[15] And not the kind of force only partially contemplated in the League of Nations Covenant: "This force must be of adequate dimensions, capable of immediate application, and under the control of those whose self-interest will ensure its utilization."[16]

The popularity of Eliot's view, and the corresponding unpopularity of world organization, challenges the narrative of the origins of the United Nations (U.N.) that scholars have told for decades. Since the events themselves, historians and political scientists have detected little contradiction between world leadership and world organization, between the projection of power internationally and the international control of power. They treat the U.N. as the elaboration of Roosevelt's Four Freedoms Speech, the Lend-Lease Act, and the Atlantic Charter, even though none of these statements mentioned an international organization with universal membership.[17] By casting the events of 1941 as mere precursors to what came later, scholars pass over the pivotal period when U.S. elites went from mocking world organization to thinking it vital. The turn to world organization needs to be explained, not assumed to emanate naturally from America's rise to power.[18]

That explanation begins in 1941 with the pervasive perception that world leadership precluded world organization. When planners and intellectuals devised the first blueprints for U.S. political-military supremacy, they envisioned America and Britain forming a police force with hardly any role for other powers and peoples—which is to say, most of the globe. Unambiguously, they valued projecting power to the exclusion of controlling power. Years later the U.N. would be founded on the same objective.

World Leadership without World Organization

In the month after Luce wrote "The American Century," Harold Vinacke, a political scientist from the University of Cincinnati, posed a question: "When the United States has its thousands of airplanes, its mass army, properly mechanized, and its two-ocean navy, what are they to be used for?" The outline of an answer was becoming clear to Vinacke, and it involved much more than defending the Americas. In March, after months of debate, Congress passed the Lend-Lease Act, an unprecedented grant of executive authority to open the spigots of aid to Great Britain and any other country the president deemed vital to U.S. defenses. The American political system was now acting on the premise that the security of its hemisphere depended on the balance of power in Europe and Asia. This novel axiom, Vinacke wrote, liberated U.S. policy from its "territorial and geographic basis," rendering it "world-wide rather than hemispheric in outlook."[19]

Would the global outlook vanish into thin air after hostilities ceased? Vinacke thought not, for the country was acquiring a new consciousness of itself and its place in the world. The United States, in Vinacke's estimation, was resolving to "use the power which it possesses to create world conditions satisfactory to it rather than prepare to adjust itself passively to world conditions as created by others." These "others" meant not only the Triple Axis of Germany, Italy, and Japan. Great Britain so coveted an alliance with the United States that Vinacke believed the Americans would "call the tune"—so long, he added, as they accepted the duties of leadership that they had heretofore refused.[20]

Vinacke went on to head the Japan section of the Office of War Information. After the war, he returned to the University of Cincinnati to teach. He had, it is safe to say, no singular significance in the making of American foreign policy. Hence the significance of "What Shall America Defend," his article in the *Yale Review*. Its very obscurity indicates the distance that the aspiration to world leadership traveled in a few short months. Vinacke was just one of a panoply of elites who, by the spring of 1941, saw the United States emerging as the supreme political-military power. And they said so in public. They filled newspapers, magazines, and journals with discussion of the new world order, in the ubiquitous phrase of the moment, that America could build and lead.[21]

America's largely self-appointed planners understood the limited capacity of their government's bureaucracy to undertake farsighted research in the midst of the present crisis, although in February the State Department did establish the Division of Special Research, through which it later conducted postwar planning.[22] But those who addressed postwar matters did not all intend to be ersatz policymakers, aiming solely to influence the state. They also appreciated the power of civil society, in its own right, to define the parameters of thought and action in American and international society. In mobilizing for a new world order, American elites and citizens followed a venerable tradition of internationalist groups across the North Atlantic, dating to the advent of the peace movement in the final years of the Napoleonic Wars and intensified by the proliferation of philanthropic foundations in the twentieth century. "Everyone is planning a post-war world," CFR planner Isaiah Bowman observed, not entirely happily.[23] So many postwar groups formed in 1940 and 1941 that it became difficult to survey planning work as a whole. Several organizations assembled bibliographies of postwar proposals, the multiplicity of bibliographies replicating the original problem.[24]

Anticipations of the American Century were not confined to a few personages, like Luce or Roosevelt, on whom scholars have dwelled.[25] In the first four months of 1941, many foreign policy elites publicly articulated a new goal: the acquisition of global political and military supremacy by the United States, working in tandem with Great Britain but without a wider world organization.

ALTHOUGH A NUMBER OF officials and intellectuals began to envision postwar U.S. supremacy toward the end of 1940, the prospect still verged on being fanciful. It remained more a perceived necessity than a program to be implemented, more *should* than *could*. One reason was geopolitical. In the later months of 1940, Germany and Italy, working in concert with the Soviet Union, extended their rule of Europe, making allies of Hungary, Romania, and Slovakia. The Luftwaffe rained bombs on London. Japan took advantage of France's weakness to move troops into northern Indochina, before invading the rest of the French colony in 1941. These military setbacks hardly augured greater U.S. participation in the postwar world, nor did America's halting response to them. At the end of 1940, the Roosevelt administration had to decide how far to escalate its support for the British Empire. Under the Neutrality Act of 1939, the United States allowed Britain to buy war materiel from Americans but required Britain to pay in cash and carry the cargo away from U.S. ports. Both halves of the "cash and carry" policy were losing relevance as Britain hemorrhaged the dollars it required to purchase U.S. arms and faced mounting Nazi attacks on shipping across the Atlantic.[26]

The impasse convinced Roosevelt to act boldly. In a series of speeches surrounding the new year, he proposed that the United States become the "great arsenal of democracy" by equipping the front lines against the Axis without requiring immediate compensation. Roosevelt made his first declaration of America's postwar aims in his annual address to Congress on January 6, 1941. Against the "new order of tyranny," he propounded the Four Freedoms—of speech and worship, from want and fear—to be realized, he repeated for each, "everywhere around the world."[27] "At least the Crusades of a thousand years ago had a more limited objective," griped Edwin Borchard, the noninterventionist international lawyer.[28]

As the historian Anders Stephanson points out, the maximalism of the Four Freedoms contradicted Roosevelt's coexisting tendency to accept dictatorial and totalitarian governments as legitimate members of international society, provided they eschewed the lawless "gangsterism" he ascribed to the Nazis.[29] Either of Roosevelt's positions, however, supposed a novel U.S. interest in policing the balance of power centered in Europe, despite the president's frequent appeals to hemispheric security. As Raymond Leslie Buell observed to his colleagues in Luce's Post-War Committee, Roosevelt "supposedly imposes a hemispheric limitation on U.S. intervention, but this means very little. For under his own definition the U.S. would be justified in using force to destroy hostile land bases in other continents, and this doctrine can lead us to the defense of British and even Red Sea ports before we are through."[30]

In order to supply the fight against the Axis, Roosevelt sought the assent of Congress, as he had not done over the destroyers deal. He wagered that noninterventionists, if brought into the open, would suffer a crushing defeat. He was right. The Lend-Lease Act, debated in January and February and passed in early March, removed the cash-and-carry restrictions and empowered Roosevelt to designate future recipients of aid. Under international law, no neutral could assist a belligerent as America was aiding Britain. Interventionist lawyers thus decided that America was not a neutral. Led by Quincy Wright, the political scientist and international lawyer, they popularized the category of *nonbelligerent* to characterize the U.S. position.[31]

By shedding the vestiges of neutrality, Roosevelt freed up interventionists to think and speak about the kind of world for which the Anglophone Allies stood. Even before the Lend-Lease Act passed, Borchard lamented that noninterventionists had been "out-shouted."[32] After the act's passage, commentators widely acknowledged that the United States was at war in all but name. "America is arming on a great scale and is manifestly intervening in the war," Walter Lippmann noted.[33] U.S. military spending was on its way to constituting 13.1 percent of gross domestic product in 1941, dwarfing its 1.5 percent level for most of the 1930s.[34]

Having all but achieved their proximate goal of getting the United States into the war, interventionists now considered the United States destined to define the future of international order—a volte-face from six months prior, when the fall of France sent planners scurrying to figure out how much of the Western Hemisphere they could preserve in a world led by Hitler. Five days after Luce's essay came out, Vice President Henry Wallace declared that whatever the outcome of the war, America's responsibility afterward would be "enormously increased." "The wisdom of our action during the first three years of peace," Wallace said, "will determine the course of world history for half a century."[35] Speaking in the thick of the Lend-Lease debate, Wallace risked antagonizing opponents in Congress, but he went ahead anyway. A few weeks later, the Lend-Lease Act passed, and Wallace proceeded to double the lifespan of his imagined U.S.-led peace. Now he called on the country to "build a Pax Democratica which will bless us and the whole world for a century to come."[36]

As prominent politicians spoke broadly of a new postwar vocation for the United States, middle-ranking elites gave more sustained attention to the subject. When the American Academy of Political and Social Science held its annual meeting in early April, the guiding theme was America's future as the premier world power. The columnist and political scientist Max Lerner urged the United States to "assume the world leadership which she must assume if that will help to achieve some degree of world order."[37] Another speaker, Otto T. Mallery, struck a similar note. A New Deal economist with the National Resources Planning Board, Mallery averred that "destiny offers to the United States the ultimate balance of power and of resources in the world after the war." The outstanding question was, "What will the United States do with this power and treasure?"[38]

Likewise, Buell convened a roundtable of elites for *Fortune* magazine in mid-February and found a sea change from the previous year. At the start of 1940, members of the roundtable, like planners in the State Department, had wanted the United States to maintain its traditional neutral rights and mediate in the European war "in favor of a just peace."[39] Now, however, all but two of the group's twenty-six economists, businessmen, diplomats, academics, and journalists presumed that Britain would and must win the war and thereby create an opportunity for the United States to "play a decisive role in formulating the next peace." Once the war devastated land armies, America and Britain could use their "supremacy on the sea and in the air" to police the postwar world, Europe very much included. One of the dissenters in the group captured the consensus that worried him: "The assumption has been made by the majority here and with surprisingly little dissent that America is going to emerge from the present conflict rich, strong, ready, and eager to take on those duties and obligations to distribute its largess throughout a stricken world and at the same time play the major part in underwriting New Orders on three or four continents."[40]

This consensus was capacious in ambition as well as conception, leaving many questions open. If America were to police the world, could it manage solely through naval and air power, or would it require a large standing army? Even less clear were the economic and social principles of the new order, a subject that elicited individual idiosyncrasies and domestic political cleavages. Mallery, having asked how America should use its power and treasure, answered with the promotion of reciprocal trade agreements and the universal right of recreation. (A champion of playgrounds since the Progressive Era, Mallery went on to found the International Recreation Association during the Cold War in an effort to bring nations together.)[41] For every Luce or businessman Wendell Willkie who envisioned U.S. leadership heralding the next era of free trade, a New Dealer like Wallace spoke of America "insuring to all humanity those minimum living standards" to banish hunger from the earth.[42] Wallace's counterpart in unofficial circles was Vera Micheles Dean, the director of research for the progressive-minded Foreign Policy Association and a rare Jewish woman ensconced in the Northeast policy elite. Dean wanted to redress the way the last postwar settlement had privileged political and territorial arrangements over the social and economic "standard of living" of the masses. She proposed a new slogan of "human welfare" and later promoted this agenda as a founder of the U.N. Relief and Rehabilitation Administration.[43]

But the common denominator of postwar discussions was not welfarism. It was rather that whatever shape international society took, the United States should be the one to mold it. As Buell wrote to the Luce Post-War Committee, "Despite the demand for Peoples Charters and new social orders, the immediate issue of this war is Power."[44] On this score New Dealers and anti–New Dealers agreed. Dean herself argued that by failing to assume world leadership, the United States had doomed the Treaty of Versailles and nearly forced Americans to live within their continental boundaries. This, above all, was what had to change. "It must be recognized that this conflict will determine the political, social, and economic shape of the world in accordance with the general philosophy of life formulated or practiced by the victor," she wrote. In the "struggle for world order," America had to win, then lead.[45]

The implications were not lost on noninterventionists in Congress, who saw a future of endless warfare for the United States. "If we enter the war today to save the British Empire, we will be involved in war for the rest of our lives," Senator Robert A. Taft cautioned. He predicted that the United States would find constant cause to enter European wars if it placed its effective frontier on the English Channel.[46] Historian Charles Beard agreed, warning the Senate Committee on Foreign Relations that interventionists sought to "make over Europe and Asia, provide democracy, a bill of rights, and economic security for everybody, everywhere, in the world." Such enthusiasms Beard denounced as "the childish exuberance of the Bolshevik internationalists who preach the gospel of one model for the whole world."[47] For the final time, it turned out, opponents of U.S. global supremacy stood up in Congress as a political force.

But they did not stand tall. Senator Hiram Johnson had trouble convincing his noninterventionist allies to testify against the Lend-Lease proposal. Liable to be denounced as isolationists, they feared for their reputations.[48] Noninterventionists were winning the debate they wanted to have, but not the one that moved increasing numbers of Americans. Noninterventionists' principal argument against entering in the war was that North America was impregnable against any power or combination of powers that might attack from across the ocean.[49] Most interventionists conceded the point but did not think it mattered. More than the safety of territory, interventionists sought a new global order for which the United States would set the rules. In reply, noninterventionists sounded the familiar alarm that rather than right the wrongs of Europe and Asia, America would become entangled in age-old patterns of power politics and war. But what if the United States could wield power so great as to bend the rest of the world to its will? What if it alone could "build and outproduce the whole of Europe," as Lippmann foresaw in rebutting a proposal for a negotiated peace from noninterventionist Montana senator Burton Wheeler?[50]

Accused of favoring entanglement in Old World politics, interventionists answered, in effect, that America would become too mighty to entangle. This proposition differed fundamentally from the one President Woodrow Wilson had offered in 1919—that the League of Nations would constitute a "disentangling alliance" that would get rid of rivalry and war, thus Americanizing the world.[51] Like Wilson, the interventionists of 1941 conjured an Americanized world, but not by means of organizing the world to act collectively in the interest of the whole. The world would be Americanized because America, unfettered, would dominate it. "The cure," as Luce wrote, "is this: to accept wholeheartedly our duty and our opportunity as the most powerful and vital nation in the world and in consequence to exert upon the world the full impact of our influence, for such purposes as we see fit and by such means as we see fit."[52] *As we see fit:* America Firsters were not the only ones who put America first.

Indeed, until the autumn of 1941, interventionists evinced little interest in reviving an international political organization after the war. They emphasized projecting power, not controlling it, highlighting the strong hand America would enjoy vis-à-vis the British Empire and any other international grouping. It was therefore possible for Luce, writing in the name of internationalism, to mention international organization not once in his "American Century" essay. Likewise, in April 1941, interventionists formed a new citizens group called Fight for Freedom to advocate an immediate declaration of war, and despite calling for a "new world order" the group scarcely referenced international organization.[53] It was the struggle for supremacy between America and Germany that would "decide the future of the world for a thousand years as Hitler has said."[54] Those who bothered to speak of international organization usually condemned it. "Why is it that the members of the Group are so opposed to the League?" one postwar planner asked his colleagues in the CFR.[55] When a *Time* editor pitched a story idea on the League of Nations and the World Court, the editor immediately had to add, "(Don't laugh.)"[56]

Even the most dedicated supporters of the League prioritized the achievement of world leadership first and world organization a distant second. The Commission to Study the Organization of Peace (CSOP), formed to publicize postwar plans, mustered only the vaguest public pronouncements through 1941. Its members deferred world organization to the distant future, following a "transition period" of American-British leadership. By January 1941, the transition period preoccupied CSOP's Subcommittee on International Organization, headed by Wright.[57] CSOP came out in June in favor of a "joint American-British sea and air force, with the necessary bases and ser-vicing facilities, strong enough to police the seas and to localize outbreaks of violence in land areas." This arrangement would last "at the initial stage, or," rather differently, "as long as may be necessary."[58] In other words, one member complained, CSOP envisioned a "rather indefinite dictatorship by Britain and America."[59]

As the U.S. policy elite decided to pursue global supremacy, international organization constituted no better than an afterthought. At worst, it seemed to embody the naive hopes of a generation of American diplomats and intellec-tuals. As Francis P. Miller commented to the CFR planners, "One of the great fallacies of American thought during the last twenty years was that war could be eliminated by 'incantation.'"[60] Force, not incantation; armed supremacy, not world organization—these dichotomies prevailed through most of 1941. They might well have been maintained throughout the war. For Americans planning the shape of things to come, world leadership and world organization did not go together. Each ruled out the other. And the one U.S. elites wanted was world leadership.

As the Lend-Lease debate revealed, noninterventionists lost their war before they lost its final battle at Pearl Harbor. They did not lose because they opposed world organization and other peaceful, cooperative modes of engagement—which interventionists, too, either opposed or paid little mind at the time. Noninterventionists lost because they sought to restrict U.S. military commitments to what seemed necessary to defend the United States proper. It was this position that interventionists attacked and stig-matized as "isolationism," seeking to make it, as Luce put it, "as dead an issue as slavery." A dead issue, an obvious anachronism, was just how a range of politicians and commentators cast isolationism in 1941 as they read the new concept onto the past in an attempt to write nonintervention out of the future.

Tellingly, those who propagandized against isolationism offered no co-herent narrative of how the creed figured in history. Everyone spun his or her own tale of when isolationism had reigned and who had expounded it. Some dated isolationism to the founding of the republic and saw it diminishing ever since.[61] For others, isolationism recurred, receding during crises and rushing back in times of peace.[62] Many located isolationism's heyday in the interwar period. Lippmann, for example, blamed twenty years of "sepa-ratism, isolationism, disarmament, pacifism, and cynicism" for bringing on the Second World War and sapping the Anglo-American powers of the will and arms to fight.[63] Others agreed but blamed Republicans alone, not Democrats. Another claimed that in the interwar period "everybody was an Isolationist, regardless of party."[64] Florida senator Charles Andrews had it both ways in the same speech. The United States, he maintained, followed an uninterrupted "policy of passive isolationism" from 1921 onward, yet somehow "no President, except possibly Harding, has ever been an isolationist while in office."[65]

Interventionists scarcely quibbled over their vastly different interpretations of history. Whenever and however isolationism was supposed to have flourished, what mattered was that it belonged to a bygone age. If so, the American people did not need to consider the merits of isolationist arguments. They had only to recognize that isolationism was an archaism and bury it in the ash heap of history. Likening isolationism to childhood, Vice President Wallace implied that the passage into world leadership was natural, necessary, and irreversible. "We of the United States can no more evade shouldering our responsibility than a boy of eighteen can avoid becoming a man by wearing short pants," he said. "The word 'isolation' means short pants for a grown-up United States."[66] Harsher still was William C. Bullitt, the U.S. ambassador to France and patient-turned-collaborator of Sigmund Freud. Back home from Paris, he accused isolationists of suffering from a "gruesome form of dementia praecox which causes men who cannot bear to face the harsh reality of the real world to regress mentally and to traverse backward, in search of a lost paradise, all the stages of their existence."[67] Whereas Wallace optimistically depicted a graduation out of isolation, Bullitt revealed the corollary. Those who refused to advance went backward, losing agency, rationality, and relevance.

If the United States chose not to take up arms on a global scale, it would wither away: U.S. foreign policy elites won the argument for world leadership by arguing against "isolationism." Yet now that they wished to ascend to world leadership and define the structure of international society, the question became what that structure should entail if not world organization. It was this question that postwar planners intended to answer. "The job is a staggering one," Assistant Secretary of State Adolf Berle recorded in his journal as the State Department prepared to assemble an official committee of planners.[68] Fortunately for him and his department, experts outside of government stood ready to help.

Planning to Lead by Leading the Planning

For a century before 1941, Anglophiles the world over dreamed of joining together in a single, globe-spanning polity. They hoped the "English-speaking peoples" would manifest their racial unity in a loose federation that would lead even the misfortunate non-English speakers toward peace and freedom.[69] They counted supporters not only in the British Isles but across the white settler Dominions of Britain's Commonwealth of Nations: from Australia and New Zealand to South Africa to Canada and Newfoundland. In the United States, however, their ranks were thin. Despite increasing Anglo-American intimacy since the turn of the century, Americans could not see themselves partnering officially with Great Britain or its Common-wealth. Although some advocates of the League of Nations envisioned that Anglo-American power would underwrite it, few sought a formal or exclu-sive alliance with Britain, much less with elements of its empire.[70]

Yet in 1941 Anglo-American unity vaulted to the forefront of U.S. poli-tics. "The question of any sort of union between Britain and America had never been discussed in the same way before," Whitney Shepardson, a di-rector of the CFR, told a crowd at the CFR's London counterpart, Chatham House, in July.[71] Shepardson observed that Anglophiles in the United States had "gone beyond the stage of speculating on what the future might look like if wishful-thinking people had their way." The journalist Clarence Streit was making waves with his book, *Union Now with Britain,* which proposed that the United States and the British Commonwealth immediately combine into a single federal polity.[72] The idea of Anglo-American unity, Shepardson said, had "advanced to a stage where it has become an acute political question," receiving ample consideration from Shepardson's colleagues at the CFR and the public at large.[73]

Shepardson knew whereof he spoke. For three decades, since thriving as a Rhodes Scholar at Oxford University, he had been one of those "wishful-thinking people," devoting himself to the furtherance of Anglophone unity, at least when not discharging his duties as an international business execu-tive. Shepardson headed the American branch of the Round Table, a transna-tional society for the promotion of the Commonwealth, and wrote frequently for the *Round Table* journal.[74] After Pearl Harbor, President Roosevelt sent him to London as a special assistant to the U.S. ambassador and named him the first secret intelligence chief of the Office of Strategic Services, the forerunner of the Central Intelligence Agency (CIA).[75] But it was in the year before Pearl

Harbor that Shepardson found his moment. Of the various possible configurations for postwar U.S. policy, there was little question which had the most appeal—to the point that the CFR planners talked about creating a subcommittee called Relations between English-Speaking Peoples, before deciding that there was no need because they were giving the subject ample consideration as it was.[76] At last, other Americans seemed to want what Shepardson had long sought: a world order run by the Anglo-Saxon nations, aligned in a permanent partnership.

Better yet, the United States would take the lead, effective immediately. Shepardson, as chairman of the CFR's Political Group, saw to it that America would lead the peace by first of all leading the planning. He and several other planners had attended the Paris Peace Conference in 1919 and learned that the more detailed proposals of the British proved more influential.[77] This time the United States would come prepared. In the summer of 1941, Shepardson visited the United Kingdom to strengthen ties with British planners and found the roles reversed already. As he reported back to the CFR, British peace planning had not "reached as concrete or specific a stage as in the United States," even though America was not yet a belligerent.[78] Delighted, Shepardson did not consider whether the progress of U.S. planning, based on calculations of the nation's own interest, implied that the wave of Anglo-American enthusiasm might recede as quickly as it surged.

BY 1941 SHEPARDSON'S COMMITMENT TO Anglophone unity was decades in the making. Harder to explain was why so many of his colleagues suddenly shared his passion. Why, from January into the autumn, did *the* framework for American postwar policy become a close partnership with the British Commonwealth? Shepardson aside, the answer cannot be reduced to Anglophilia, which some scholars have featured in explaining Americans' willingness to aid Britain at the risk of war.[79] Anglophilia had never before sufficed to generate wide-ranging interest in practical proposals to join the United States with the other "English-speaking peoples."

The newly Anglo-minded planners worked in dozens of loosely connected bodies, mostly located between Boston and Washington, DC. Their sole coordinator was the Princeton-based American Committee for International Studies, which, despite the energetic efforts of its chairman, the military strategist Edward Mead Earle, performed its job lightly, mostly by circulating information. In February 1941 Earle's committee reported on the emerging consensus among the groups. The committee saw little need for more studies of U.S. relations with Latin America. "A purely hemispheric policy offered no satisfactory basis for policy," the committee wrote. "More significant was the growth in Anglo-American cooperation—or, more broadly, the grouping together of the United States, the British Commonwealth, and Latin America."[80] At the suggestion of Quincy Wright, the committee planned a large conference on postwar North Atlantic relations, and it came to fruition in Prouts Neck, Maine, in September.[81]

Inside the U.S. government, by contrast, "clear authority for planning action is still lacking," economist Alvin Hansen reported to the CFR's Economic and Financial Group on returning from Washington, DC, in mid-February. When it came to planning the future, the Roosevelt administration strained to prepare for the war that was still to come.[82] As Hansen noted, a handful of interdepartmental committees were studying postwar trade patterns in Latin America. But larger considerations of international order, integrating political, military, and economic aspects and extending beyond the Western Hemisphere, fell to CFR planners as well as dozens of unofficial organizations taking the initiative on their own.

These planners foresaw a new world order of Anglophone unity for reasons more robust than Anglophilia. For one, developments at home and abroad had clarified the likely outcome of the war, removing the obstacles to American-British leadership that planners had previously confronted. In the closing months of 1940, as the last chapter described, the CFR's Economic and Financial Group had drawn up the Grand Area of Anglo-American preeminence to counter a German-dominated greater Europe. Back then, however, the planners still worried that Germany might defeat Britain and establish a grand area of its own. And even if Germany lost, the Political Group objected that Britain—and not the United States—would be the senior partner of a postwar alliance. Facing a kaleidoscope of plausible outcomes, the planners wondered aloud how far into the future they could really plan.[83]

These doubts vanished at the start of 1941. Now the planners felt they could see years beyond the war. Shepardson opened a series of animated meetings of the Political Group by asserting the "importance of considering relatively long-term national objectives."[84] The group was impressed by the deluge of public proclamations of America's stake in the peace, referencing Roosevelt's Four Freedoms Speech in particular. Moreover, it saw a power structure taking shape across the Atlantic along the most optimistic lines of Grand Area planning. Germany appeared likely to end up confined to the European Continent, if not defeated completely. The rest of the world would belong to the Anglophone powers, their fleets intact, as they waged a warlike peace with Nazi Europe.

Indeed, this projected Anglo-Nazi standoff was the cold war that mattered at the time. The Soviet Union figured peripherally in Americans' postwar thinking before Germany attacked it in June 1941. Until then, the Soviet Union was a neutral toward the war, more so than the United States was. Because the Soviet contribution to world trade was scant, the CFR planners ignored the country when they expanded the U.S. defense perimeter from the quarter sphere to the Grand Area. And for several months after Germany launched its invasion, it appeared that the Soviet Union might be swiftly conquered as Hitler intended, far from emerging as a mighty factor in the postwar world.

Japan, despite being a member of the Tripartite Pact, was also far subordinate to Germany in U.S. postwar thinking and planning. It was Japan that had alarmed war planners for decades, because it posed a threat to ill-defended U.S. territory in Alaska, American Samoa, Guam, Hawaii, and the Philippines. Japan would indeed attack those territories in 1941 and 1942. Yet the nonterritorial threat from Germany was what shook the American political system. Japan had to invade all of French Indochina in July 1941 in order to compel the U.S. Congress to fortify the Pacific, most notably by sending B-17 bombers to the vulnerable Philippines.[85] Meanwhile, even as the Roosevelt administration imposed a near-total embargo on Japan in the summer, postwar planners in the CFR were counting on incorporating Japan into their U.S.-led Grand Area. Until November 1941, for example, Bowman believed the United States could woo Japan away from the Axis by recognizing Japanese control in Manchuria in return for its withdrawal from mainland China.[86] Eurocentrism rendered East Asia peripheral to the planners, and racism perhaps allowed them to view Japan as infinitely malleable.

It was against Nazi Germany, prior to Pearl Harbor, that Americans developed the cold war concepts they would apply to the Soviet Union in the late 1940s. Germany ruled western Europe throughout 1941, bombing Britain before turning east. In the Nazis U.S. elites confronted an implacably expansionist, totalitarian adversary that divided the world into two armed camps, each standing for its own political, economic, and social order.[87] And they decided that the United States, leading the Free World—the name of an

This propaganda poster, created by the U.S. Office of War Information in 1942, echoes the words of Abraham Lincoln's famous "House Divided" speech in 1858 to tie the main currents of American history to the interventionist vision of a "free world." Courtesy of the Northwestern University Library.

interventionist association and publication established in 1941—must possess a preponderance of power over the slave world.[88] In its inaugural issue in October, *Free World* magazine dedicated itself to the cause of "universal struggle" between democracy and fascism, and included the Soviet Union on the side of the anti-fascist resistance. "As long as the aggressor is not definitely beaten," it announced, "there can be no peace."[89] Peace was empty of meaning in a world locked in actual war or warlike enmity between two irreconcilable orders.

Such geopolitical projections provide an important part of the explanation for Americans' interest in leading the world through a formal and exclusive partnership with the British Commonwealth: the idea reflected the probable centers of postwar power as of early 1941, extrapolating the wartime status quo forward. However intent on leading the postwar world, the United States still needed to integrate itself closely with Great Britain, and the greater Commonwealth, in order to do so. America was arming, but Britain was fighting. Its fleet, not the U.S. Navy, stood between Hitler and North America. Furthermore, Britain possessed an imperial system that seemed to be proving itself vital in the war against the Axis and equally vital to the preservation of order after the war—especially if, as planners envisaged, the United States could jointly man British bases. As Roosevelt wrote privately, using words drafted by Undersecretary of State Sumner Welles, "The British Isles, the British in those Isles, have been able to exist and to defend themselves not only because they have prepared strong local defenses but also because as the heart and the nerve center of the British Empire they have been able to draw upon vast resources for their sustenance and to bring into operation against their enemies economic, military and naval pressures on a world-wide scale."[90] In 1941 Roosevelt and other policy elites concluded that the United States had a strong interest in preserving something like the British "world-system," as the historian John Darwin dubs it: the global network of military bases, the common allegiance to laws and norms, the circulation of finished goods and raw materials—and the desire to stay supreme over any rival.[91]

Shifting power realities in 1941 did not work only to elevate Britain in America's esteem. One reason why U.S. elites converged around an American-British framework was that *American* came before *British:* they believed the postwar United States would be the senior partner in the relationship, a prospect that had seemed dubious during World War I and the interwar period.[92] The CFR planners replaced "Anglo-American" with "American-British" in their discussions in the spring of 1941.[93] Buell coined "America-British leadership."[94] The perception that U.S. power had surpassed Britain's was shared, and welcomed, across the Atlantic. "Pax Americo-Britannica" and "Americo-British world order" was how Arnold Toynbee, the dean of British internationalism, characterized the future for which he hoped.[95] In mid-May, the *Economist* urged its British readers to accept that "we are the weaker, and the less numerous partner." Going forward, it wrote, "the ultimate decision must rest with the ultimate power, and that, increasingly, lies over the oceans."[96] The Roosevelt administration appreciated the reversal of position and immediately put the U.S. advantage to use, pressuring Britain to implement liberal reforms. The administration used the Lend-Lease negotiations that commenced in 1941 to extract a British pledge to eliminate commercial discrimination across the empire.[97] Roosevelt went on during the war to ask Britain to relinquish control of India and hector France to place its colony of Indochina under international trusteeship.[98]

Both Anglophilic sentiments and geopolitical realities, then, drove U.S. elites to single out the British Commonwealth as America's primary postwar partner. Yet those factors do not explain why many planners eyed an exclusive American-British partnership, ruling out meaningful participation by others. Postwar planners did not simply apply the last generation's Wilsonian universalism wherever the Nazis weren't; American-British partnership was not the League of Nations writ small. In the eyes of U.S. planners, some of whom designed and promoted Wilson's League, this time was different: world order required a single dominant power solely responsible for orchestrating it.

ARMED FORCE, "we know now," is essential to any international objective, George Fielding Eliot underscored as he presented his plan for American-British leadership to the Political Group in February. Force had to be overwhelming in scale and capable of rapid deployment, or else it would be "useless."[99] Eliot had no doubt that the League experiment fell into the latter category. Nor would another broadly based international organization fare better. The obstacles were insuperable: the diversity of interests and outlooks, the diffusion of responsibility, the absence of superintending authority. Unlike a general association of nations, "Anglo-American sea-power is in fact a world-wide power capable of immediate application," Eliot claimed, "and seems likely to be the only power answering that description."[100]

Of all the planners, Eliot ranked alongside Miller as the most zealous advocate of Anglo-American exclusivity, of involving none but Anglophone peoples and powers in any postwar project. Yet no one really disputed the basic vision of a "new international order under American-British auspices," as the Political Group phrased its objective for the postwar world in June.[101] This, in addition to Anglophilia and geopolitics, was what propelled ideas of Anglophone unity into popularity: the promise that American-British leadership, because of its exclusivity, might succeed in creating international order where international organization had failed. For the CFR planners, the joint armed power of America and Britain, and no one else, would keep order among nations and do so under terms favorable to the hegemons and the demands of their liberal and capitalist systems.

Hamilton Fish Armstrong, in the fourteenth of his forty-four-year reign as the editor of the CFR's magazine, *Foreign Affairs,* aptly characterized the planners' prescription. "The primary responsibility for the maintenance of international order would rest upon the United States and the British Empire for an indeterminate period following a Nazi defeat," he wrote. Such an arrangement need not forbid the nominal participation of others—a fact that loomed larger later in the year. For now, however, the planners were thinking all about the essentials, America and the Anglo constituents of Greater Britain. "Whether this responsibility is discharged openly or whether it is under the guise of enforcing the decisions of a new or revived League of Nations is of secondary importance from a technical military point of view," Armstrong continued. "The important thing is that the two powers must be in possession of such facilities as will ensure their ability easily and effectively to deal with any possible situation which might arise."[102] Miller applied his characteristic candor to the tactful phrasings of Armstrong. "Small states," Miller stated, "were parasites on the international body politic." They had nothing to contribute to the maintenance of international order and only lived off whatever order was provided by the strong.[103]

The planners were not, however, eager to give up all hope of ending war. They wanted to think of themselves as extending the work of prior internationalists, themselves not least. But the most they could realistically imagine was to scale down war to a series of policing operations undertaken across the globe by the American-British enforcer. One could of course define, or dress up, policing ("intervention," in later nomenclature) to be something other than war. But to a remarkable degree the planners resisted the temptation as they discussed their views. They decided to exclude "the ultimate eradication of war" from their list of basic U.S. interests, lest they evoke, one planner explained, a "false pacifism."[104] Instead they recommended that Roosevelt encourage Americans to "dedicate their intelligence to the supreme task of establishing a stable world order"—one of many articulations of U.S. aims as building order rather than building peace.[105]

As they reached the conclusion that the United States should maintain world order through superior force, planners did not shrink from stating U.S. objectives in the language of supremacy, domination, and taking the offensive. Their terminology provided more than rhetorical flourish; it highlighted what was novel about their analysis. Americans had long thought of themselves as leading the world toward better things, but only now did leadership appear to require the global preponderance of military power. The first mention of the term *supremacy* in CFR memorandums came in October 1940, when the Economic and Financial Group called for an "integrated policy to achieve military and economic supremacy for the United States within the non-German world."[106] By 1941 planners spoke frequently of achieving domination. Hanson Baldwin, a *New York Times* military analyst and cochair of the CFR's Armaments Group, matter-of-factly described the planners' proposal as consisting of "world domination by the United States and the British Empire acting in close and continuous collaboration."[107] For Miller, both the scope and the purpose of the new mission rendered the United States as an empire. "Washington was now the center of a civilization reaching to Australia and South Africa," he said. "America had to accept its imperial destiny, give up its defensive attitude, and accept its responsibility."[108]

In pursuit of domination, Baldwin favored a posture of "aggressive defense," citing Lippmann's proposals to rapidly accumulate military bases.[109] Eliot dispensed with the pretense of defense: "Defensive war is the worst kind of war." As he saw it, American-British leadership would be "a policy essentially offensive in character," replacing "a purely defensive one geared to the Western Hemisphere."[110] (That dominance over the entire Western Hemisphere embodied defense—the position of many noninterventionists as well—itself marked a shift from the late 1920s and early 1930s, when popular and congressional criticism of U.S. intervention in Nicaragua and Haiti led the administrations of Herbert Hoover and Roosevelt to adopt the Good Neighbor Policy.)[111] In a memorandum in May, Eliot laid out his "doctrine of advanced bases." First, he instructed, "never allow the enemy to gain possession of a base from which he can attack your vital centers." Second, "seek to obtain for yourself advanced bases from which the enemy's vital centers can be attacked." These principles collapsed the distinction between offense and defense. "Even from the purely defensive viewpoint," Eliot affirmed, "it is always better to keep the enemy at a distance from one's own vital centers."[112] Pure defense thus mandated the same strategy as offense. As dramatic as Eliot's doctrine sounded, it simply generalized the basis on which the United States sent Lend-Lease aid to Britain.

Unlike hemisphere defense, the posture of offense or aggressive defense had no geographical limit but applied most immediately to Europe. Adopting the terminology of classic balance-of-power politics, planners spoke of the postwar American-British alliance possessing a "reservoir of power to hold the balance" on the Continent.[113] Their allusion was inexact; especially as 1941 wore on, they proved more inclined to establish a superior authority to eliminate balancing forces altogether. By September the CFR's Armaments Group foresaw America and Britain disarming Germany— some thought permanently—and dismantling the production of military aircraft all over western Europe. The group hoped the Anglophone powers would deploy force "unstintingly at the first indication of any rearmament attempt."[114] At the same time, the leading powers would act as they saw fit; the planners eschewed, with scant discussion, any legal commitments to obligate America or Britain to act in case of rearmament or aggression. Self-interest, not law, received the planners' trust.

As the Armaments Group studied how to organize the police force, Eliot and retired major general Frank McCoy, who served as president of the Foreign Policy Association throughout the war, found a model in British imperial policing.[115] They suggested that America and Britain rely on air power to shuttle around small, elite land forces, as the British used in the North-West Frontier Province of India and nominally independent Iraq.[116] Such an airborne army could overcome two obstacles imposed by U.S. domestic opinion: it could comprise "a small number of highly-trained troops and not a mass citizen army," as Miller observed, and it could avoid the widespread bombing of civilians.[117] After Pearl Harbor, the idea of a combined American-British police force would win little support from heads of government, but it nonetheless stood as an early example of enduring patterns of thought. One was the idealization of air power as a substitute for citizen armies, the airplane thereby adapting global policing to democracy. Another was the reduction of Europe from a subject to an object of great-power politics, to a status previously reserved for colonial and neocolonial territories. Hitler had initiated this transformation by seeking in eastern Europe his version of the subjugated American West or British Raj; now American planners anticipated extending the principle throughout the Continent, right through Germany itself.

Yet if Europe drew the lion's share of the planners' attention, it was only because of Europe's importance to the balance of power. The planners did not limit postwar American-British military responsibilities to the North Atlantic or any other discrete space, nor against the defeated Axis states. They sought to secure a preponderance of power wherever power lay. Miller called for an American-British "Navy and Air Force (with necessary bases and servicing facilities) strong enough to meet any other combination of forces."[118] "It is obvious," wrote Armstrong, summarizing the views of his colleagues, that America and Britain "must be in control of the necessary air and naval bases which will enable them, acting jointly or in close cooperation, to contain any possible hostile force."[119] No doubt Armstrong had the Axis powers in mind as the primary hostile force, but he directed his strategic maxim against "any possible" adversary. Using the very word *contain,* Armstrong prefigured the doctrine of containment against the Soviet Union during the Cold War and a litany of states thereafter.[120] The objective, born in 1941, was to maintain armed primacy, not merely police the fallen Axis.

This objective guided the Armaments Group in its principal task for the year: mapping the military bases from which the American-British alliance would enforce postwar order. The planners quickly discovered that if the British Empire did not exist, they would have to invent it. Eliot posited that outside North America global supremacy required three vital centers for naval and air bases: the Caribbean, the Mediterranean, and the South China Sea.[121] Fortunately, as he noted, America and Britain currently possessed most of the needed bases. The group stressed that Britain must retain and expand its control over the Mediterranean in particular, by acquiring positions in Casablanca, Mogador, and Sicily.[122] The United States should not only support Britain in this effort but potentially jointly occupy the bases. Throughout the year, the planners debated whether bases would be apportioned between the two powers or run by a genuinely integrated force.[123]

Combining U.S. forces with existing British positions would not suffice. The group wanted an archipelago of new bases in the Atlantic and the Pacific. Most important were naval bases "for the purposes of Atlantic and European domination," especially in the north (in Newfoundland and in Greenland, Denmark, and Norway) and along the approach to South America (in the Cape Verde Islands or West Africa near Dakar, and perhaps in Natal in eastern

Brazil). The planners could not be as precise about the Pacific, where American belligerency and British survival struck them as less assured. They nevertheless contemplated new bases off the coast of Alaska and along the Malay Barrier, running from present-day Malaysia and Singapore to Indonesia, well beyond the U.S. Navy's outpost in the colony of the Philippines.[124]

In plotting world domination (by their own reckoning), the CFR planners moved decisively past both hemisphere defense and world organization, the two positions around which U.S. foreign policy had revolved in the preceding decades. A Pan-American perimeter denied U.S. interests in world order. A league of nations denied the United States the means to order the world. These were fateful conclusions, and novel ones, not anticipated at the beginning of the war. As Shepardson told British planners, the CFR's Armaments Group "started as a Disarmament Group searching for the solution of the problem of how best to disarm, but from there had gone on to the idea of the need to maintain security, for a longer or a shorter period, by American and British arms."[125]

But charting a new course would not be as simple as marking down bases on a map. In May Bowman, the chair of the Territorial Group, posed a challenge that went beyond the Armaments Group's purview. "How could the taking over of Dakar and Singapore be justified on the basis of a Western Hemisphere doctrine?" he mused. "If freedom of opinion and of choice were cut out of the Monroe Doctrine, it would then resemble the Nazi doctrine very closely."[126] As Bowman implied, American-British leadership could not be, and especially could not appear to be, solely about maintaining armed supremacy over all potential rivals. Such a goal was not necessary for the defense of the United States, so it had to sound morally justified. In order to address this presentational problem, the planners turned again to the British Empire, in which they found a ready-made model for covering the stark coercion of superior force with the veneer of liberal freedom.

THROUGHOUT 1941 the United States and Nazi Germany squared off in the arena of global public opinion, each staking a claim to lead the world toward a superior form of life. Roosevelt issued the Four Freedoms explicitly for this purpose, proclaiming his vision to be "the very antithesis of the so-called new order of tyranny which the dictators seek to create with the crash of a bomb."[127] Roosevelt's postwar planners understood the need to develop an affirmative concept to counterpose to the Nazi New Order. Of course, there was no going back to the Versailles settlement and the League of Nations, but a compelling substitute would have to inspire the peoples of the United States and the world. They therefore endeavored to expand American-British policing into a full-fledged, Anglo-ruled international society that advanced freedom as well as stability.

In a series of memorandums from May to September, Shepardson's Political Group laid out sweeping proposals to institutionalize postwar cooperation with the British Commonwealth of Nations.[128] The planners began by rejecting not only the halfhearted "associated power" relationship from World War I but also a "complete defensive alliance with the British Commonwealth by formal treaty." Even this radical measure failed to provide a sufficiently positive and comprehensive vision. Instead they decided that American-British leadership should take the form of a "permanent political tie-up," involving the "unified use of sea and air power" for global policing but not stopping there. Also included would be a "cooperative policy on trade, raw materials, shipping, commercial aviation, currency, and investment" and "general collaboration on such matters as health, nutrition, migration, resettlement, and the development of backward regions," all implemented as far as the non-German world extended.[129] That is, the Anglophone nations would take over the entire apparatus of international governance centered in Geneva—a process that wartime events had already initiated, sending the League of Nations' Economic and Financial Section to take refuge in Princeton courtesy of Rockefeller Foundation largesse.[130]

In early June, at the peak of Anglophone feeling, the Political Group went so far as to draft an act of Congress that would grant near-citizenship to citizens of the British Commonwealth around the world. It appointed the Canadian-born historian and CSOP chairman James Shotwell to be the framer of this quasi-constitutional document, whose purpose, as stated in its preamble, was to "extend the Freedom of the United States of America to Citizens of the British Commonwealth of Nations." Shotwell's draft conferred almost every right, short of the right to vote and hold political office, on what it dubbed "the 'defenders of freedom' throughout the English-speaking community." By this Shotwell meant the white citizens of the Dominions; the group immediately excluded Indians and other residents of Britain's crown colonies. Under the act, in other words, white English speakers across the Dominions would receive the unrestricted right to immigrate to and reside in the United States, where they could conduct business and own property like any citizen.

Far from seeking to remake the world in the image of America and its federalist system, the planners intended to remake the United States in the image of white settler colonialism. They found inspiration in turn-of-the-century fantasies of uniting whites across the noncontiguous Anglosphere. These fantasies layered modern notions of race on the ancient Greek practice of extending citizenship rights to members of other city-states. Through "racial isopolitan citizenship," as the political scientist Duncan Bell terms it, nineteenth-century Britons saw an opportunity to create a supreme globe-spanning polity at the vanguard of civilization.[131] In 1941 U.S. policy elites in New York eyed a similar opportunity, albeit one with risks. Arthur Sweetser, a journalist close to the League of Nations Secretariat, wondered aloud whether the act "might not be interpreted by the rest of the world as a move toward Anglo-Saxon domination." But the group sided with Miller, his riposte preserved by the meeting minutes: "Noting that a common language was the principal basis of community, Mr. Miller did not care what other peoples might call the action." As a matter of fact, the group regarded the act merely as the beginning of Anglophone integration. It hoped the extension of American freedoms to white Anglos everywhere would constitute a "symbolic first step toward that long-term American-British association which the Group had debated for months."[132]

But despite wishing to institutionalize American-British cooperation, the CFR planners ultimately decided to rely not on formal legal obligations but rather on the commonality of interest and sentiment they believed to exist among the Anglophone powers. They had learned from the League experience that binding duties would matter little once the time for action came. So they shrunk from advocating on-paper commitments requiring America and Britain to act against aggression. (And they gave no consideration to measures for restraining the big two from *committing* aggression.) Although political scientist Walter Sharp, the group's research secretary, proposed that conferences between the American and British powers should "exceed advice or recommendation and assume an executive character," he admitted his inability to "envisage just what such machinery would look like or how it would operate."[133]

The group's final blueprint called for the American-British security council, as it were, to reach decisions through a "round-the-table consensus of views," without holding a vote.[134] There were to be no safeguards against abuses of power. What could an abuse of power even mean in a scheme that reserved to a few states the prerogative to do as they saw fit? The planners were now miles from the League of Nations and other internationalist prescriptions. For all the hierarchies it inscribed, especially in the colonized world, the League had created formal standards by which abuses of power could be conceptualized and claims advanced in its name, as they were by the thousands.[135] It was this possibility that the idea of American-British leadership obliterated.

Even though they sought to imbue American-British partnership with elements of the Geneva system, then, the planners did not so much modify the League template as scrap it. They did consider retaining the International Labor Organization and the League's technical sections, in which experts studied and implemented economic, social, and humanitarian programs.[136] They also contemplated extending to all colonial territories a modified version of the League's mandates system, which provided limited international oversight of colonies taken from the defeated German and Ottoman powers in World War I. Through a new mandates system, with U.S. participation, Americans could trade and invest across the colonial world on equal terms with the colonial powers.[137] But as a model for high politics, for keeping the world orderly, the League was the opposite of a model.

Rejecting the League of Nations, the planners also declined to take the other locus of prewar U.S. foreign policy, the Pan-American system, as a point of departure. In making the leap from hemispherism to globalism, they did not understand themselves as extending the Monroe Doctrine to the world. If any part of the Western Hemisphere captured the planners' imagination in 1941, it lay to the north, not the south. Anglophone Canada, the CFR planners repeatedly argued, deserved Lend-Lease aid and new programs of economic assistance and cultural exchange, all of which would build on the bilateral Permanent Joint Board of Defense, created in the previous August by President Roosevelt and Canadian prime minister Mackenzie King.[138] The planners reasoned that whereas Nazi influence in Latin America remained an omnipresent worry, Canada deserved special treatment because it was "the one nation of the Hemisphere that is opposing Hitler with the force of arms."[139] And not by coincidence: the folk-minded planners figured that "Canada's population of twelve million, half of whom are of British descent, would certainly be more congenial in partnership with the United States than would Latin America with its 120 million, chiefly of Latin or Indian descent."[140]

In short, the CFR planners hewed neither to League-style internationalism nor to traditional Pan-Americanism. They looked elsewhere for guidance—to the intra-imperial machinery of the British Commonwealth. In the Commonwealth they found a successful model of global order that, making no pretense of universal participation, maintained close informal cooperation among the white Dominions even as settler nationalism drove them formally apart. After World War I, Great Britain and its Dominions formed the Commonwealth and convened at regular conferences empowered only, as the planners noted, to "advise and recommend." The Commonwealth system, enshrined in the Statute of Westminster in 1931, therefore showed how mere consultation might prove effective among like-minded nations. The planners believed they knew why the system worked while the League did not: "The English-speaking people have a genius for extemporizing order."[141] Much as this Burkean genius had produced the domestic common law, so too would it develop procedures of international cooperation in response to concrete situations.[142] Lest their theory seem far-fetched, the planners felt the process was well under way in the destroyers deal and Lend-Lease program.[143]

The planners also studied a second model for postwar cooperation, largely drawn again from the Anglophone world: the intergovernmental machinery used by the Allies in World War I to coordinate their war effort.[144] Like the Commonwealth conferences, which they helped to inspire, inter-Allied bodies possessed no executive authority but secured concerted action. The Allied Maritime Transport Council, the Inter-Allied Food and Munitions Councils, and the Supreme War Council—all these instruments of wartime alliance impressed the CFR planners as being superior to universal world organization, including in times of peace. "It is now generally recognized," they wrote, "that one of the tragic errors of statesmanship in 1919 was the abrupt scrapping of this inter-continental machinery."[145]

Similarly, in Luce's Post-War Committee, Buell detected that the coordinated effort against Nazi Germany was giving rise to a new era of "Americo-British" supremacy modeled on the British Commonwealth and the Allied war councils. "Under Lend Lease," Buell observed at the end of 1941, "a vast web of administrative relationship is quietly being built up between Britain and the U.S.—a relationship which has not yet been described or analyzed by any periodical for the benefit of the American public." He estimated that three thousand British officials, from every department of government, were already present in New York City and Washington, DC. Just as the Imperial War Cabinet of 1915 had supplied a template to establish the British Commonwealth, so perhaps the Lend-Lease program was "creating a nucleus of Americo-British power which will dominate the post-war world."[146]

It was this nucleus that mattered most to U.S. planners even as they began, in the summer and autumn, to pay attention to other features of international society. The CFR Political Group contained some of the most prominent League of Nations boosters in the country, but in 1941 they stood convinced that world organization would not produce an acceptable world order. Only the armed supremacy of the United States could do so, in partnership with the British Commonwealth and carrying on the torch of British world leadership. All of a sudden, the record of nineteenth-century British diplomacy looked better than Americans had thought at the time. In column after column, Walter Lippmann reinterpreted the Monroe Doctrine as an Anglo-American alliance directed against the Holy Alliance, ignoring that Americans had invoked the Monroe Doctrine against Great Britain as much as any other power.[147] The British, Lippmann wrote, "have organized the largest security that the world has known since the Romans, and with all their mistakes they have extended more widely the area of law and order than it was ever before extended on earth."[148]

More candidly, Buell acknowledged that Americans had condemned British supremacy so often before, but he condemned their condemnation. Americans had suffered from a "colonial inferiority complex," Buell decided.[149] They blinded themselves to the truth that nineteenth-century Britain "maintained almost single-handed the nearest semblance to world order known in modern history."[150] Although the United States had an opportunity to partner with Britain in 1919, its president failed to appreciate the world-ordering role of the British Navy. Wilson's League of Nations inevitably turned into a "fruitless search for a substitute for the Pax Britannica."[151] This time would be, had to be, different. The United States would accept no substitute, except perhaps a Pax Americana.

The Apogee of American-British Leadership

In 1941 anti-isolationism acquired a positive program. Its adherents had grasped for some way to enforce world order during the 1930s and the

Phoney War, when collective security failed and the most they could ask of the United States was that it refrain from selling arms and extending loans to aggressor nations. Now they identified the United States as the ultimate arbiter of global politics, the leader of an order that would overpower that of the Axis and of any possible future rival. "It may change our entire way of living," as one Midwestern businessman put it, "but if there has to be one top dog in this world we are going to be that top dog and not Adolf Hitler."[152] Henceforth the United States would project military power beyond the Western Hemisphere and, in principle, wherever armed strength and its sources could be found. At the same time, anti-isolationists figured that U.S. supremacy should take the form of a close partnership with the British Commonwealth. This was not a perfect fit. American-British internationalism was neither wholly American nor fully internationalist. Looking back, one might dismiss the plans of 1941 as vivid imaginings that would never have become policy.

To the contrary, a version of the Anglo new order might well have come to pass if the geopolitical configuration that generated it had endured. The United States and the British Commonwealth were in fact developing a robust material and ideological partnership to contain a Nazi-led Europe, with America serving as the arsenal of democracy, just short of belligerency, and the Soviet Union remaining neutral. Even when those conditions started to change in the second half of 1941, as the German Army swept eastward to invade the Soviet Union, U.S. foreign policy elites did not yet judge a wider international political structure to be worthwhile or reconcilable with U.S. supremacy, as Chapter 4 will discuss. At the highest levels of the U.S. government, officials shared the interest of planners and intellectuals in exclusive American-British institutions for leading the postwar world.

As a British planner found in April, the State Department was thinking along joint American-British lines much like the CFR members who worked for it. Dispatched to the United States to ascertain American thinking about the peace, historian Charles Webster discovered to his surprise and pleasure that U.S. policy elites "realize the longer and deeper issues better than many Britishers."[153] After speaking with four of the CFR planners in New York, Webster found officials in Washington equally congenial. Even the typically Anglophobic Berle "obviously thoroughly believed in Anglo-American cooper[ation] after war," Webster recorded in his diary.[154] Although the State Department was not yet ready to establish a postwar planning committee of its own, research director Leo Pasvolsky was already formulating plans to do so, having maintained close contact with the CFR throughout the war. By the autumn, officials began to lobby Roosevelt to endow the State Department with the sole authority for official postwar planning—part of a scramble within Roosevelt's anarchic bureaucracy to secure such a role.[155]

Webster's observations had even more validity than he knew. Each aspirant to head up postwar planning within the U.S. government sought to follow the CFR's lead. In July, when William Donovan founded the intelligence office that would later evolve into the CIA, he made a priority of setting up a World War I–style "inquiry" and brought in several academics from the CFR, unsuccessfully inviting Armstrong to be his second in command.[156] For his part, Vice President Wallace, the vocal anti-isolationist, headed the Economic Defense Board, charged with procuring and managing strategic resources, and invited CFR planners to a series of dinner meetings at the Hay Adams Hotel in Washington.[157] At the first dinner, on May 3, Wallace welcomed thirteen members of the CFR and six other experts in order to discover "the direction in which our minds are moving."[158] That direction followed all the major lines of CFR planning as Wallace translated into military terms the meaning of his speeches pledging a Pax Democratica to raise the living standards of the worldwide "common man."[159]

First and foremost, the United States must not fail to lead as it had after the last war, when it left the fate of the world to a general peace conference and the ineffectual League of Nations. "This time," the group agreed, "the instrument of execution will be an American-British agreement," and "we must not again say things that we won't underwrite." To wit, America and Britain would police the world via sea and air power for years after the war. The group proceeded to list fourteen essential "strong points" around the globe to be placed under joint control.[160] And it emphasized that America and Britain should pursue the fastest and closest possible "fusion" of their political and economic as well as military institutions. As it turned out, the Anglophilic CFR planners had no trouble making common cause with the relatively anticolonial Wallace. Suspicion of British aims provided a rationale for American-British partnership too: anticipating that Britain would otherwise resort to currency controls and bilateral trade arrangements, Wallace and company wanted to forge a union straight away.[161]

The CFR planners urged Roosevelt to issue a declaration of postwar principles that would "dramatize" American-British cooperation, firing the public imagination as the League ideal did in World War I.[162] On August 14, 1941, the president obliged. Eager to prevent an Anglo-Soviet carve

THE Atlantic Charter

THE President of THE UNITED STATES OF AMERICA and the Prime Minister, Mr. *Churchill*, representing HIS MAJESTY'S GOVERNMENT IN THE UNITED KINGDOM, being met together, deem it right to make known certain common principles in the national policies of their respective countries on which they base their hopes for a better future for the world.

1.   *Their countries seek no aggrandizement, territorial or other.*

2.   *They desire to see no territorial changes that do not accord with the freely expressed wishes of the peoples concerned.*

3.   *They respect the right of all peoples to choose the form of government under which they will live; and they wish to see sovereign rights and self-government restored to those who have been forcibly deprived of them.*

4.   *They will endeavor, with due respect for their existing obligations, to further the enjoyment by all States, great or small, victor or vanquished, of access, on equal terms, to the trade and to the raw materials of the world which are needed for their economic prosperity.*

5.   *They desire to bring about the fullest collaboration between all nations in the economic field with the object of securing, for all, improved labor standards, economic advancement and social security.*

6.   *After the final destruction of the Nazi tyranny, they hope to see established a peace which will afford to all nations the means of dwelling in safety within their own boundaries, and which will afford assurance that all the men in all the lands may live out their lives in freedom from fear and want.*

7.   *Such a peace should enable all men to traverse the high seas and oceans without hindrance.*

8.   *They believe that all of the nations of the world, for realistic as well as spiritual reasons, must come to the abandonment of the use of force. Since no future peace can be maintained if land, sea or air armaments continue to be employed by nations which threaten, or may threaten, aggression outside of their frontiers, they believe, pending the establishment of a wider and permanent system of general security, that the disarmament of such nations is essential. They will likewise aid and encourage all other practicable measures which will lighten for peace-loving peoples the crushing burden of armaments.*

FRANKLIN D. ROOSEVELT

WINSTON S. CHURCHILL

August 14, 1941

This poster, issued by the U.S. Office of War Information in 1943, celebrates the signing of the Atlantic Charter by Franklin D. Roosevelt and Winston Churchill on August 14, 1941. Courtesy of the National Archives and Records Administration.

up of eastern Europe—"the Russians are making peace commitments like beavers," Berle fretted—Franklin D. Roosevelt met Winston Churchill off the coast of the British Dominion of Newfoundland.[163] From the seas, the two navy men issued the Atlantic Charter, originally called the Eight Points to evoke Wilson's Fourteen Points. It was the first official statement of U.S. postwar aims, proclaimed by America and Britain alone even as Panzer tanks closed in on Leningrad. Roosevelt's and Churchill's eighth and final point called for the disarmament of nations that may threaten aggression, "pending the establishment of a wider and permanent system of general security." On this basis, historians have interpreted the Atlantic Charter as a momentous step toward the revival of world organization.[164]

To Roosevelt it was nothing of the kind. When Churchill proposed to endorse an "effective international organization," Roosevelt struck the phrase. He told the prime minister that only America and Britain, not some world body, could keep peace in the aftermath of war.[165] Roosevelt's own adviser, Welles, protested, disheartened by Roosevelt's casual suggestion that "nothing could be more futile than the reconstitution of a body such as the Assembly of the League of Nations," in Welles's paraphrasing. Welles thought an assembly could be established in a second postwar era, after a transitional period run by America and Britain. The body, he maintained, could act as a "safety valve" through which small nations could voice their complaints or associate themselves with the great powers. Welles's idea won Roosevelt over by 1943, as Chapter 4 will describe, but for now, Roosevelt did not budge. Perhaps a new league might become useful someday, he said. Until then, the United States and Great Britain would exercise trusteeship over the world and no other nation could take part.[166] He refused to pledge the United States in favor of world organization, even as a distant prospect.

In Africa, Asia, and the Middle East, the Atlantic Charter excited subjects of empire who insisted that its pledge of self-determination applied to them.[167] The document figures in historical memory as an anticolonial pronouncement.[168] But one might equally ask how *colonial* the Atlantic Charter was. The charter marked the zenith of American interest in joining with the British Empire to police the world. In substance, it comported with Secretary of the Navy Frank Knox's call, two months later, for American-British domination of the seas one hundred years hence. "You may say it is a dangerous power when controlled by so few," Knox said, "and there is truth in that reflection. But, feeble and inadequate as may be the impulses in American and British hearts for the common good and the advancement of civilization, and likely as it may be that this power will sometimes be abused, it is far safer thus than if that power should be permitted to pass into the hands of aggressive nations who seek their own selfish aggrandizement."[169] Knox almost elaborated the counterargument within the argument itself. A more perfect union of national prerogative and global responsibility, of exceptionalism and internationalism, would not need to make excuses.

4

INSTRUMENTAL INTERNATIONALISM, 1941–1943

THE WORLD WAS A DANGEROUS PLACE IN which America had to take up arms: no one needed to convince Edward Mead Earle of that. Before Henry Kissinger, Hans Morgenthau, and a cavalcade of émigré realpolitikers transplanted the dark lessons of Weimar democracy to the United States, academics like Earle, born and raised in New York City, readied the soil.[1] In the mid-1930s Earle established a "grand strategy" seminar in Princeton, New Jersey, while in New Haven ambitious scholars set up the Yale Institute for International Studies. Although both institutes dedicated themselves to the study of power politics, only after the fall of France did the strategists morph into advocates of U.S. global supremacy and critics of the bugaboo they called isolationism. Earle, in particular, became a full-throated interventionist spokesman, taking his message to the pages of *Political Science Quarterly* and *Ladies' Home Journal* alike. He told Americans to attain a "primacy of our own" in order to preserve a "universal concept of international order," previously underwritten by British arms.[2]

The Yale Institute, meanwhile, produced the most elaborate geopolitical argument against hemisphere defense and for U.S. participation in the power balances of Europe and Asia. This was Nicholas J. Spykman's *America's Strategy in World Politics,* published in 1942 but mostly written in the year after the fall of France.[3] Spykman contended that German and Japanese domination of Eurasia would deprive the United States of the raw materials it needed for industrial military production. He also maintained that this specific threat merely proved a general truth. "States," he wrote, "can survive only by constant devotion to power politics." After the present war, Spykman wanted the United States to police Europe and Asia as Britain had formerly done, continually intervening with superior force to ensure an acceptable political equilibrium. The irrelevance of a universal organization like the League of Nations almost went without saying. At most, Spykman envisioned a number of separate regional councils or a great-power conclave along the lines of the nineteenth-century Concert of Europe.[4]

In so arguing, the academic strategists occupied the vanguard of foreign policy thinking in 1940 and 1941. Yet in another respect they marched increasingly out of step with private planners and public intellectuals. Earle and Spykman used power politics not only as a framework of analysis but also as a language of legitimation. They wanted the populace to accept the same severe conclusions they had drawn. Blaming liberalism for imbuing Americans with an excessive faith in law, morality, and world organization, Earle and Spykman attempted to recast power politics as the most American of pursuits. Just as the U.S. founders had sought to check and balance power domestically, they argued, so would balanced power prevent tyranny internationally.[5] Yet insofar as the strategists envisioned the United States as the preeminent balancer, they implied that American power might constitute a tyranny. Spykman did little to dispel this implication. He appraised U.S. behavior in the Western Hemisphere harshly; "our so-called painless imperialism has seemed painless only to us," he wrote. And he stated baldly that Adolf Hitler was seeking the kind of *Lebensraum* in Europe that the United States had long enjoyed in the Americas.[6] The academic strategists, however attuned to the need for public legitimation, offered a bleak message: seek maximum power, imperialistic though it may be.

Quincy Wright thought this "realism" (as it was just coming to be called) would never work. Already in August 1940, Wright wrote Earle to explain why—in the process articulating a new rationale for world organization. Although he claimed the mantle of Wilsonianism, Wright did not express confidence that power politics could and should be overcome. He heartily approved of Earle's assault on "isolationism," and at that moment Wright was struggling to work out his own preferred vision of world order in the Commission to Study the Organization of Peace (CSOP). Instead Wright outstrategized the strategist, arguing that Earle's methods subverted his aims. The American public, Wright wrote, would never agree to play power politics,

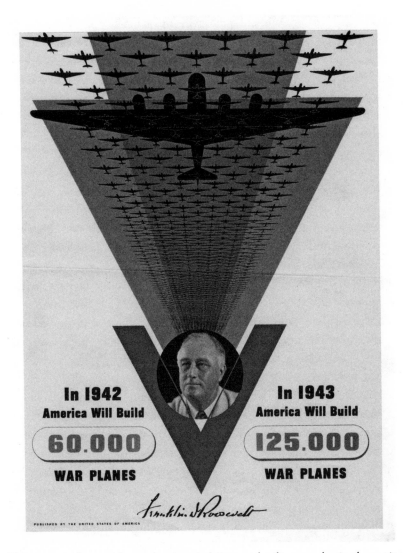

This propaganda poster boasts that America's increased military production has set it on the path to victory in World War II. Courtesy of the National Archives and Records Administration.

a system of shifting alliances suited to the princes of seventeenth-century Europe. "The United States is, I think, positively precluded from the balance-of-power politics with its existing constitutional and democratic structure," he judged.[7] The only *practical* alternative to isolationism, the only way to ensure that Americans would permanently punch their weight on a global basis, was world organization. Without quite giving up on the internationalist dream of a peaceful and lawful world, Wright developed an instrumental rationale for what remained of the Wilsonian program. Absent international organization, America could not lead the world. If only to secure its own supremacy, Wright's logic implied, the United States had to claim the mantle of internationalism—to appear, at least, to organize world politics around principles other than power alone.

Wright was prescient. At the time he originally wrote to Earle, and for twelve months more, most officials and intellectuals followed the academic strategists in dismissing any idea of a new League of Nations. They did envision an international body of a different kind—an intimate and exclusive partnership among the Anglophone nations. Yet such American-British hegemony seemed appealing because it promised to provide international order as no wider formula could. Whether endorsing an empire of the Anglo-Saxon race or the century of the common man, or some of each, U.S. policy elites were one in seeking to participate in—indeed to dominate—power politics and no longer to transcend it through universal methods. Through most of 1941, world supremacy and world organization appeared to preclude one another. Particularist and universalist prescriptions remained poles apart.

It was Wright the idealist who anticipated the eminently realistic logic by which world organization came to appear consistent with, even essential to, U.S. supremacy. Beginning in the second half of 1941, advocates of supremacy perceived the force of Wright's criticism and the appeal of his solution. They worried that the primacy of America alone would appear as brute domination. U.S. supremacy looked even more imperialistic if it were exercised in tandem with Britain, no matter how tenderly its supporters described the traditions of Anglo-Saxon law and liberty. It would look that way first of all to non-Anglo powers, especially the Soviet Union. Surprised when the Nazis attacked the Soviets in June 1941, and again when the Red Army proved its mettle over the following months, American planners started to envision the Soviet Union as a potentially significant postwar player, one that might seek to counter blatant American-British hegemony.

Yet why not simply bring the Soviet Union into the fold, reviving the Concert of Europe for the twentieth-century great powers? Why include small states, roundly dismissed as obstacles to international order? Wright had suggested the answer: U.S. global supremacy would otherwise offend Americans themselves. It was principally to legitimate U.S. supremacy domestically that international organization entered the agenda in late 1941 and 1942. By working through a universal body, with every nation a member, the United States would seem to lead an enlightened world order, bound by rules of law and respecting the equality of others. This, at any rate, was the lesson that interventionist elites drew from their own self-diagnosed failure to pitch supremacy without organization. By 1942 even Earle was criticizing Spykman's book for advocating "irresponsible force, irresponsibly controlled."[8] Arnold Wolfers of the Yale Institute likewise wondered whether, "given the temper of the American people, it may even prove impossible to organize Anglo-American cooperation . . . except under the more universal auspices of some league or association of powers."[9] Members of both Earle's seminar and the Yale Institute went on to advise the U.S. government to create the United Nations (U.N.).[10]

Solving the problem of legitimacy, however, raised a further challenge: how to reconcile the practice of power politics with the appearance of transcending it. Postwar planners felt the contradiction keenly. Through most of 1942 they groped for some way to square the circle, hoping to yoke world supremacy to world organization without yet knowing how to do so or whether it could, in fact, be done. In this they followed the path not so much of Woodrow Wilson and his Inquiry as of British prime minister David Lloyd George and his War Cabinet, which during World War I had sought to reconcile the popular demand for a league of nations with the imperatives of British world leadership.[11]

To the extent that scholars have tried to explain why the United States opted to create a world organization, they have missed the domestic concern to which the U.N. was primarily addressed. Historians both celebratory and critical foreground the kind of international environment that the U.N. was intended to produce: in one version, a peaceful, open, rules-based order; in another, a world safe for capitalism.[12] Political scientists, too, tend to privilege international benefits in debating why states cooperate with international organizations: "realists" minimize the significance of such organizations whereas "liberal institutionalists" counter that organizations help states to collaborate with each other and coordinate their interests.[13] Both camps ascribe to states a narrow rationality determined by the international system and insulated from domestic political contestation and ideological formations.[14] Neither can explain why the United States wanted the U.N. in the first place—why, amid a ferocious war, officials and intellectuals preoccupied themselves with the problem of domestic legitimacy and developed a new concept of internationalism, embodied in a new international organization, as the solution.

The Inadequacies of the Anglosphere

Through the first half of 1941, a chasm separated U.S. global supremacy and universal world organization as postwar possibilities. In the Council on Foreign Relations (CFR), postwar planners took turns lambasting the moribund League of Nations, which they associated with pacifism.[15] Arthur Sweetser and James Shotwell, the two greatest supporters of the League system within the CFR's Political Group, were the nonexceptions that proved the rule. Sweetser, previously a fixture in the Secretariat and Information Section of the League, declined to defend the organization's relevance in matters of high politics, arguing only to retain the financial and economic experts assembled under its auspices.[16] Shotwell showed less enthusiasm still. Despite chairing CSOP, he concluded it was "far better to emphasize the liberties of mankind against the menace of a Gestapo and let the problems of international government work themselves out later."[17] The CFR planners determined that any future world organization would have to follow a "transitional period" of unspecified duration after the war.

Over the second half of the year, however, global supremacy and international organization came together, less because the latter gained in appeal than because the former lost some of its own. At first, welcome developments in the war compelled planners to consider broadening their blueprint for an exclusive partnership between the United States and the British Commonwealth, in that order. As Great Britain defended its home isles against the Luftwaffe and received mounting Lend-Lease aid, planners began to imagine that Nazi conquests could be rolled back within Europe rather than merely contained to the Continent and parts of North Africa and the Middle East. Perhaps the United States could avert a postwar cold war that would pit the Anglosphere against the Nazis' New Order. Instead it could usher in a unified "one world," as Wendell Willkie would title his best-selling travelogue two years later.[18] Such an outcome seemed far from assured, but its mere plausibility sufficed to compel the CFR planners to apply the globalist lessons of the fall of France on a truly global scale. Yet expanding the U.S.-led order did not automatically imply expanding international institutions beyond American-British control. The U.N. would emerge as a second-best option, called forth to secure legitimacy at home as much as abroad.

Toward One World, under America and Britain

The CFR's Economic and Financial Group exemplified one set of concerns that drove the Grand Area Anglosphere to expand. Since the fall of France, the economists had developed comprehensive recommendations for postwar U.S. foreign policy by assessing the requirements of a liberal-capitalist international economy in the context of zero-sum geopolitical competition with a German-dominated Europe. In September 1940 they had devised the Grand Area, an Anglo-led, politically and economically integrated combination of the Western Hemisphere and the British Empire. On the basis of prewar trade patterns, they calculated the Grand Area to provide the minimum "elbow room" needed to maintain U.S. hegemony and liberal capitalism in the Western Hemisphere and economic superiority over a German-dominated Europe.[19] This integrated political-military-economic sphere—a kind of global liberal autarky—could absorb export surpluses through trade and ensure adequate raw materials for defense.

In 1941 the Grand Area grew grander as the planners sought first to increase the American-British advantage over Nazi Europe and then to incorporate Europe itself into the U.S.-led order. The Economic and Financial Group clarified that the Grand Area contained swaths of Africa and Asia, including the whole of the "British Commonwealth and Empire, the Dutch East Indies, China, and Japan."[20] Its members also insisted that the Nazis should be prevented from gaining control of the Near East and North Africa, areas previously thought to be lost causes, and of the Soviet Union, which had been left out. By May the Grand Area was growing from a self-contained economic unit into what planners now called a "nucleus" of an integrated world economy.[21] Within six months, U.S. strategy in the prospective cold war with Nazi Germany advanced from containment to rollback, to use the terminology of the following decade.

Rather than redo their studies, the economic planners moved their goalposts. They shifted from minimum requirements to maximal objectives, casting the latter in the language of necessity. Quietly contradicting the group's original calculations, economist Winfield Riefler concluded that "the existence of the German 'grand area,'" confined to Europe, "would be fundamentally incompatible with the American economic system."[22] Riefler would soon be appointed as Vice President Henry Wallace's chief adviser on the Economic Defense Board, and his views found support elsewhere in the government.[23] Lynn Edminster, a special adviser to Secretary of State Cordell Hull, publicly announced in May that the United States sought to "establish and maintain the largest possible sphere in the world within which trade and other economic relations can be conducted on the basis of liberal principles."[24] Having already determined, after France fell, that the United States needed to lead a globe-spanning order, U.S. elites sought every opportunity to enlarge the Grand Area. After mid-June, the CFR planners ceased to discuss the Grand Area except as a stopgap measure that awaited the incorporation of Europe after a full Nazi defeat.[25] Thus the traditional American preference for global intercourse overtook the emergency planning for liberal autarky, but the former bore the mark of the latter: global intercourse now entailed global armed policing.

Seeking universal economic integration, the planners considered creating international institutions that would lubricate global capitalism. As several noted, because of the trend toward the governmental direction of economic processes, even a liberal economic order would require some degree of coordination by political authorities.[26] From September to December 1941, the Economic and Financial Group formulated plans for an international currency stabilization and lending authority in which governments would cooperate to finance the reconstruction of industrial economies and the development of what it termed backward areas. Three years later, this authority became the International Monetary Fund and the World Bank, established at the Bretton Woods conference in New Hampshire. The outcome owed partly to the direct efforts of the Economic and Financial group's cochairmen, Alvin Hansen and Jacob Viner, who were wartime advisers on the Federal Reserve Board and in the Treasury Department, respectively, and influenced the leading official negotiators at Bretton Woods, John Maynard Keynes for the United Kingdom and Harry Dexter White for the United States.[27] The work of the CFR planners constitutes one point of origin of the postwar monetary and financial system and the U.S. commitment to reconstruction and development.[28]

On balance, however, the economic globalism of the CFR planners scarcely diluted their commitment to American-British world leadership. Nor did it lead them to envision a full-scale international political organization, which, they recognized, represented a much more controversial proposition than economic institutions. In fact, they conceived of the World Bank specifically for the purpose of cementing Anglo-American cooperation and dominance. As Riefler characterized the group's objective, "We must establish interpenetration between the European economy and that of the rest of the world, and we want the United States and the United Kingdom to be running it."[29] For the CFR economists, the foremost rationale for promoting global development after the war was to address the balance-of-payments deficit that Britain would face. The British Isles were hemorrhaging foreign reserves and invisible exports, a problem exacerbated by the State Department's demands to dismantle the imperial preference system in compensation for Lend-Lease aid. Once it engaged in postwar reconstruction, Britain seemed certain to struggle to finance heavy imports, particularly from the United States.

After bringing British economists into the CFR for a series of meetings, Hansen sailed to London to discuss the problem at a conference of government officials and experts from Chatham House and other bodies. He reported back that Keynes favored the continuation of bilateral exchange controls after the war; the United States would agree to buy British exports, and Britain would return the favor.[30] But Hansen and the other planners preferred a multilateral approach, which was also acceptable to Keynes. By building up the world economy, they thought, the Anglophone powers could create a market for British exports without having to negotiate and maintain clearing agreements, which might strain Anglo-American relations. For this reason the economists devised plans to guarantee private investment in underdeveloped regions through an international lending authority, controlled either wholly or two-thirds by American and British directors.[31]

Given the expansionist aims of the CFR's economic planners, one might be tempted to join some analysts in arguing that the perceived imperatives of capitalism propelled America's assumption of global political-military responsibilities and its recasting of international institutions.[32] Yet politics cannot be reduced to economics so neatly, even when one looks no further than the CFR economists. The Economic and Financial Group embedded political considerations into its calculations at every turn. In the immediate aftermath of the German conquest of France, it deemed a quarter sphere area to be adequate for the U.S. economy alone, reversing itself only when interventionists and noninterventionists alike demanded the defense of the entire Western Hemisphere. Then it devised the Grand Area not merely to maintain liberal capitalism by absorbing export surpluses but also to outcompete Nazi Europe through greater self-sufficiency in trade and raw materials. In a cold war with the Nazis, geopolitics and economics would be intertwined. And neither factor would require an international political organization outside the monopoly of America and Britain.[33]

MOREOVER, the economists did not clamor the loudest to expand the divided-world Grand Area to one-world globalism. It was instead the more

openly politically oriented CFR planners who pushed for fully global supremacy and, eventually, world organization. From March 1941 onward, the
CFR's three other committees—the Armaments, Political, and Territorial
Groups—attacked the strictures of the Grand Area despite continuing to treat
it as the most realistic basis for planning. They put the economists on the
defensive, forcing them to repeat that the Grand Area represented a mere
minimum.[34] When Riefler deemed a German Europe to be incompatible
with the American economy, he was accommodating the criticisms of *Foreign Affairs* editor Hamilton Fish Armstrong.[35] Armstrong and his colleagues
in the Political Group worried that the Grand Area assumed the present war
would give way to a destructive and uninspiring armed standoff with the
Nazis, a peace in name only that would "go on until Germany either was
defeated or ruled the world."[36] They first articulated their objection at the
end of 1940, recommending that the United States police the Western Hemisphere and let Britain take the east. In 1941 their objection remained but
their prescription flipped: America should defeat the Nazis within Europe and
lead everywhere. Francis P. Miller, the Anglophilic interventionist, put the
issue bluntly as ever. He doubted that democracy could long survive within a
limited area. "The goal of democracy," he said, "must be world conquest, a
world-wide victory for its ideal." (Democracy was "not aggressive in spirit," replied Harvard University Soviet expert Bruce C. Hopper, either in agreement
or in disagreement.)[37] Even while the Axis powers controlled Europe, and before the Soviet Union entered the war, U.S. postwar planners chafed against
their own plans for global supremacy, deeming them not global enough.

At the same time, planners remained staunchly American-British in their
conception of the postwar political structure. That began to change after
Operation Barbarossa introduced the most important international rather
than domestic consideration to provoke a rethinking of formal American-
British exclusivity: the entrance of the Soviet Union into the Grand Alliance
and potentially the peace settlement. When Hitler ordered his Wehrmacht
east, surprising American officials and analysts no less than Joseph Stalin,
postwar planners in the CFR immediately, if vaguely, detected that they
might need to adjust their Anglophone framework. The entire CFR staff met
three days later on June 25 and recognized that wartime events could outstrip
their plans. Until now, Armstrong remarked, the group had thought only in
terms of "Anglo-American naval and air strategy." Economist Percy Bidwell
confessed that the Grand Area studies, based on prewar trade patterns, had
been mistaken to ignore the Soviet Union altogether. More important than

international trade, it turned out, was industrial capacity.[38] (One planner had actually imagined in February that the postwar Soviet Union could pose an obstacle to American-British dominance, but he feared a "German-Russian bloc" that would fuse German technicians and Russian labor.)[39]

After Germany launched Operation Barbarossa, however, the CFR men and government officials saw that an exclusively Anglo-American settlement might create enemies. In the State Department's postwar research division, a report in July warned of the emerging "United States Empire" in the Atlantic and the Pacific. "Any fundamental so-called lasting or enduring peace settlement must avoid planting, by a great expansion of our own world power, antagonisms which would render this country vulnerable in the future," the report stated.[40] Undersecretary of State Sumner Welles likely had this concern in mind when, on July 22, he gave a speech calling for the complete destruction of Nazi Germany and the creation of a new "association of nations."[41] It was the closest a major administration official had come to endorsing world organization, although neither Welles's superior, President Franklin D. Roosevelt, nor colleagues like Assistant Secretary of State Adolf Berle shared Welles's sentiment.[42]

By September the CFR planners gave full expression to the international rationale for broadening, in some fashion, the American-British concept. As League of Nations enthusiast Sweetser summed up, "alliance begets alliance." In a memorandum to the State Department, written on behalf of the CFR's Political Group, he warned that "Anglo-Americanism, if not carefully directed, may be made to appear as an attempt at world hegemony and Pan-Americanism as an exclusivist or divisive effort."[43] But this appearance might yet be averted. Combine the "Pax Anglo-Americana" with a new world organization, Sweetser proposed, and the latter could rescue the former. By involving other states in some sort of activities—Sweetser barely outlined what those might be—America and Britain could dominate without seeming domineering.

In other words, the Political Group valued world organization for its symbolic power. Common participation would evoke common control. The planners gave no more than an afterthought to which functions a new league would actually perform. While the Americans and British would "handle the *Realpolitik*," Sweetser suggested, the general organization might deal with economic, social, and technical matters. "The *substance* of such an organization is obviously a far more complex problem," he added, and left it at that.[44] What mattered was how the organization, whatever form it took, could cleanse American-British hegemony for the rest of the world.

International legitimation therefore constituted a significant rationale for widening the formal structure of the postwar order. It would remain so throughout the war. By itself international legitimation nonetheless falls short in accounting for policy elites' sudden interest in world organization during the last third of 1941. Although planners sought to remedy their neglect of the Soviet Union after the German invasion, they remained far from certain that the Soviets would survive the onslaught, much less win the war. If the Soviet Union lost, they recognized, the war would leave Eastern Europe in a shambles. In that case, postwar reconstruction would require even closer cooperation between the United States and Britain than the planners had anticipated.[45] In October the CFR planners questioned whether the Soviet Union would even be a party to the peace settlement. Regardless, all agreed that, as Miller wrote, "the negotiations that determine the outlines of the world to come will be between Americans and British."[46] American-British exclusivity continued to underpin the planning.

In any event, even if the Soviet Union had obsessed American planners, they could have sought to incorporate the Soviets alone into the postwar power structure, to form a concert of the Big Three. But in 1941 the CFR planners never contemplated turning the American-British concept into an American-British-Soviet one. Why, then, did they ponder including all other states besides America and Britain? Neither the territorial enlargement of U.S. postwar aims, nor the advent of the Soviet alliance, suffices to explain the surge of interest in world organization starting in the autumn of 1941. The answer lay closer to home.

The Problem of Public Opinion

Virtually from the moment they determined that the United States should possess supreme power in the world, foreign policy elites identified domestic political opinion to be a paramount challenge and an immediate priority. The exigencies of war did not prevent them from monitoring and strategizing about public opinion as they planned the American-British Grand Area; on the contrary, for all interventionists talked of a new interdependence in world affairs, it was the United States' insulation from the conflict, unique among the great powers, that afforded them the room to worry about their own public as frequently as they did the Wehrmacht. Self-consciously, then, U.S. policy elites sought to figure out how "power might commend itself to the American public in other ways than as an expression of traditional imperialism," as Miller put it.[47] What they offered in 1940 and 1941 were mainly two exceptionalist nationalisms, American and Anglo-Saxon, deployed equally in the secretive CFR planning and in prominent essays by Walter Lippmann, Henry Luce, and others. Interventionist elites also lessened the appearance of "traditional imperialism" by touting the potential of mobile sea and air power to replace occupying land armies (or, in Luce's case, by barely referencing military force at all). Contrasting naval freedom with oppressive armies had been part of the repertoire of the British Empire since the eighteenth century; to judge from the passage of the Lend-Lease Act and the quickening march to war, such a formula might suit a Pax Americana as well. Not for nothing did Whitney Shepardson estimate, in July 1941, that U.S. public opinion would sooner accept an exclusive postwar partnership with the British Commonwealth than a universal league of nations.[48]

But when Roosevelt and Prime Minister Winston Churchill announced joint Anglo-American war aims, their Atlantic Charter failed to impress one of its primary audiences: Americans at home. In Congress, noninterventionists like Senator Hiram Johnson assailed the declaration for creating a de facto "offensive and defensive alliance between the United States and Britain."[49] Senator Robert A. Taft denounced the charter as asserting "complete power over the territorial disposition of the world," since it forbade territorial changes except where approved by the peoples concerned and required only the Axis powers to disarm.[50] Senator Arthur Capper, while expressing abhorrence of Hitler, believed America's bid for postwar domination would subvert its freedom and independence. "I am opposed to our attempting to police all Europe, Asia, Africa, and the Seven Seas," he told radio listeners, "and to our paying the costs of all their wars."[51] In terms once called internationalist, these critics objected to U.S. embroilment in power politics across the globe.

It was not only committed noninterventionists who bridled at the Atlantic Charter. In the postwar planning commission of the Federal Council of Churches, the members were split over whether America should enter the war, but they knew what they thought about the charter. John Foster Dulles, the chairman of the Protestant ecumenical group and the future cold warrior, judged that the charter envisaged "Anglo-Saxon military and economic hegemony" that would freeze the status quo. In this regard, the charter fell "far short" of Wilson's formula. It smacked of a victors' peace whereas Dulles and his commission wished America and Britain would create "international organs having the power to make decisions in which others will participate as a matter of right."[52] In a private letter, Dulles was indignant at the hypocrisy of Roosevelt for promising, in the charter, to "seek no aggrandizement, territorial or other." Dulles foresaw that ample aggrandizement "will be a fact," and he listed the ways in which it already was: "We have acquired for ninety-nine years far-flung naval bases in the Atlantic. We have taken over Greenland and Iceland, and through the guise of developing commercial aviation we have driven the German and Italian airlines pretty much out of South America and are developing there what in reality are United States military air bases. We are greatly developing naval and air bases in the far distant Pacific islands and in the northwestern extremes of Alaska. These, coupled with our two ocean navy, will put us in a position to dominate the Far East." These developments, undertaken after the fall of France and before Pearl Harbor, left Dulles with no doubt that "the United States will come out of this period with a combination of naval power, air power and strategic bases controlling both the Atlantic and Pacific Oceans and South America to an extent that we will have acquired a dominant position in the world comparable to that of England during the last century. It seems to me that this is in fact 'aggrandizement, territorial or otherwise.'"[53] If the values of prewar internationalism were dying, they were not quite dead. At the birth of U.S. world leadership, prominent Americans found the prospect imperialistic.

American-British advocates were unable to deny the poor reception of their idea. Lippmann admitted as much in his column, although he continued to tout the unity of the "English-speaking peoples" through the rest of 1941.[54] In the CFR the postwar planners changed course. Noting that the charter "fell like a dead duck" upon Congress and the public, they doubted that exclusively American or American-British arrangements could ever be made acceptable.[55] Sweetser led the Political Group in penning a stinging rebuke to the Atlantic Charter, less for its content than for its optics. As the group wrote to the State Department: "An *imperialistic* connotation may all too easily be given to the projected American-British policing of the seas, not only by Axis propaganda-mongers, but by perfectly sincere people as well."[56]

As the Political Group saw it, Roosevelt and Churchill relied too narrowly and overtly on the presumed superiority of their nations. Such exceptionalism needed internationalism too—a sense of law, equality, and peace offered by Woodrow Wilson's Fourteen Points but missing from Roosevelt's Eight Points. Whereas Wilson had promised universal disarmament, at least eventually, Roosevelt envisaged the victors remaining "heavily armed themselves—for an indefinite period," Sweetser noted. Although Wilson had wished to reincorporate the defeated powers into the world community, Roosevelt appeared to condemn them to permanent subjugation. Worst of all, Roosevelt said nothing about international political organization, which Wilson had put at the center of a program to overcome power politics. In short, Roosevelt had just committed the United States to a military alliance too naked to command popular support. Sweetser delivered a harsh verdict to the State Department: "It would be harder to sell the 'Atlantic Charter' to the American people than it was Wilson's program."[57]

Having heaped scorn on the concept of world organization for the past two years, American policy elites now began to discuss whether to create one. On August 26, less than two weeks after the enunciation of the Atlantic Charter, the CFR planners held extensive discussions on international organization for the first time since the fall of France.[58] Soon officers in other postwar groups also noticed a change. As the Federal Council of Churches' liaison in Britain reported in September, "Nearly all the best people in America are thinking in terms of the all-in association of nations of the League of Nations kind."[59] In October leaders of the Woodrow Wilson Foundation, an educational group dedicated to perpetuating Wilson's ideals, likewise noted "very definite indications of the return to public interest and favor of both Mr. Wilson and the program for which he stood."[60] Through the rest of the year, the CFR's Political Group entertained proposals for international organization alongside its exclusively American-British schemes. In the Armaments Group, planners went so far as to contemplate an international police force, possibly including "token" German units, that would impose disarmament on central and western Europe.[61] The Economic and Financial Group, for its part, figured it ought to allow one-third of the directors of its postwar development and finance organization to come from states other than America and Britain.[62]

This was a subtle but significant shift, triggered by domestic considerations more directly than external ones. Postwar planners feared that under the formula of the Atlantic Charter, the American public would recoil from world leadership, perhaps from international involvement altogether, once the war concluded. What necessitated world organization was the "critical importance of beginning here and now to re-educate the American people up to their international responsibilities," historian Henry Wriston commented to the rest of the Political Group. The best antidote, Wriston continued, was to involve the United States in international institutions and joint obligations in relatively uncontroversial areas, eroding public resistance through symbolic acts of cooperation.[63] Now, only weeks after they got the official American-British declaration they wanted, postwar planners and thinkers determined that stark global supremacy might be an impossible sell. Instead of working toward a better pitch of the Atlantic Charter, they determined that no words could prettify the "imperialistic connotation" of American-British exclusivity. For so tall an order, the United States would have to create a new world organization, however undesirable in its own right.

In reaching this decision, postwar planners cited "public opinion" as their main reason. What they meant by this term requires explanation. Most literally, the planners were referring to momentary mass preferences, as represented in opinion polls and public expressions. Some evidence from such sources did suggest that American-British supremacy faced a legitimation problem that was unlikely to go away. Influential commentators had criticized American global supremacy ever since interventionists like Lippmann, Luce, and journalist Dorothy Thompson floated the prospect early in 1941. These critics, like the senators who were dismayed by the Atlantic Charter, consistently identified armed supremacy with imperialism broadly defined. Months before the charter was released, Freda Kirchwey, the editor of *The Nation,* condemned the American Century as a "new brand of imperialism" cloaked in sweet words.[64] Norman Thomas, a leader of the Socialist Party and the Keep America Out of War Congress, denounced a fast growing "imperialist feeling in the United States of America . . . altogether lacking until the last four months."[65] Not to be outdone, the *Christian Century,* the periodical of mainline Protestantism, shuddered that schemes like Lippmann's would involve the United States in "the greatest imperialistic venture in history."[66]

The critics likened U.S. global supremacy both to nineteenth-century European empire and to the contemporaneous New Order of the Nazis—evils united in Thomas's reference to "that British Nazi poet, Rudyard Kipling."[67] But they required few other semantic innovations in order to make their case. They simply appealed to the long-standing internationalist values of equality, democracy, and disarmament among nations. As Kirchwey contended, U.S. global preeminence would contravene "honest internationalism," despite Luce and company's effort to appropriate the term and cast their opponents as isolationists. "The fact is," she wrote, "no democratic basis for national dominance can be found in any formula, no matter how you slice it. It cannot be found because it does not exist."[68] Kirchwey ruled out U.S. global supremacy root and branch, writing with the confidence of someone who expected her assumptions to make intuitive sense to her readers.

Yet most elites did not draw the same implication from the hierarchical nature of American supremacy. Kirchwey lacked the social position of Luce; Thomas was no Roosevelt; and Taft and the noninterventionists were losing ground in Congress. More typical of the criticism than Kirchwey's outright rejection was the accommodative stance of Max Lerner. A columnist and political scientist, Lerner detected the peril that Kirchwey did, stating that Luce's vision of an American Century would anoint "American imperialism," antithetical to democracy, around the globe. But he wanted to think that world leadership and participatory democracy could be reconciled. By entering into some sort of "partnership" with countries in Europe, the Far East, and Latin America, he wrote, the United States could fulfill "our great role of leadership" after all.[69] It was this logic that Roosevelt's planners adopted in the wake of the Atlantic Charter: a symbolic internationalism could cleanse imperialism, squaring it with the democratic impulses that were the wellspring of public legitimacy.

Taken as a whole, then, opinion surveys and political commentary indicated no great rejection of U.S. supremacy or American-British leadership. Postwar planners feared "public opinion" out of proportion to actual opinions expressed by the public. In their many discussions of the problem, they rarely cited an existing political force that menaced their plans. And when they did mention opinion polls, they found them more encouraging than not. As several CFR planners remarked in September, recent Gallup polls indicated that majorities of the public eschewed postwar disarmament and now regretted America's abstention from the League of Nations.[70] Although the Atlantic Charter did not fire the public imagination, neither did most Americans dismiss it as an instrument of American-British imperialism. In late August, as postwar planners lambasted the charter, a poll showed that 42 percent of Americans approved of Roosevelt and Churchill's program whereas 17 percent disapproved.[71] The outstanding reaction, perhaps, was none at all: 41 percent had no opinion. In another poll five months later, upwards of 80 percent could not name one provision of the charter.[72] Indifference might have disappointed the planners, but it does not explain their about-face.

When planners expressed anxiety about *public opinion* they did not, in the main, mean the term literally. *Public opinion* sometimes denoted mass preferences and utterances but also signified ethico-political legitimacy in the national political sphere. Under this second meaning, U.S. elites understood the public to be fundamentally opposed to power politics—the defining quality of prewar internationalism, now associated with isolationism. Whatever the polls said for the moment, the public seemed liable to recoil from international responsibilities once the fighting stopped.[73] Assistant Secretary of State Adolf Berle had this conception in mind when he worried in his diary that "the American public, with its natural aversion to war and its natural inclination to optimism," might welcome Hitler's promises of peace.[74] The America First Committee also appealed to the peaceful proclivities of ordinary Americans but, contrary to Berle, warned against the U.S. government concluding an undemocratic and imperialist peace. Sounding like prototypical nineteenth-century internationalists, the committee declared: "The long range aims and policies of our country must be determined by the people through Congress. We hope that secret treaties committing America to imperialistic aims or vast burdens in other parts of the world shall be scrupulously avoided to the end that this nation shall become a champion of a just and lasting peace."[75] From the standpoint of traditional internationalism, interventionists faced an uphill battle in making U.S. participation in global politics acceptable.

But a fix was available. Instead of separating from political entanglement, the United States could redeem the world through intervention aimed at transcending power politics. Wilson had proposed just this alternative through his "disentangling alliance" of the League of Nations. Yet his United States, in 1919, seemed too weak both to remake the world and to stay politically and military above the fray. Two decades later, the United States finally possessed the material power to make Wilson's vision more credible—except that Wilson's heirs no longer wished to do so. In the wake of the Atlantic Charter, postwar planners pioneered a third way: gesture rather faintly at ending power politics while implementing power politics on a global scale. A simulacrum of Wilsonianism could flatter the public's sensibilities, making supremacy safe for democracy.

And the flattery would extend beyond the public's sensibilities. The language of "public opinion" served a third and final function, in addition to denoting expressed preferences and connoting general norms. It allowed interventionists to express indirectly their own anxiety that their vision might be as imperialistic as their critics charged. Perhaps those "perfectly sincere people" whom the CFR planners fingered included themselves. Projecting their qualms onto the public, interventionists could voice, and contain, their cognitive dissonance. For in envisioning U.S. political-military preeminence, they were violating their own values as internationalists long committed to the transcendence of power politics. To a blistering detractor who thought great-power dominance was the way to "imperialism," not "permanent peace," Shotwell replied only that he had a "strong conviction that liberty loving people will not make themselves over into international police forces for any length of time."[76]

Occasionally interventionists registered the contradiction, sounding indistinguishable from noninterventionists. Several CSOP members, for example, protested Shotwell's plans as constituting a "rather indefinite dictatorship by Britain and America."[77] When several dozen Anglophone academics and officials convened at Prouts Neck, Maine, for the Conference on North Atlantic Relations—seeking to implement the Atlantic Charter, promulgated three weeks earlier—one objected that his colleagues envisioned an "Anglo-American Holy Alliance." He complained that the group was assuming the benevolence of American and British power, but nations on the other end might react as Americans and Britons had received Klemens von Metternich and his monarchs.[78] If internationalism seemed to be morphing into its opposite, however, that was not how advocates of global supremacy wanted to see it. After the Atlantic Charter held up a mirror, they needed a new way to justify supremacy to themselves.

IN THE FOUR MONTHS BETWEEN THE announcement of the Atlantic Charter and the Japanese attack on Pearl Harbor, the idea of world organization rose from the dead, but not via a linear resurrection. American policy elites did not revalue the League of Nations, originally conceived and still perceived as a vehicle for expressing public opinion and controlling military power. To the contrary, a new world organization gained appeal as a device for *managing* public opinion and *projecting* military power. Planners hoped to synthesize the substance of American global supremacy, in partnership with Britain, with the form of league-style universalism.

How, exactly? Once brought down to specifics, how would world organization convey a sense of common participation without involving common control? How would it seem more serious than the League about meting out armed sanctions and yet be less binding upon the great-power enforcers? Such questions only began to be posed in 1941 as the paradigms of American-British policing and world organization jostled against one another. Two days after Pearl Harbor, Shepardson acknowledged that his Political Group should "make up its mind whether the object of this collaboration was to perpetuate an American-British hegemony or to provide a nucleus of a general system of collective security."[79] Shotwell conveyed the same ambivalence in addressing the public as chairman of CSOP. "The postwar world," he cautioned, "will not be ready for anything so splendid as the immediate establishment of a stronger and more universal League of Nations." Perhaps such a new league would follow, after the United States and Great Britain exercised "chief responsibility" for setting the terms of peace.[80]

However abstractly, U.S. policy elites forged a powerful argument before the nation entered the war: the United States had to lead the postwar world, and world organization might make it happen. As Sweetser wrote, "it would be one kind of world with America active, another with America inactive."[81] When Japanese planes bombed a U.S. naval base in Hawaii on December 7, 1941, turning the United States into a formal belligerent, the attack on Pearl Harbor caused nowhere near as deep a shock as the fall of France. America's place in the world had been reconceptualized over the previous eighteen months. Even the war of position in American politics had largely been won. As the interventionist senator (and future ambassador to the U.N.) Warren Austin noted a month before Pearl Harbor, Americans had resolved to "transform a country which had become almost entirely isolationist and pacifist into the most powerful military country on earth."[82] Austin was correct that a true transformation had taken place. And when he cast the prewar United States as "entirely isolationist and pacifist," he exhibited the deeper achievement of advocates of global supremacy: casting domination of an entire hemisphere as total disengagement, thus turning armed preeminence into the only option. What Pearl Harbor did was to make manifest that the contest was over. The America First Committee dissolved just days later, declaring its principles to have been right but its cause to have been lost.[83] Noninterventionists got behind the war effort.

Far from reexamining their assumptions after Pearl Harbor, postwar planners affirmed them. On December 15, geographer Isaiah Bowman, who chaired the CFR Territorial Group, wrote to Armstrong and exulted that the United States "must accept world responsibility." In the past, he admitted, the nation had been "rather timorous in our approach to this question," and in his view justly so: "We are not imperialistic in outlook. We have no desire to dominate the world." To seek domination was wrong, Bowman implied—as he argued that the United States must seek domination. "The measure of our victory," he concluded, "will be the measure of our domination after victory."[84]

"The Kind of a World We Want"

Two weeks after the United States entered the war, President Roosevelt approved the establishment of a fully governmental planning committee to pick up where the CFR had left off.[85] The State Department's Advisory Committee on American Foreign Policy first convened on February 12, 1942, in Welles's office.[86] As Roosevelt's man in the department, Welles led the committee into 1943, guiding discussions and pronouncing when a consensus on a subject had been reached. He also went over the head of Secretary of State Cordell Hull to keep Roosevelt apprised of the committee's work. More than anyone, it was Welles who convinced the skeptical president to get behind a world organization by March 1943 and persuade Great Britain and the Soviet Union to follow suit.[87]

In public Welles positioned himself as the second coming of Woodrow Wilson. Standing at Wilson's tomb in November 1941, he became the first member of Roosevelt's inner circle to endorse U.S. participation in a postwar world organization. Americans, he said, "must turn again for light and for inspiration to the ideals of that great seer," Woodrow Wilson. "How rarely in human history has the vision of a statesman been so tragically and so swiftly vindicated."[88] High praise, yet faint; a prophet sees but does not do. From the start of the planning, Welles held up the League of Nations as an antimodel. What was needed, he said, was a "completely fresh approach."[89] Welles expected that a decade after the war's end "we would not have arrived in any Utopia"; rather, "the same old jealousies and fears and hatreds and tensions would be reasserting themselves."[90] Led by Welles, State Department planners set out to determine how the United States could project its full power in a world prone to war.

That they inherited the assumptions of the CFR's planning was no coincidence: the State Department brought in the CFR planners themselves. Before Pearl Harbor, officials looked forward to drawing upon "the best brains outside the government" when they took planning in-house.[91] Thus when the new, official planning group was assembled, it was not quite new nor fully official. CFR planners chaired two of the four original subcommittees: Norman H. Davis, the CFR president, headed the Subcommittee on Security

Problems, and Isaiah Bowman took over the Subcommittee on Territorial Problems. Hamilton Fish Armstrong, too, proved an influential member and coordinated with the CFR planning staff, which continued to operate throughout the war. The State Department brought in several other outsiders as well: Anne O'Hare McCormick, a *New York Times* columnist; Myron Taylor, a former executive of US Steel; and later Clark Eichelberger and James Shotwell, two leading organizers of anti-isolationist intellectual elites.[92]

Early in 1942, with the United States finally in the war and assured of its standing in the peace, the diplomats and experts recruited by the State Department treated America's supremacy as an established fact. Extending the ambition of the CFR group, State Department planners foresaw the whole postwar world unified under U.S. leadership. Gone were the elaborate geographical calculations performed in the year after the fall of France to determine how much of a divided world the United States should seek to lead. Now globalism was axiomatic, requiring no justification. American interests and responsibilities "embrace the whole world," Bowman confirmed.[93]

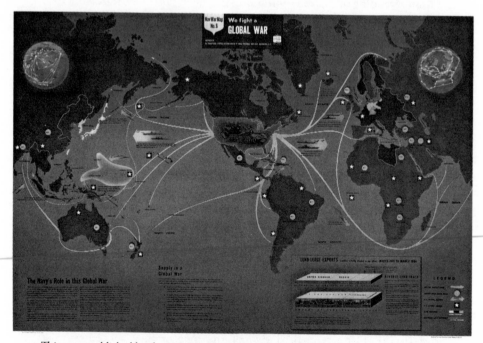

This map, published by the U.S. Navy in 1944, displays the global extent of America's naval operations at the height of the war. Courtesy of David Rumsey Historical Map Collection.

Unhappy news came in from the battlefield in the first half of 1942. Behind Field Marshall Erwin Rommel's Afrika Korps, the Nazis took the offensive in North Africa. Japan tore through the Dutch East Indies and captured the British stronghold of Singapore. In Washington, DC, however, the planners imagined a prostrate postwar world looking to America for leadership. "The peoples now sunk under the pressure of the enemy forces would really need leadership with respect to everything," Bowman commented in March. "It had been so in 1918 and 1919. Their minds no longer were self-reliant and independent, and they looked desperately for someone to give orders." By wrecking the old order, Hitler appeared to have wiped clean the slate of history, only it was the United States, not Germany, that would define the future. In discussing the problem of minorities in Europe, for instance, Welles remarked that although people tended to look down on the transfer of populations as a harsh practice, "the next generation would not feel that way, and we must look a long way ahead." Bowman concurred. "People were getting used to the idea of moving minorities," he said, "because Hitler had carried the process so far."[94]

If "the kind of a world we want," in one planner's phrase, seemed within reach, one obstacle stood out above the rest.[95] It was not the Soviet Union or international communism. Although some worried about Russian domination of eastern Europe, and thence Germany and western Europe, such fears stayed in the background of their discussions through 1942, while the Soviet Union still battled for survival. By contrast, the problem of American "public opinion" preoccupied the State Department planners as much as it had their predecessors in the CFR. Few meetings elapsed without someone interjecting that everything they were working toward depended on the public overcoming its traditional aversion to extrahemispheric political and military action. "Our very biggest problem may be at home," Bowman said, to Welles's affirmation on behalf of the group. "How should we go about keeping our present sense of responsibility, so prevalent today throughout the American public—keep it into and throughout that postwar period?"[96]

Opinion polls were heartening to a degree. "Every poll of opinion," Welles noted, showed the public willing to enforce peace and join an "international organization with teeth."[97] But no amount of data could quell the planners' anxiety, convinced as they were that "isolationism" might always surface. Shotwell, now part of the State Department group, wrote the very first draft for world organization that the planners considered. He did not mention the Soviet Union. Instead he began by exclaiming that "the present war has caused a major revolution in American thinking with reference to the problem of national security"—and yet claimed sentences later that "the innate longing of Americans for their old-time isolation is probably as strong as ever."[98] Understanding global supremacy to have dubious American credentials, postwar planners sought to reconcile their project with the values of the U.S. public and political system.

This was the planners' most salient concern as they decided to create a new world organization. On March 7, 1942, the Subcommittee on Political Problems, composed of the principals of the larger committee, ended its inaugural meeting with Welles stating that the planners "should definitely assume that an international political organization would be established." The planners had barely addressed what such an organization would look like. For most of the meeting, they mostly discussed when to hold a peace conference, and despite feeling that the last conference in Paris had tried to solve too many problems at once, they concluded that the United States should orchestrate a peace conference during rather than after the war, lest "our national *will* to handle the peace problems, with all their difficulties, might be dissipated."[99]

At the next meeting, on March 21, they reiterated the point. Only one aspect of international organization merited discussion: the need to set it up quickly so as to lock internationalism into the public mind and keep isolationism down. If world organization were delayed, "American opinion might not be in support of our program to the extent necessary 'to put it across,'" warned the lawyer Benjamin Cohen, from Roosevelt's brain trust. Intensive work now "would give time for ideas to crystalize favorably prior to the armistice." Welles agreed. "Postponement of international organization," he said, "might give American opinion time to veer away from necessary international participation."[100] The matter was decided, Welles affirmed: the United States should establish a world organization and do so before the war was through.

Having accepted the bare idea of world organization, the planners turned next week to its structure, which they thought might be erected during the war. The outline of what became the U.N. Security Council can be traced to this March 28 meeting. Here the planners figured out how to reconcile great-power privilege with the universal form of world organization. Three objectives guided them: establishing an effective policing apparatus directed by the great powers, making the small powers feel included, and ensuring American freedom of action and the ultimate approval of the U.S. Senate.

The solution, they decided, should begin by vesting real power to make decisions solely in the U.S.-led Big Four, including Britain and the Soviet Union and perhaps France or China. As a small body possessing the force of arms, it could take decisive action as the League of Nations Council could not. Yet this could and should be accomplished without kicking out the small powers. The aim should be that of "instilling the fullest possible sense of participation," said the CFR's Armstrong. A sense of participation could be *instilled* because it was essentially to be a simulacrum of participation. The planners mused that four or five small powers, each representing a region on a rotating basis, could sit on the new council as long as they were stripped of the veto power that all representatives had enjoyed under the League's unanimity rule. Perhaps the Big Four would also "hand pick" the delegates sent by these nations in order to assure their suitability. When Berle objected that the plan sounded like the "sterile intellectual mold of the Council and Assembly of the League of Nations," Bowman assured him of the contrary. The Big Four would retain control in a "quiet intangible organization" behind the scenes. All the planners desired was some method whereby "all states could be given recognition and given opportunity to regard themselves as participants in the decisions made." "Speaking frankly," Welles summed up, "what we required was a sop for the smaller states: some organization in which they could be represented and made to feel themselves participants."[101]

In mid-July Welles formed a new Subcommittee on International Organization, chaired by himself, in order to formulate a draft constitution to present to Roosevelt. After some hesitation, the planners decided to retain a successor to the League of Nations Assembly so that defeated powers and small states could "meet and ventilate their grievances."[102] Shotwell had spent much of the interwar period promoting criteria for defining aggression in order to make collective security obligations more binding, but now he led the way in rejecting any such thing. The planners jettisoned the requirements of the League of Nations Covenant, contained in Articles 10 and 16, that obligated member states to apply sanctions. This time, the great powers would enjoy full discretion to identify aggressors and decide whether and how to act.[103] Rather than attempt to strengthen international law and the judicial settlement of disputes, the planners sought to subordinate them to great-power politics. Certainly, the planners agreed, an international court was no place to decide matters of war and peace. Shotwell decried "the American tendency (in contrast to the British) to lump together all kinds of international disputes within a juristic framework. The identification of acts of aggression was a political matter which could only be handled by a politically constituted agency." At one point he suggested discarding the Permanent Court of International Justice in order to revert to the informal methods of arbitration ascendant before World War I.[104] Shotwell stood ready to undo the attempts of internationalists, over more than two decades, to judicialize international politics by setting up a court and promoting or requiring its use to resolve differences.

Shotwell's reference to an outmoded "American tendency" underscored how far ideas of internationalism had traveled over the past decade and especially within the past two years. U.S. elites now looked upon international society from a position of paramountcy, and they grew as jealous of political discretion as the British had been in the last war. Ironically, this evolution brought about a more suspicious attitude toward the British government itself. The heroic Britain of 1941, standing between Hitler and America, never completely disappeared, but the planners increasingly viewed Britain as a postwar competitor standing between American capital and the colonies. Welles, for example, wanted to disabuse the British of any assumption that the United States was fighting to save their empire. Even a remodeled British Empire, he said, would be a "valuable asset" only if it operated on a broad basis of international partnership.[105]

As U.S. diplomats tried to convince Britain to end imperial preferences in return for Lend-Lease aid, State Department planners studied the colonial world in the autumn of 1942 and found American power and world organization to be congruent there as well. Rather than seek to decolonize subject peoples, a course that would free each new state to close its borders to liberal capitalist exchange, the planners opted to internationalize colonialism. In the heady period between the autumn of 1942 and the spring of 1943, before great-power negotiations began in earnest, Welles and his planners hoped to extend to all colonies a strengthened mandates system with U.S. representation on regional councils.[106] They even entertained proposals to bring the current mandates under "direct international administration" where U.S. officials could serve.[107] Once again Americanization and internationalization went hand in hand: the new trustees administering French North Africa, Roosevelt told Welles, might well be American.[108] The plans would prove difficult to implement, but the torch of world leadership had clearly passed from London to Washington, DC. By the beginning of 1944, Roosevelt delighted in finding himself "unquestionably better prepared than the British" regarding proposals for the postwar world—a reversal, he pointed out, of Wilson's fate.[109]

As Roosevelt's planners contemplated what kind of world they wanted, they emphasized the global projection of American power and worried chiefly that the American people would stand in the way. World organization emerged as a means to this end, as a device for suppressing what they perceived as the public's default disinclination to sustain global supremacy. Yet the planners' instrumental attitudes toward world organization should not obscure the genuine, hierarchical ideal that the organization symbolized for them. In the coming epoch of American leadership, the United States would exercise control but every nation would speak. The small powers would "ventilate" in the American forum, the U.N., bestowing recognition upon the order America gave them even as they blew off steam.

One of the planners put the matter concisely at the end of an early, winding meeting (described by Welles as "'jumping around' too widely") full of uncertainty about how to redraw the map of Europe. "The endurance of our terms of settlement would be the great test," said Anne O'Hare McCormick, the *New York Times* columnist. America needed to see "popular acquiescence in those settlements." Welles approved. "If the people agree to their destiny as we see it," McCormick continued, "we can expect the peace to last."[110] Whatever course the United States chose—no matter how arbitrary the choice—would be the only way, and all others should be expected to follow. That others might act differently, and fail "the great test," the planners did not discuss.

From Four Policemen to the United Nations via American Power

Postwar planners thought they could determine the fate of the peoples of the world, but for some time they struggled to convince their boss to entertain their big idea, a new world organization, at all. In the year following the declaration of the Atlantic Charter, Roosevelt inserted China and the Soviet Union into his vision of American-British world orderers, but he refused to go further. In April 1942, Welles sent him a sketch of a "United Nations Authority." Adding five regional representatives to Roosevelt's Four Policemen, the authority would eventually expand into a full world organization. But Welles found his proposal "summarily turned down at the highest level."[111] According to everyone who discussed postwar matters with Roosevelt in 1942, the president felt firmly that the Big Four should dictate the peace.[112] The United States, Great Britain, the Soviet Union, and perhaps China—they would police the world and "all other nations save the Big Four should be disarmed," Roosevelt told the Soviet foreign minister.[113] Roosevelt was not about to relinquish control of war and peace to another League of Nations with a hundred signatories to satisfy.

Then Welles showed him that he did not have to. In a two-hour meeting in January 1943, Welles laid out how the postwar planners had squared great-power control with universal participation.[114] Embedded in a world organization, the United States could exert *more* control than in an informal four-power concert. Welles's draft, like the eventual U.N. Charter, required every member nation to make its forces and facilities available to the great powers. By internationalizing colonies and strategic bases, the organization opened the world to American access.[115] Welles's detailed exposition might have converted Roosevelt; by 1943, too, Roosevelt was more willing to make territorial settlements and more suspicious of Soviet intentions, deciding to revive France as a counterweight rather than disarm it completely.[116] Roosevelt clearly did not metamorphose into an advocate of subordinating American power to international law and multilateral procedures. In March he proposed a new world organization to the British for the first time and spoke in Wellesian terms. The Big Four would make "all the more important decisions," the president said. Once a year or so, the universal assembly would meet, but not to take action. Small countries, the president said, would merely "blow off steam."[117]

From 1943 to 1945 Roosevelt convinced his allies to sign up to a new world organization, which neither Churchill nor Stalin, thinking along regionalist lines, had favored.[118] Without the initiative of the United States, nothing like the U.N. would have come into being. But the subsequent negotiations over the veto power, and related provisions on which historians have focused, shed dim light on why the United States made a top diplomatic priority of establishing the organization, an objective that ranked as high as any other in the horse-trading at Yalta and other summits.[119] As the historian Warren Kimball points out, Roosevelt himself regarded subsequent disputes over the veto as a triviality, relevant mainly for domestic political reasons.[120] More illuminating is the moment of conception, revealing in particular that the American decision to create the U.N. is explicable only as part, and a subordinate part, of the American decision to seek global political-military supremacy.

As they first envisaged a new world organization, officials and intellectuals assumed other powers would go along with American prerogatives in the future. They never debated the merits of multilateralism versus unilateralism, having designed an organization that would minimize the burdens of the

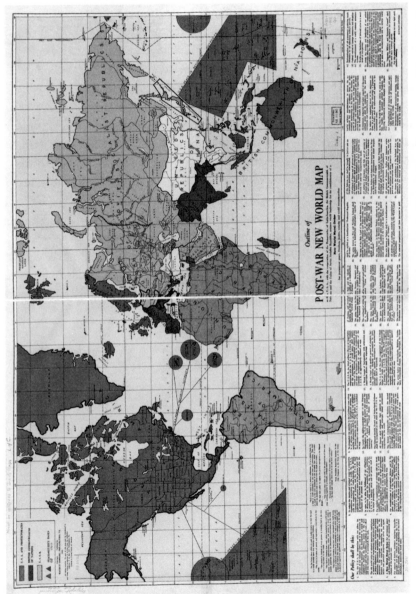

This map, produced in 1942, outlines one vision of a postwar world in which the United States "assumes world leadership." Courtesy of the Library of Congress.

former. In a few instances, however, they indicated a preference if events should force a choice. "The United States must exercise power after this war," Buell reflected in March 1942, as the officials he advised made the decision to set up a new world organization. "It must not allow its initiative to be vetoed by other countries but it must be willing to allow other United Nations to associate themselves with us in the exercise of this power."[121]

Buell was not alone in prizing America's freedom of action. On the Board of Economic Warfare, the vice president's New Deal lieutenant, Milo Perkins, laid out a ten-page wish list of gifts that the United States could bestow upon the postwar world. "We have power," Perkins wrote. Foreseeing that some nations would not go along with this power, he insisted the United States must exercise leadership nonetheless. Perkins concluded, "If we attempt active participation in postwar world affairs before ridding ourselves of the fear that an indecisive position might displease certain nations because it sets forth frankly what we want, we shall end by pleasing nobody and by bringing ruin to ourselves. This nation from its beginning has stood for certain basic ideals; we must work boldly for their world wide fulfillment and let the chips fall where they may."[122] Multilateralism where possible, unilateralism if necessary: with this formula Perkins asserted American sovereignty over international society.

5

THE DEBATE THAT WASN'T, 1942–1945

ARNOLD TOYNBEE HAD NOT VISITED the United States in a decade when Rockefeller Foundation money brought him back in the autumn of 1942. But Toynbee, officially the director of studies at Chatham House, and unofficially the dean of British internationalists, knew exactly whom to see.[1] He spent two weeks meeting with postwar planners in the State Department and another week in New York with the Council on Foreign Relations (CFR). Then he circulated around the country, renewing acquaintances with Raymond Leslie Buell, Edward Mead Earle, and Quincy Wright, among other postwar-minded semiofficial elites. He failed in his attempt to establish formal exchanges of personnel between planners in America and Britain; Leo Pasvolsky, chief of research in the State Department, brushed the request aside, determined to keep control in American hands.[2] Yet when Toynbee reported back to the Foreign Office, he had nothing but good news to deliver.

Finally British diplomacy was seeing the realization of one of its foremost objectives since 1914: rousing the United States fully into world politics. Toynbee found his American counterparts preparing a massive campaign of public education in the evils of "isolationism" and the corresponding virtues of projecting U.S. power in the postwar world. Toynbee himself doubted the need for such a campaign. Most everyone he met seemed as committed to world leadership as they were anxious that the rest of the country would recoil.

"I was frequently told that Isolationism is dead," Toynbee reflected, "but just as often that it is likely to rise again in some new avatar or metamorphosis." Toynbee believed the former was true but the latter revealing. He concluded that American internationalists were mobilizing not to defeat extant opposition but rather to create a "bulwark" against any resistance that might arise later.[3] In nominally rallying around participation in international organization, they worked to legitimate U.S. global supremacy.

Toynbee noted a second curiosity about his American friends, this one as welcome as the first. In the past year, American internationalists like Vice President Henry Wallace had made grand if vague pronouncements about the future disposition of the colonial world, alarming British officials already contending with the U.S. demand for the destruction of the imperial preference system in consideration for Lend-Lease aid.[4] For all the talk of instituting international control over colonized territories, however, Toynbee reported that as discussions became concrete, Americans became pliable. When informed that internationalization would hinder the progress of subject peoples toward self-government, Toynbee's American interlocutors "nearly always" proved ready to combine some sort of international supervision with existing colonial administrations.[5] They might well decide merely to update the mandates system devised by the British government in World War I, Toynbee forecast presciently. Here, too, the great internationalist ferment seemed more symbolic than substantial. Fearing supposed isolationism, Americans fixated on *whether* their country would accept internationalism. They pushed to the background what kind of internationalism it should be.

For understanding America's effort to win the peace as it helped to win the Second World War, Toynbee's observations provide a better point of departure than much of the scholarship that has followed. Adopting the intellectual frameworks of wartime interventionists, historians and political scientists have structured their analyses around the assumption that in creating and joining the United Nations (U.N.), the United States seized its "second chance" to lead the world.[6] In 1945 internationalism supposedly triumphed over a contemporaneous adversary—isolationism or something like it, which having thwarted American participation in the League of Nations might well have won out again. The result was a "vociferous public debate," to quote one historian.[7] Americans, both in the elite and at the grass roots, weighed multilateral and institutional solutions to global problems as never before and, after democratic debate, committed themselves to internationalism.

The triumph thesis takes at face value the self-presentation of advocates of U.S. supremacy, with the effect not only of flattering their political agenda but also of failing to appreciate the significance of the mobilization around internationalism. The debate at the war's end was loud but not competitive. To extend Toynbee's insights, advocates of the U.N. arrayed themselves against the idea of isolationism rather than actual people who disagreed with them. When the Senate ratified the U.N. Charter by a vote of 89–2, the outcome reflected the paucity of outright opposition all along. Dominant from the start of 1942, the new, anti-isolationist internationalists faced nothing like the political uncertainty of the previous two years, when challengers organized themselves and put forward plausible proposals for U.S. policy during and after the war. Nor did internationalists welcome disagreements within their ranks. They intentionally suppressed the discussion of alternatives at every turn, lest internal divisions play into the hands of imagined isolationists. It made little difference whether they were government officials or nonpartisan activists: U.N. proponents framed the decision around *whether* to embrace world leadership and world organization (internationalism) or abstain from the world (isolationism), dampening consideration of *how* to take part in world affairs. The anti-isolationist internationalists stood to gain by claiming victory in a contested and participatory debate—an "experiment in democracy," as one activist titled her memoir—but such claims are dubious.[8]

What transpired from 1943 to 1945 was less a debate than a campaign of legitimation. Viewed in this way, it acquires stakes that justified the effort. By mobilizing in the name of internationalism, foreign policy elites turned U.S. world leadership into an unanswerable position in American politics. *This* outcome, unlike the vote to ratify the U.N. Charter, was not assured. From 1940 to 1942, a small set of political and intellectual elites, concentrated in the two hundred miles between New York City and Washington, DC, drew up the first plans for postwar U.S. political-military leadership. Aware of their own insulation from popular and partisan politics, they persistently worried that the American people, and their representatives in Congress, would refuse to go along; armed supremacy might be judged un-American and uninternationalist, as many had criticized the Atlantic Charter. The attack on Pearl Harbor allayed this fear only partially. Despite the near unanimity in favor of prosecuting the war to a decisive end, winning the war did not necessarily imply that the United States should police the world afterward. There might have ensued a vigorous public debate over whether and how postwar America should use its unprecedented military, political, and economic power to keep the peace and shape international affairs. Global supremacy might have faced attacks from both standpoints from which Americans had historically opposed power politics: a hemispherism that eschewed Old World political-military commitments and a universalism that sought to control and transcend balance-of-power and great-power politics.

Yet the attacks never came. The harshest critics of President Franklin D. Roosevelt's foreign policy, led by Ohio senator Robert A. Taft, rose to the floor of Congress to discuss (and mostly applaud) the U.N.[9] Some argued, from the other direction, that only a genuine federation among nations could tame international rivalry and prevent another war, but world federalists remained marginal, lacking significant support in either political party.[10] The outstanding fact was the approval of America's global preeminence and the absence of much-anticipated objections.[11] "We tell ourselves that we have emerged from this war the most powerful nation in the world—the most powerful nation, perhaps, in all history," an exultant President Harry S. Truman remarked in a radio address given one week before Japan's surrender.[12] Truman added that the nation's ideals of self-government and dignity ultimately explained its armed strength. The president found little need to justify global supremacy. As World War II ended, global supremacy functioned as a foundational good against which other values would be measured. Implausible before the war, it now appeared as the consummation of American history.

It was no such thing; too much intellectual and cultural work had to be performed in order to make global supremacy seem natural. It was this work that wartime interventionists carried out in the name of internationalism and the U.N. Promulgating a narrative in which American foreign policy swung between the poles of internationalism and isolationism, they demolished the intellectual resources that had countered armed supremacy. Their narrative expelled noninterventionists from the ranks of internationalism and the sphere of legitimate discourse. The *restraint* of American power became the height of introversion and selfishness. By extension, no vision for a better world could fail to include the United States as the supreme power and defining agent. Once opposed to nationalism and defined by the transcendence of power politics, internationalism came to denote U.S. world leadership above all. Thus interventionists did not merely argue that an internationalism without U.S. supremacy would be undesirable; they rendered the prospect conceptually impossible, articulable only outside the terms of American political discourse.

"Stop Isolationism Now"

Hamilton Fish Armstrong, Norman H. Davis, Whitney Shepardson, James Shotwell, and Arthur Sweetser were among the few dozen people responsible for planning the postwar policies of the nation whose economy would emerge from the war as large as that of the rest of the world combined. In 1942, in their time away from planning the world to come, they hired the public relations firm of Thomas Fizdale, Inc. To be precise, it was the Woodrow Wilson Foundation, of which they were directors, that employed Fizdale to develop a plan of action for the rest of the war years. In the view of the foundation's leaders, Wilson had failed for one key reason: the American people did not understand his ideas. Internationalists back then mounted no attempt to educate the public, Thomas Fizdale recalled inaccurately. By contrast, "there was propaganda as vicious as Goebbel's [*sic*] for isolationism," he continued anachronistically. Who better than a public relations man to tell the foundation how to balance the imagined scales by unloading its substantial coffers, which were already funding former League of Nations enthusiasts in the Commission to Study the Organization of Peace (CSOP)? The time had come to put academic studies aside, the foundation resolved, and "go to work for 'Internationalism' now."[13]

By the war's end, U.N. advocates would claim to have defeated their isolationist opponents in a competitive democratic debate. Yet a competitive debate was manifestly not what the Wilson Foundation prepared for in 1942, nor what it got afterward. Despite referencing Goebbels-esque isolationist propaganda from the last war, Fizdale did not identify a single adversary in the present. He placed no emphasis on devising superior arguments. Instead he assumed the forces of internationalism possessed free rein to influence a passive public. Through the latest techniques of persuasion, the foundation could reach "that greater mass of Americans . . . who prefer 'soap operas' to Wagner."[14] Exhibiting the popular Freudianism that informed midcentury public relations, Fizdale wanted the foundation to blanket the public in print, radio, and film with quasi-religious dogma.[15] Give the people a "catechism in internationalism," Fizdale urged.[16]

The foundation needed little persuading. It threw itself into the anti-isolationist crusade over the next three years, producing a widely read pamphlet called "Our Second Chance"; helping Twentieth Century Fox release the Academy Award–winning film *Wilson*, a biopic that dramatized the League of Nations fight, and publicizing the great powers' Dumbarton Oaks proposals for world organization even before the State Department did.[17] In all these activities, the foundation's president explained at the outset, the goal was to present Wilson as an American hero with a "prophetic gift" and as a "symbol of international organization."[18] Such gauzy language did not indicate diffuse cultural objectives. Through canonizing Wilson, the foundation's officers envisioned winning a legislative fight and elevating anti-isolationist internationalism above the arena of political contestation. Prophet Wilson, whatever his resemblance to Woodrow Wilson, offered his flock a chance at redemption and lent world leadership an unimpeachably internationalist and American pedigree. His revelations grounded the origin myth of U.S. global supremacy.

THE WOODROW WILSON FOUNDATION WAS one hub in a large network of public officials and citizens' groups that sought to convert ordinary Americans to anti-isolationist internationalism. As scholars have suggested, it would be a mistake to privilege the agency of either the government or private foundations in generating support for postwar American leadership. Not only did officials and nonofficials pursue the same objectives; often they were the same people. At various moments in 1942 and 1943, for example, historian James Shotwell planned the U.N. in the State Department; formulated the Woodrow Wilson Foundation's public-relations campaign; set up, through the Carnegie Endowment for International Peace, "international mind" alcoves in public libraries and ten International Relations Centers for coordinating pro-U.N. groups in the West and the Midwest; and arranged for the Carnegie Endowment and CSOP to host an NBC radio series, "For This We Fight," which secured one-quarter of listeners nationwide.[19] Some scholars apply the term "parastate" to nominally private organizations in order to highlight their loyalty to the American state.[20] If anything, the label may err in still suggesting the ultimate centrality of officialdom, at least for the period prior to the expansion of the national security bureaucracy in the late 1940s. The unofficial Americans United for World Organization approached the State Department, not vice versa, to ask how it should promote the Dumbarton Oaks proposals negotiated by the Big Four.[21]

The Roosevelt administration, for its part, appreciated that civil society groups could make for "very helpful allies" in the fight for public opinion, provided that they were "discreetly guided" along the right path, as one of

Pasvolsky's staff wrote early on.[22] To that end the State Department launched perhaps the most determined effort in its history to engage the American public. After the Big Four committed themselves to creating a postwar international organization in the Moscow Declaration of October 1943, the department established the Division of Public Liaison, dedicated to civil society outreach.[23] Under Edward Stettinius, the US Steel executive who replaced Cordell Hull as secretary of state, State Department officials gave more than five hundred speeches in every major U.S. city and distributed millions of promotional pamphlets between the release of the Dumbarton Oaks proposals in October 1944 and the start of the San Francisco conference that drafted the U.N. Charter the following June.[24] Most significantly, the department invited forty-two domestic interest groups and nongovernmental organizations to participate at San Francisco. It even listened to them, heeding their requests for the U.N. Charter to reference the protection of human rights and establish an Economic and Social Council that could consult with nongovernmental organizations.[25]

From this record, one might conclude that the State Department largely made good on its stated aim of conducting a "democratic foreign policy."[26] But democracy is easy to support on issues about which few people disagree. More remarkable than the state's willingness to reach out to civil society groups was that it could comfortably do so due to a broad anti-isolationist consensus. After Pearl Harbor, interventionists encountered a receptive public and no organized opposition. In July 1942 Sumner Welles's planners in the State Department issued their first fortnightly summary of American public opinion on postwar problems and noted that the already small "isolationist minority" had shrunk further since the United States had joined the war. As they pointed out, a staggering 73 percent of Americans now supported U.S. participation in postwar international organization, according to Gallup surveys, up from 50 percent the year before and 33 percent in 1937.[27] Public approval remained around the three-quarter mark through 1945, a level pollsters considered to be tantamount to unanimity in a diverse country.[28] To say there was little debate over world organization is to understate. Participation in the postwar U.N. ranked as one of the least contentious issues in American politics.

Critics of the League of Nations before Pearl Harbor did not fail to notice that popular sentiment had deserted them. "The American people seem hell bent on some kind of league, alliance, or what have you," historian Charles Beard lamented as delegates met in San Francisco.[29] But few former noninterventionists headed down Beard's road to marginality. Most supported the U.N., following the lead of senators Taft and Arthur Vandenberg. One reason was precisely that public sentiment seemed insurmountable. Despite later claiming that Pearl Harbor "ended isolationism for any realist," Vandenberg initially thought the attack vindicated noninterventionists who warned that Roosevelt would provoke his way into war.[30] But ultimately he accepted another interventionist argument: any world war would inevitably draw in the United States, as had now happened twice.[31] Whether or not interventionists had been right on principle, their political success made them right in practice.

Furthermore, noninterventionists found little to dislike in the modest design of the new world organization. When shown the State Department's plan, Vandenberg marveled that "it is so conservative from a nationalist standpoint."[32] Why not sign on? U.S. planners had discarded the provisions of the League of Nations that imposed collective security obligations on the United States. "The San Francisco Charter has no 'Article X,'" Shotwell observed, and "there is a conscious avoidance of defining aggression."[33] With the most controversial elements of world organization abandoned before another controversy could begin, many noninterventionists could accept the U.N. without completely reversing their previous views. Beard decided that the Dumbarton Oaks proposals were not worth opposing vocally even though they strengthened the great powers and created a "talk shop for endless discussions." "Dumbarton Oaks really commits us to nothing," Beard wrote to noninterventionist international lawyer Edwin Borchard. "It declares national sovereignty in unmitigated terms."[34] As the *New York Herald Tribune* commented in an editorial, the charter represented "a kind of least common denominator of what is today practically acceptable to all."[35]

For some supposed isolationists, the U.N. was too weak rather than too strong. Taft, the onetime noninterventionist leader and future Cold War critic, declared early on, in 1943, that the United States should join a universal commitment to use economic and military force to prevent aggression; an international body would decide whether to deploy sanctions by a majority vote.[36] As Raymond Leslie Buell observed to his colleagues in the Post-War Committee of *Time*, *Life*, and *Fortune* magazines, Taft's willingness to countenance global military policing made it absurd to call him an *isolationist*, a term defined by one's stance on the use of force against aggression. Insofar as Taft envisioned U.S. military force summoned by an international agency, his multilateralism went further than Roosevelt's ever did.[37] The least-common-denominator approach of the architects of the U.N. achieved exactly what it set out to do: offer a symbol to attract the widest possible number of Americans. "For some time," the *Washington Post* observed in July 1945, "it has been evident that opposition to the United Nations Charter in the Senate has virtually collapsed."[38] It is no wonder that Citizens for Victory, set up in 1942 to succeed the Committee to Defend America by Aiding the Allies, fizzled out almost as soon as it began. With the America First Committee having disbanded, and with nothing to take its place, the group could not find enough "isolationists" to impugn.[39]

THE DEARTH OF OPPOSITION CALLS INTO question analysts' search to explain why internationalism won the debate in World War II. The bigger puzzle is why internationalists staged a debate at all. Why mobilize around U.N. participation when hardly anyone—two senators, in the end—opposed it? The purpose was summarized by the wartime slogan of the Woodrow Wilson Foundation–backed League of Women Voters: "Stop Isolationism Now."[40] Despite the lack of identifiable isolationists, the *idea* of isolationism proved spectacularly generative. It animated internationalists and transformed their agenda, more, in fact, than they knew.

By no means, however, were they ignorant of the public support they commanded. They pored over scientific surveys in newspapers, magazines, and journals like *Public Opinion Quarterly,* founded in 1937. Not content to leave polling to the pollsters, the Roosevelt administration developed sophisticated techniques for measuring and interpreting popular sentiment, first through the Office of War Information and then through the State Department's Office of Public Opinion Studies. Led by political scientist H. Schuyler Foster Jr. for twenty-two years starting in 1943, the latter office produced tens of thousands of surveys scrutinizing the attitudes of interest groups and the aggregate public to every international question.[41] Political leaders paid attention. Roosevelt devoured weekly surveys of opinion polls and newspaper editorials.[42] Welles remarked to his postwar planners that "every poll of opinion" indicated the public's desire to enforce the peace and join a world organization.[43] Suffice it to say that advocates of postwar supremacy understood the paltry numbers of their antagonists.

But they had the luxury of looking ahead, of finishing the postwar planning undertaken from the start of the war in Europe. The Woodrow Wilson

Foundation's public relations man put it well. The goal, he implied, was not to persuade John Doe. Mr. Doe was persuaded already. Now his persuasion had to be entrenched, his reservations expelled: "Mr. Doe must be *made sure.*"[44] Thus, from 1942 to 1945, foreign policy elites railed against "isolationism" as or more frequently as before.[45] Nothing seemed so frightening as the prospect that after the war Americans might "retreat to isolationism" (Roosevelt), "return to isolationism" (columnist Walter Lippmann)," "swing back to isolationism" (journalist and State Department planner Anne O'Hare McCormick), "try isolationism once again" (Minnesota senator Joseph Ball), and so forth.[46] Given the actual state of popular sentiment, this anxiety produced its share of hyperbolic scenarios. At the end of 1942, for example, a Midwestern CFR official warned colleagues that isolationists had gone underground. They were merely biding their time, being "experienced in the art of guerilla warfare."[47] Isolationism's absence only proved its strength.

Such contortions notwithstanding, fear of isolationism was ubiquitous and expressed privately and publicly alike. Not only an epithet, deployed to discredit noninterventionists, *isolationism* structured the mental map of wartime internationalists. They believed and absorbed their own myth. Despite their recent coinage of the term, they took isolationism to be a self-conscious, organized force that had rivaled internationalism for decades and thwarted American participation in the League of Nations. Wartime internationalists defined their very identity in opposition to isolationism, pushing into the background *internationalism's* previous antonyms of nationalism, imperialism, and power politics. This conception—of internationalism as anti-isolationism—structured the entire nondebate, as it were.

It was left to the few remaining opponents of U.S. postwar plans to note how stultifying the anti-isolationist framing was. "The terms internationalism and isolationism are being used by the proponents of the new world order as representing two opposing schools of thought," noted Congressman Frederick C. Smith, a Republican from Ohio. Smith complained that the country's ruling class held internationalism to be "of a highly, magnanimous and benevolent nature, which if adopted will bring to all the nations so much mutual goodwill and affection for each other that the causes of international strife will disappear. On the other hand, isolationism, so these forces tell us, is a wicked thing and by its very nature just the opposite of internationalism, greedy and malevolent in the extreme." Before he could lay out his objections to specific plans, Smith felt compelled to repudiate what had become conceptual common sense: "I must pause to object to the monopoly which the administration seems to feel it possesses of being the sole judge as to what really constitutes so-called internationalism as well as so-called isolationism."[48] A debate conducted in such terms was no debate at all.

In addition to writing off opponents of military entanglements, wartime internationalists refused to air alternative schemes for world organization that might divide them and benefit isolationists, who, however dormant, seemed liable to erupt at any moment. Noting how rarely the anti-isolationists attempted to conceptualize international organization, one historian blames the leadership of the American Association for the United Nations, including Shotwell, for collaborating with officials and suppressing differences of opinion within the movement.[49] This argument implies that with different leadership internationalists outside of government might have offered more alternatives for world order and more criticism of the administration's plans. But what if conceptual sterility was the point? Obsessed with defeating isolationism, wartime internationalists fetishized world organization, attributing significance to its bare existence while remaining agnostic as to its form.

WHEN THE LEAGUE TO Enforce Peace (LEP) formed in June 1915, two years prior to America's entry into World War I, it began by formulating a four-article treaty to which its members wanted all nations to adhere. Soon it became America's largest civil society group favoring world organization, although the specifics of its platform divided even the international lawyers who were its main constituency.[50] The LEP had no counterpart in World War II. On the other hand, the internationalist movement, highly conscious of itself as such, maintained political unity precisely because of its "lack of any apparent long-term or coherent policy of action," as one member complained.[51] It preserved consensus by confining public discussion to the broad outlines of a world organization with universal membership, some sort of economic and policing powers, and perhaps competencies to oversee the administration of colonies.

The most popular "internationalist" tract was *One World,* a travelogue manifesto penned by Wendell Willkie after his globe-spanning trip in the autumn of 1942. Willkie, the 1940 Republican presidential nominee turned interventionist ally of Roosevelt, urged Americans to eschew all manner of imperialisms in the postwar world. Positioning himself against "narrow nationalism," he opposed racial exploitation at home and preached partnership abroad, particularly with the peoples of Asia who were throwing off the colonial yoke. But despite calling on the U.N. to become a "common council in which all plan together," Willkie ventured no further details.[52] More important than proposing an institutional structure for cooperation—where common council would become either the right of all nations or the charity of a few—was picturing the global masses, from Cairo to Chongqing, sharing the desires of ordinary Americans and looking to the United States for leadership.[53]

Like Willkie, the experts in CSOP, chaired by Shotwell, declined to offer public blueprints for world organization. One member, University of Toledo president Philip C. Nash, reminded Shotwell that "it was in June 1915, three years before the Armistice, that the League to Enforce Peace was making a fairly definite picture of the Covenant of the League."[54] Was the present commission tardy by comparison? Shotwell was unmoved. Although CSOP began to circulate drafts for a new world organization internally, these were not publicized until 1944 and closely resembled State Department plans, to which CSOP members like Shotwell had directly contributed.[55] Two years into the U.S. war effort, public debate over postwar world order was less advanced than it had been two years *before* American entry into World War I. In August 1943 Henry Luce told the Post-War Committee of his magazines that he wanted to support some scheme for world organization but could find none in circulation.[56]

Thus the Big Four governments had a free hand to release their own plan, as they did in October 1944 following the Dumbarton Oaks Conference in Washington, DC. The conference proposals were widely seen as a formula for great-power domination, drafted exclusively by the great powers themselves. Unlike the League of Nations Covenant, the proposals lodged responsibility for international peace and security exclusively in an executive council with five permanent members and not in a universal assembly. The power-political nature of the proposals troubled even the U.S. postwar planners who had shaped them. At the end of October, officials from the State Department, the military, and the CFR convened in Princeton, New Jersey, for a special meeting.[57]

New York Times military analyst and CFR planner Hanson Baldwin opened the session on security by predicting "widespread criticism in public debate" given that the great powers "virtually arrogated to themselves the exclusive right to keep the peace." Pasvolsky, perhaps the chief American architect of the U.N., reinforced Baldwin's concern by highlighting the realpolitik premises of the Dumbarton Oaks proposals. The new organization, he said, would possess little capacity to discipline the great powers. Peace would depend "almost exclusively on the ability of these super-powers to exercise a considerable amount of self-restraint."[58] The U.N. would work, if it did, by creating the conditions for a more organized "balance of power"—the bête noir of nineteenth-century internationalism and a phrase that other planners proposed to strike from their vocabulary.[59] The more they talked about Dumbarton Oaks, the more the planners expected a popular backlash. Although they often attributed the potential backlash to "isolationism," they simultaneously appreciated that something else was at issue: not whether but how the United States would participate in world politics.

The planners' prediction did not prove entirely unfounded. Politicians and commentators universally acknowledged Dumbarton Oaks's big-power bias. Republican governor Thomas Dewey, in the thick of his presidential campaign against Roosevelt, initially excoriated the Dumbarton Oaks plan as the "rankest form of imperialism" in which the strong would coerce the weak.[60] No less than Hans Morgenthau, a founder of the realist school of international relations, blasted the architects of the new world order for going to the opposite extreme of his customary Wilsonian whipping boy. Morgenthau wrote that the Dumbarton Oaks framework attempted to build international society on a bedrock of "power alone," bereft of the common moral standards appreciated even by the statesmen of the Holy Alliance.[61] Columnist Walter Lippmann also contrasted the emerging U.N. with the League of Nations but cheered the former because it repudiated the latter. In two books, widely read and reprinted, Lippmann appended Soviet Russia to his American-British condominium from 1941, and he judged the Dumbarton Oaks agreement to exemplify his un-Wilsonian "nuclear alliance" of the major powers.[62] Never mind the issue of "how to have the small powers 'represented,'" Lippmann told his readers; in practice the big powers would consult members of their sphere of influence anyway, so each American, British, or Soviet vote would in fact represent a broad consensus.[63] If the British-led League of Nations had often honored the formal equality of states in the breach, the Dumbarton Oaks plan so mocked the principle that Lippmann could claim only that representation would be virtual.

The unmistakable hierarchies of Dumbarton Oaks might have inspired formidable opposition, especially from the self-styled Wilsonians whom Lippmann decried. Yet widespread reservations translated into vanishingly few rejections. After Dewey's initial outburst, the two presidential campaigns concluded a pact between advisers Cordell Hull and John Foster Dulles to keep the Dumbarton Oaks plan out of the election.[64] Pro-U.N. elites ramped up their anti-isolationist activism nonetheless.[65] They did draft amendments to the Dumbarton Oaks proposals that were mostly incorporated in San Francisco: Shotwell's CSOP and Dulles's ecumenical Protestant group called for the creation of commissions on human rights and trusteeship.[66] But these changes were understood to be ornamental.[67] No one insisted on them as a condition for supporting for the U.N. Charter. Internationalists intended to establish *some* world organization, and Dumbarton Oaks qualified.

Why did the Dumbarton Oaks agreement command such thorough assent? For one, however distasteful it looked, few internationalists disagreed with it on fundamentals. Having reconciled themselves to power politics in 1940 and 1941, internationalists wanted a security organization dominated by the United States and the great powers. They had decided that the League of Nations had failed principally because it relied on peaceful, legalistic conciliation and could not impose its writ. So long as states refused to cede their sovereignty to a world government, this lesson inevitably worked to bolster the great powers, who alone could furnish military force.

Accordingly, it was in attempting to create a robust "international police force" that semiofficial and unofficial internationalists made their most significant innovation in the design of world organization.[68] Starting in 1943, CSOP members and CFR planners discussed methods for putting at the disposal of the great-power council a standing air force, constituted by the U.N. itself rather than each member state, that could deploy rapidly from bases all over the world in order to beat back aggressors.[69] These proposals, which came out of the exclusive American-British policing schemes of 1941, invested each of the great powers with a veto (except on disputes to which a great power would be a party), before the Dumbarton Oaks proposals did likewise. Because they contemplated a supranational rather than multilateral air force, the imagined world police suffered from being either so large and robust as to threaten state sovereignty or so puny as to be militarily ineffective. Ultimately the founding states of the U.N. arrived at a weaker solution—a quota system, never implemented, by which nations would designate some of their own forces for immediate dispatch upon orders of the U.N. Security Council.[70] If the most influential nonofficial internationalists had their way, the U.N. Charter might have put into effect more great-power dictatorship, not less.

Moreover, to the extent that internationalists disagreed with aspects of the charter, they were unwilling to call for its rejection. In a strategy of self-suppression, they muted serious divergences of opinion until the Senate rati-fied the U.N. Despite objecting to an absolute great-power veto, for example, Shotwell followed the principle he spelled out in 1942 that set the tone for the entire nondebate: "I think it is much more important to clarify the Amer-ican mind with reference to the inescapable fundamentals than to confuse it with a multitude of plans."[71] Shotwell's principle convinced a growing faction of world federalists—who became a substantial minority akin to the position of pacifists during the First World War—to support the Dumbarton Oaks agreement despite their desire to strengthen the U.N. General Assembly and elevate it over the Security Council.[72] Only after the U.N. Charter came into being, and especially following the detonation of the atom bomb, did dis-senters organize into the United World Federalists and campaign to revamp the charter.[73]

Alternative visions for the postwar international order, beyond the drastic measure of world federalism, were imaginable and imagined. A number of intellectuals put forward distinctive proposals that drew on commitments of prewar internationalists to law, disarmament, and world opinion. Manley O. Hudson, a judge at the Permanent Court of International Justice, led a group of experts in outlining "The International Law of the Future," which in-cluded creating an obligation among all states to settle disputes between them of a legal nature in the world court.[74] Hudson's plan, along with one by dip-lomat Hugh Gibson and Herbert Hoover, the former president and prewar noninterventionist, called for the victorious nations to reduce their military establishments after the defeated Axis powers were disarmed. "No State should be permitted to arm itself merely as it pleases," Hudson said.[75] Political philosopher Gerhart Niemeyer attempted to square the inevitability of leader-ship by the great powers with opposition to militarism everywhere. "If we really fight for democracy," he wrote, "victory will be won only in the hour that sounds the end of power politics." To that end he envisioned a series of strong regional councils that would balance responsibilities among the great powers and give significant influence to the small powers. He also proposed to create a world council, composed solely of individuals outside governments, that could pronounce on any issue based on a "universal frame of reference," without having political interests to represent or political functions to per-form.[76] More mechanically minded was Ely Culbertson, a famous bridge player, who detailed a plan to allot quotas on armed force. Under his scheme, an international force would have slightly more military strength than any individual nation—22 percent of the global share, as opposed to 20 percent for the United States, 15 percent each for Britain and the Soviet Union, and so on—so that no nation could achieve world domination and neither could the world organization.[77]

But none of these or other proposals garnered the active support of party politicians or pressure groups on anything like the scale of the LEP plan during World War I. The specter of isolationism—powerfully invoked against noninterventionists throughout the war—served to quiet internationalists in their moment of supposed triumph. Roosevelt issued a stark warning to this effect in his State of the Union Address in January 1945, on the heels of his fourth election victory. The ailing president, unable to come before Congress, made his words clear enough from the White House. He blamed critics of the League of Nations Covenant from the last war for abetting the "retreat to isolationism." "Perfectionism, no less than isolationism or imperialism or power politics, may obstruct the paths to international peace," Roosevelt avowed.[78] In assaulting perfectionism, Roosevelt assaulted, in the name of internationalism, the internationalism of the previous generation. Once meaningful differences of opinion were reduced to a perfectionist impulse, not worth comprehending on their own terms.

Roosevelt was only echoing the lessons of a spate of new narratives of the League fight published in the closing years of the war. These authors set the terms of historical memory for decades to come, and they distorted their subject matter to fit the assumptions and agenda of anti-isolationist internationalism. When they turned to the League fight for guidance, they did not examine the intellectual alternatives promulgated by contemporaries. Instead they effaced those alternatives. In their telling, the League fight pitted internationalists against isolationists, pure and simple. As the *New York Times* summed up the two hours and thirty-four minutes of Twentieth Century Fox's *Wilson,* "The League is but a symbol of international accord, and the opposition to it—with Senator [Henry Cabot] Lodge as the villain—is just an inchoate obstructive force."[79] The *Times* critic praised the film nonetheless for inspiring millions of Americans with its subject's ideals.

More complex narratives acknowledged divisions among the internationalists of World War I, only to condemn them. If the League fight did not simply pit internationalists against isolationists, it *should* have done so: writers switched from description to judgment and condemned advocates of particular plans for world organization for declining to line up behind world organization, period, whatever its content. Ruhl J. Bartlett's *The League to Enforce Peace,* still the most detailed history of that organization, glossed over the LEP's manifest legalism, presenting its activists as intellectual allies of Wilson who hurt their own cause by quibbling over details.[80] Thomas A. Bailey, one of the most influential diplomatic historians of midcentury America, blamed Wilson instead, to the same effect. First in *Woodrow Wilson and the Lost Peace,* and then in *Woodrow Wilson and the Great Betrayal,* Bailey reproached the president for spurning mild reservations to the Treaty of Versailles. Stubborn and tactless, Wilson failed to unite internationalists, assuring victory for isolationists. The lesson was clear. This time America should cast off isolationism and "assume that world leadership which had been thrust upon her," almost irrespective of the form this should take.[81] Although Bailey assumed world organization would accompany world leadership, his anti-isolationist standpoint subordinated the former to the later.

In this way the internationalists who staged the nondebate of World War II constructed the needless debate of World War I.[82] Projecting the internationalist / isolationist dichotomy onto the past achieved three functions at once. It stigmatized opposition to U.S. global supremacy as selfish and provincial isolationism. It discredited debate among internationalists as perfectionism, the handmaiden of isolationism. And it legitimized supremacy by giving it credentials in the American past. The opportunity for postwar leadership could be represented as a second chance, not a first, offering redemption rather than deviation. Yet simply by virtue of imagining a second chance to defeat isolationism, Americans were creating something new.

Cooperation for Domination

Although internationalists staged a debate against a phantom enemy, their nondebate proved to be world-historically productive. It settled what Sumner Welles, a few weeks after the D-Day landings, called "the real question before the American people today." This was whether, after winning the war, "they wish to make the fullest use of the strength which is theirs."[83] This strength, Welles noted, dwarfed that of any other nation in the world. As the United States helped to set up the institutions of postwar international society in the final years of the war, its political class perceived and constantly proclaimed that America had ascended to primacy among nations and must maintain primacy over all others in the interests of national security and world order. The pursuit of cooperation and domination proceeded together.

President Truman mapped the path to a "just and lasting peace" before Congress in October 1945: "We must relentlessly preserve our superiority on

This map, produced by the U.S. Navy in 1945, forecasts a global network of major American bases after the war had been won. Courtesy of the David Rumsey Historical Map Collection.

land and sea and in the air."[84] Truman was blunt, but no one could deny the reality of American global military supremacy as victorious U.S. troops streamed across central Europe and East Asia. In the closing months of the war, "magazine and newspaper editorials, radio commentators, government officials, and corporate advertisements constantly reminded Americans that their nation was the greatest power on earth," the historian John Fousek writes.[85] Martial greatness now seemed the ultimate proof of American greatness.

From the British embassy in Washington, DC, the loss of world leadership to the Americans within six years was acutely felt. In a lengthy stock-taking of U.S. opinion, chargé d'affaires John Balfour informed the incoming Labour Party government that Anglo-American relations were heading toward a "new order of things." The Americans still regarded British strength as essential to the interests and values of the United States. They still wished Great Britain to occupy a "highly important position as the bastion of Western European security and as the focal point of a far-flung oceanic system." But the prestige that Britain acquired in the lead-up to Pearl Harbor, Balfour reported, had been "largely eclipsed" by the burdens that warfare had imposed on Britain and, he might have added, the bounty that it had bestowed upon the United States. Americans clearly expected their British ally to "take her place as a junior partner in an orbit of power predominantly under American aegis."[86] Or as Prime Minister Winston Churchill told the House of Commons, "The United States stand at this moment at the summit of the world."[87]

Churchill was right, both in placing the United States at the summit and locating his own country and the Soviet Union down below. Although the term *super-powers* would be coined in 1944 to characterize the Big Three, the United States ranked first among unequals.[88] To think of the Cold War as a "bipolar" contest obscures America's vast advantage in global terms.[89] In 1945 U.S. factories served up as much manufacturing output as the whole rest of the world.[90] While postwar reconstruction would later narrow that gap, no one knew whether and how far such reconstruction would succeed. The United States alone required no postwar reconstruction, only a conversion to peacetime of its booming war economy. For it alone, the war enhanced "the magnitude of our material resources and the supreme quality of American industrial capacity," as Welles put it.[91]

Geopolitically, too, American superiority was as marked as editorialists suggested. Only the United States could be assured of preserving its sphere of influence, the Western Hemisphere, after the war. Only the United States could project all dimensions of military power on a truly global scale. If the Red Army stood astride half of Europe (the much less industrialized half), it would be decades until the Red Fleet and the Red Air Force could deliver troops well beyond Soviet territory.[92] On taking office, Truman estimated he should get 85 percent of what he wanted from Russian diplomats, who "needed us more than we needed them."[93] Meanwhile, the United States had supplanted the British Empire as the main policeman of Asia, balancer of Europe, and creditor of the international economic system—not to mention of bankrupt Britain itself, dependent on Lend-Lease aid during the war and billions in intergovernmental loans immediately after.[94] As Luce's *Life* magazine editorialized, "Practically all Americans realize by now that they are in the game of international power politics for good, and that joint action with Britain and Russia is the best way for them to play it." The United States had been a reticent player in the past, *Life* acknowledged, but conditions were different now: "we can take care of ourselves and we have an almost unlimited stack of chips."[95]

Livingston Hartley, the Washington director of the American Association for the United Nations, summarized the position of the superpowers in testimony to Congress. The British Empire, he conceded, contained more people than the United States. The Soviet Union possessed a larger army; one day it might develop the resources to ascend to primacy. "But the United States, in this year 1945, is supreme in naval strength, air strength, industrial power, and wealth," Harley noted. It alone possessed the opportunity, here and now, to exert "leadership and unparalleled influence among the nations of the world."[96] Still, the capacity to lead the world would count for nothing without the will to do so.

IN THIS REGARD OFFICIALS AND INTELLECTUALS felt vulnerable. As we have seen, they feared a postwar reversion to so-called isolationism, and it would take less than a rehabilitation of the nonentanglement tradition in order to thwart the redeployment of U.S. land forces to Europe, where the numerical dominance of the Red Army and the potential appeal of communism could divide the "one world" for which America fought. Particularly after Nazi defeats on the Eastern Front in the summer of 1943, U.S. policymakers struggled to reconcile the goals of unifying the world order and cooperating with the Soviet Union. Through 1945 they settled on the hope that the Red Army would preside over an "open" sphere of influence in Eastern Europe, one that permitted enough economic and political freedoms to satisfy the United States but that did not compromise core Soviet security interests.[97] Whether or not they were alarmed by Joseph Stalin's designs on postwar Europe, however, U.S. elites sought to ensure their own political system was willing to exercise and maintain a preponderance of power abroad.

It was in fashioning such political will that the nondebate proved significant. Unceasing denunciations of isolationism were not necessary for ensuring a sufficient quantity of public support for membership in a postwar international organization. They did little to enrich the quality of public discussion, since advocates declined to debate alternatives. But embracing internationalism and establishing the U.N. did imbue postwar American supremacy with a legitimacy it could not have otherwise obtained. That the United States was creating a world organization furnished proof positive that it was not simply the next empire out to aggrandize itself by exploiting others. Truman, for instance, told Congress why no one could doubt America's good will in assuming "responsibility for world leadership": "Our purpose is shown by our efforts to establish an effective United Nations Organization."[98] Precisely in order to make the U.N. effective, Truman continued, the United States needed a strong military, manned via universal training and coordinated by a new peacetime Department of Defense.

Advocates of postwar supremacy seamlessly blended their cause with that of world organization. Colorado senator Edwin Johnson displayed this dynamic in an interview during the would-be U.N. fight. Johnson insisted that the Senate ratify the U.N. Charter, for "there can be no United Nations Organization without the energetic leadership of the United States. It is our plain duty to assume such leadership with confidence and determination." Johnson attempted to position world leadership as a means of realizing world organization, but the interviewer sensed the negative connotations that world leadership might still retain. He broke in, "Of course, Senator, we're talking about world leadership in the best sense." Johnson took the hint. "Yes," he replied, "I am talking about a new kind of world leadership. Not the kind that Caesar and Napoleon and Hitler had in mind, but a leadership of give and take—of cooperation and of good neighborliness."[99] Now the circle closed: world organization appeared as a method of world leadership, completing the mutual constitution of the two.

In this instance Johnson did not distinguish U.S. from Nazi world leadership by appealing to national exceptionalism. No doubt he believed America's political system and values to be superior to others'. Characteristic of political elites in this founding moment of global supremacy, however, Johnson foregrounded internationalism. He highlighted mutuality and reciprocity, participation and rules. Even Lippmann—having spent most of the war lambasting the naïveté of Wilsonian universalism and touting an American-British or American-British-Soviet concert—exclaimed that the U.N. Charter proposed in San Francisco ushered in something like an "international society under the rule of law."[100] Because the United States respected the equality of nations (internationalism), it gained the right to be superior (exceptionalism). The contradiction between internationalism and exceptionalism functioned as justification, promising to satisfy opposing values and absorbing criticism from either side.

Harnessing the legitimacy conferred by international institutions, many internationalists argued in 1944 and 1945 that the president should be able to use force solely on the authority of the U.N. Security Council, bypassing the Constitution's requirement that Congress shall declare war. Running for his fourth term, Roosevelt announced that "if the world organization is to have any reality at all," the executive must be able to deploy military force as soon as the U.N. demanded, without waiting for Congress to debate and declare war.[101] Roosevelt's position received support from six major international law experts, including Shotwell and Wright, who explained in the *New York Times* that the president could use his inherent authority to deploy force in defense of international law. Such action would represent policing, not war, and so no declaration would be necessary.[102] Roosevelt put the point vividly, likening the policing of international society to the policing of domestic society. A cop would be ineffective "if, when he saw a felon break into a house, he had to go to the Town Hall and call a town meeting to issue a warrant before the felon could be arrested."[103] Roosevelt's argument invested the U.N. Security Council with the same kind of legal and democratic legitimacy as a domestic legislature, whose elected representatives created codes of law for police to enforce.

Yet the Security Council possessed unlimited discretion to define and punish a threat to "international peace and security"; its momentary judgment defined the law. Nor were its representatives directly elected, or, in any case, representative of every nation. Nevertheless, as the symbol of international society, the U.N. possessed an ersatz legal and democratic legitimacy, skillfully deployed by wartime internationalists looking beyond the present war. Eight years after Congress had seriously considered a constitutional amendment to require a popular referendum for each declaration of war, internationalists sought to insulate the use of force from democracy. It was world organization that legitimated their project, investing global supremacy with the trappings of participatory democracy and legal order.

EVEN THOUGH WORLD LEADERSHIP and world organization went hand in hand, then, the two were not equally foundational. Just as policy elites planned for world leadership without world organization prior to the autumn of 1941, so they continued to privilege the former as they rallied around the latter through 1945. A thin commitment to internationalism could always thicken later, as some pointed out at the time. Roosevelt's speechwriter, Robert Sherwood, said in reference to the Atlantic Charter that sometimes "when you state a moral principle, you are stuck with it, no matter how many fingers you have kept crossed at the moment."[104] But what seed did internationalists plant? What "moral principle" did they announce?

That moral principle was *not* that the dictates of international law and organization should trump the will of the United States, even if only in the future. Wartime internationalists refused to confront the possibility of discord between the U.N. and the United States, partly because they had stripped from world organization any obligation for America to act against aggression unless the United States already concurred. Without confronting the real possibility of disagreement with world opinion, such internationalists could not state a principle that made internationalism more than instrumental—useful when others went along, dispensable if they did not.

A moment of semi-confrontation occurred in the post–Dumbarton Oaks meeting of postwar planners. One planner asked Pasvolsky what the United States would do if it wished to intervene against an aggressor like Argentina but a permanent member exercised a veto on the Security Council. Pasvolsky sidestepped the question. More likely, he countered, the rest of the Security Council would want the United States to use force when it would rather not. Although concluding that he personally thought the world organization should be able to judge and sanction the United States, Pasvolsky acknowledged that whether the United States would accept such subordination was "another matter."[105] In this exchange Pasvolsky went as far as anyone to place international rules above American prerogatives. Even so, he preferred to avoid envisioning a concrete scenario and expressed little confidence that the United States would constrain itself when the time came.

Other officials and planners ranked the authority of international institutions less highly than Pasvolsky. John Foster Dulles, the chairman of liberal Protestant postwar groups and an important member of the U.S. delegation at San Francisco, had an answer for the question that Pasvolsky evaded: "If a European country vetoed action to prevent aggression in the Western Hemisphere, we would be entirely free to use force."[106] Dulles, a corporate lawyer, noted that, under the charter, member states retained the right to go to war in self-defense. Should a permanent member stretch the meaning of self-defense in order to justify the use of force, "nothing can be done about it."[107] Senator Vandenberg, head of the Republican delegation, objected that Dulles implied that "we have the right to do anything we please in self-defense."[108] Once they realized this point, "the people would be disillusioned beyond words." Vandenberg did not, however, offer a different reading of the charter. In fact, he obtained Pasvolsky's permission to tell the Senate that "if the Security Council voted no and we thought action was vitally necessary we could take action on our own."[109] Before the ink dried on the U.N. Charter, American officials devised justifications for unilateral action that they or their successors would deploy later.

As suggested by Pasvolsky's willingness to inform the Senate, foreign policy elites struck similar notes in public as they did in private. Their confidential discussions at San Francisco differed chiefly in their specificity. In books, speeches, and testimony, internationalists stressed that the U.N. was a thoroughly American creation that would facilitate the projection of American power without impinging on American freedom of action. As Hartley told Congress, the Dumbarton Oaks proposals were "basically the American plan." Joining the U.N. would "place America in the lead in world affairs, fit to exert her unequaled influence, through a largely American system, to guide world evolution in accordance with American ideals."[110] Statements like this one denied any trade-off between world organization and world leadership. Quite the contrary, they positioned the U.N. as essential to the full exercise of American power.

Indeed, U.N. supporters frequently used the word *full* to characterize the extent to which the postwar United States ought to exert its own strength and follow its own judgment. In *The Great Decision,* published in 1944, Shotwell wrote that the American people must retain the "*full* opportunity to decide when, where, and how much" to contribute in the enforcement of peace.[111] What unified the "one world" that Willkie touted was that it "demands the *full* participation of a self-confident America."[112] Not least, soon after the release of the Dumbarton Oaks plan, Roosevelt gave a wide-ranging speech on foreign policy that rebuked "inveterate isolationists" and ended on an uncompromising statement of American supremacy.

Roosevelt noted that Americans could have opted to come to terms with Adolf Hitler and "accepted a minor role in his totalitarian world." But, he said, they emphatically chose otherwise: "We rejected that!" In Roosevelt's telling, Americans did not fight World War II merely to respond to the territorial attack on Pearl Harbor. Their purpose was rather to avoid a "minor role" in world affairs, to cast off constraints, internal and external, on their world power. "We shall not again be thwarted in our will to live as a mature Nation, confronting limitless horizons," Roosevelt declared. "We shall bear our *full* responsibility, exercise our *full* influence, and bring our *full* help and encouragement to all who aspire to peace and freedom."[113] As the United

States entered the postwar world, its desire to lead the world as it saw fit could not help but circumscribe international cooperation at every turn. Yet international cooperation could hardly go away. Symbolized in words and institutions, it already proved vital in cementing the nation's decision for dominance.

The Triumph of Anti-Isolationism

By June 1945 the *New York Times* had ample reason to call the U.N. a symbol that America was "in the world to stay."[114] One needed only to consult the gleaming emblem of the new world organization that hovered above the representatives of fifty nations who took the stage at San Francisco's Herbst Theater to sign the U.N. Charter. Consisting of a circular map of the world framed by a pair of olive branches, the emblem depicted unity and peace among nations—but not equality. It gave visual primacy to North America, the only continent centered on the vertical axis and facing northward (whereas the bottoms of South America, Africa, and Australasia were cut off altogether). The world owed the design to Donal McLaughlin, head of the Graphics Presentation branch of the Office of Strategic Services (OSS); Stettinius had requested a number of OSS men, fresh off promoting Dumbarton Oaks, to handle visuals for the San Francisco conference.[115] A year later, McLaughlin modified the logo by rotating the continents forty-five degrees clockwise. This version, which denied pride of place to any landmass, became the recognizable U.N. symbol of the postwar era.

But there was no mistaking the vision of American policy elites who brought the organization into being. The original emblem ably represented the centrality of the United States in the new world order and the willingness of U.S. leaders to say so. For even though policy elites created a myth of isolationism, they manipulated openly. They were not so mendacious or shortsighted as to wage a campaign of deception, which could not have incorporated a breadth of opinion shapers and might have crumbled the moment the truth came out. The remaining noninterventionists, unable to come to terms with their defeat, endlessly investigated the circumstances of Pearl Harbor, as though nefarious officials had brought on an attack and tricked the innocent public.[116] But their adversaries built something sturdier than that. Advocates of global supremacy remapped how Americans comprehended the past, present, and future of their nation in the world. Supremacy captured the concept of internationalism so thoroughly that the two appeared to be mutually implied if not one and the same.

Eleanor Roosevelt addresses the United Nations in January 1946 in London. The original U.N. emblem, centered on North America, stands above. Courtesy of Franklin D. Roosevelt Presidential Library and Museum.

Most members of the foreign policy elite preferred to smooth over this intellectual transformation, if they were more than dimly aware that it had taken place. But a few of its marginal members, at once within and aslant the mainstream, mourned as once prominent ideas escaped from view. They were not convinced by the anti-isolationists' refrain that the League of Nations failed to prevent World War II because the United States stayed out.[117] This argument held that the League had been simultaneously fundamentally faulty—based on "good intentions alone," Roosevelt jeered—and yet capable of stopping global warfare if only America had contributed.[118]

Buell, having cut his teeth criticizing U.S. and Western imperialism, found such reasoning superficial at best. He thought his fellow interventionists were fetishizing American power and world organization alike. As he wrote to Senator Joseph Ball, everything depended on "what *policies* we would have followed as a League member. We could have been as obstructive inside as we were outside." By casting the United States as the savior of world organization, interventionists assumed that the world needed American power and that American power necessarily benefited the world. To Buell's mind, by contrast, the two could easily clash. The question was *how* to organize international politics and *how* to use American power, which should be judged by its actions rather than affirmed in advance. On balance, Buell thought the campaign for internationalism was preventing a meaningful discussion. He was willing to support the Dumbarton Oaks proposals but equally feared that the agitation around them would "create the delusion that merely *joining* something solves everything." In fact, "it is only the beginning."[119]

Buell remained hopeful that global supremacy and international cooperation would develop together. It took a noninterventionist, John Bassett Moore, to extend Buell's point that American power might obstruct as well as construct. Eighty-one years old at the time of Pearl Harbor, Moore was past shifting his views with the political winds. He had been his generation's most eminent academic expert on international law, advising the State Department for decades and serving as one of the first judges on the Permanent Court of International Justice from 1921 to 1928.[120] In his opinion, "nothing could be more preposterous . . . than the supposition that the League of Nations failed to preserve the peace of the world because the United States did not become a party to it." This supposition turned America into the indispensable nation to world peace, "apparently ignorant of the fact that the United States had not only been guilty of aggressive foreign war, as in the case of Mexico, but had also added to the number of great civil wars."[121]

Moore's "apparently" suggested that U.S. elites were engaging in willful ignorance, choosing to forget. American politics no longer seemed able to register U.S. power as potentially aggressive and deserving some measure of restraint. Moore sometimes made the argument that world organization was naive, but mostly he argued that it could facilitate aggression and undermine law. That is, he criticized anti-isolationism from the standpoint of the internationalism that he had lived. He thought the U.N. gave the United States the new power to cast its rivals as enemies of the world—against whom all is permitted—and enlarge local disputes into global wars. American supremacy could be not only obstructive but also destructive, the more so if it paid false homage to international law and order.

CONCLUSION

A DISTINCTLY AMERICAN INTERNATIONALISM

GEORGE W. BUSH RAN FOR THE presidency promising to be humble in the use of American power.[1] In November 1999, the then governor of Texas used his first major foreign policy address to decry what he called "action without vision, activity without priority, and missions without end."[2] But after terrorists struck New York City and Washington, DC, on September 11, 2001, Bush would launch several such missions under the rubric of the "global war on terror," complete with occupations to remake the societies of Afghanistan and Iraq into pro-American democracies. To many commentators, Bush's bellicosity in office appeared to be a stark departure from the original vision of his campaign.[3]

Was it? It is true that prior to 9/11 Bush did not foresee waging what became a nearly limitless war. Nor did he plan to launch specific wars in Afghanistan and Iraq. Yet Bush's militarized response to 9/11 was shaped by his assumption, apparent from the start of his candidacy, that the United States should pursue armed dominance across the globe, acting as the world's ordering agent regardless of whether the United States itself faced any major threat.

In his 1999 speech, Bush named a globe-spanning set of "determined enemies" for the United States to confront: "terrorists and crime syndicates and drug cartels and unbalanced dictators." To these perennial threats to world order he added two potential challengers to America's preeminent power

173

position. China and Russia, Bush warned, could eventually dislodge the United States from paramountcy in Europe and Asia. Eurasia, in turn, constituted "the world's strategic heartland" and "our greatest priority." In Bush's telling, then, the prospects for peace were grim as the United States entered the twenty-first century, even though Nazi fascism and Soviet communism had been consigned to history's ash heap and nothing like them loomed on the horizon.

Bush never really explained why this should be so—why seeking to dominate Eurasia and police the global commons served the interests of the American people, particularly when such ambitious objectives would bring so many adversaries with them. His stance seemed just short of self-evident, warranting a few lines of rhetorical justification. "The vacuum left by America's retreat would invite challenges to our power," Bush intoned. The result would be "a stagnant America and a savage world." That was as far as Bush took the argument. The armed primacy of the United States was his unexamined assumption—and not just his. It was the baseline from which members of both political parties, and experts in Washington, DC, began any debate about America's world role.

Bush's speech stands out, however, for recognizing where the project it took forward came from: "the dark days of 1941—the low point of our modern epic," as Bush put it. In harking back to the early years of World War II, Bush was apt. It was then that global military supremacy first entered the minds, and the plans, of the officials and intellectuals who steered U.S. foreign policy. It was then that armed supremacy mounted a rapid ascent to axiomatic status. And it did so in just the terms of Bush's speech, which was titled "A Distinctly American Internationalism."

Although states often seek to enlarge their military power, to install one's dominance in the name of internationalism is something else. It effectively turns one nation's military supremacy into the prerequisite of a decent world. This kind of internationalism denies that armed force can obstruct cooperation and provoke others. It also attenuates the value of international rules and bodies. (Tellingly, Bush referred to the United Nations [U.N.] only briefly, in order to assert that he would never place U.S. troops under its command.) This kind of internationalism does not seek, first and foremost, to cooperate to solve common problems, much less to end the scourge of war. Instead it seeks to mobilize the nation to project armed power far and wide. "Let us reject the blinders of isolationism," Bush said, revealing what he was for by stating what he was against.[4] His was indeed a distinctly American concept of internationalism.

YET BUSH'S WAS NOT THE only American incarnation of internationalism, nor even the historically dominant strain. Prior to the dark days of world war, a very different concept oriented the United States in its approach toward the world. From the founding of the country to the turn of the twentieth century, American leaders consistently sought to engage in peaceful intercourse without inviting political-military entanglements in Europe and Asia. To be sure, this maxim did not stop them from conquering Native American land across North America, policing the Western Hemisphere, or seizing colonies in the Pacific. It did, however, limit U.S. involvement in much of the world's major rivalries and conflicts. It also nourished Americans' participation in efforts within the hemisphere and across the Atlantic to organize global politics and contain war. Internationalists of this kind hardly defined themselves in opposition to isolationism or a U.S. reluctance to play the game of power politics. To the contrary, any restraint the United States displayed was an asset in internationalists' cause of transforming power politics—of taming what one political scientist in 1930 called the "unholy trinity" of nationalism, militarism, and imperialism.[5]

Having inherited a commitment to engagement without entanglement, many Americans reacted cautiously to the coming of World War II, even after Nazi Germany conquered France and loomed as the dominant power in Europe while Japan rampaged through East Asia. To a cross-section of Americans, tragic new events reaffirmed a received wisdom: the worse the plight of Europe and Asia, the greater the reason to steer clear of the conflicts of distant lands and preserve the freedom and prosperity that the United States retained within its prodigious hemispheric domain.

The nationalist case for this position was straightforward, as the banner of "America First" announced. But those who resisted U.S. intervention prior to Pearl Harbor had at least as strong a claim to be acting as internationalists as their opponents did. If the United States entered the race for global supremacy, they feared, domination would replace defense as the guiding principle of policy. America would become something like an empire: arrogant, rule breaking, perpetually at war. In the long run, would an imperious

America really benefit the world? Europeans and Asians had resisted previous aspirants to mastery since Napoleon and might well thwart Germany's and Japan's bid, without the United States throwing itself into the fight. Secure between the oceans, the United States could choose a different future. It could remain at peace and cultivate within the Americas the basis of a safe and free world.

Peace, however, came at an unprecedented price after Germany conquered France and briefly bestrode Europe. For the United States to maintain a hemispheric military posture could potentially leave Europe to the worst Europeans and Asia to the worst Asians—totalitarian dictatorships harnessing the tools of industrial modernity to achieve armed conquest and subjugation. This, too, was problematic for the traditional self-definition of the United States, even though the country faced no grave and imminent threat to its physical security or economic prosperity. If the Axis powers, or any other hostile combination, were to achieve domination of Europe and Asia, the United States could no longer fulfill its mission of ushering the world into an "American," emancipated future. Much of the earth, moreover, might effectively close down to U.S. participation, at least in ways that would be compatible with liberal commerce and law. These objectives, which once dictated that the United States practice peaceful intercourse outside its hemisphere, now became militarized, requiring force to back them. For this reason many Americans decided prior to Pearl Harbor that it was worse to risk leaving Europe and Asia to a brutal fate than to risk engaging in global warfare evermore. To them, World War II was a war of choice—the right choice—and so would be U.S. dominance after victory.

Each side formulated a reasonably coherent account of U.S. interests and responsibilities. Each side developed a plausible ideological presentation of its case as American and internationalist alike. Each side also possessed significant political power at elite and popular levels, enough to make the outcome genuinely uncertain until 1941. Still, the sides did not face equal odds of success. America's foreign policy class, built up over two decades between the wars in Europe, was not about to see U.S. political, economic, and cultural influence reduced to a hemispheric husk if such a fate could be avoided. American elites expected, and felt entitled, to traverse the globe and exchange ideas, goods, and money widely. They saw themselves as part of a small cohort of people who governed the world, whether they understood world governance to be a principally American, Anglophone, white, Western, or civilizational project.

In these respects, U.S. policymakers and intellectuals in World War II continued the trajectory of American foreign policy since the turn of the twentieth century. Presidents William McKinley and Theodore Roosevelt had brought the country into the ranks of the colonial great powers. They positioned the United States as one of a handful of guardians of civilization tasked with disciplining lawless savages and lawbreaking aggressors, although the United States would exercise its police power within a hemispheric and Pacific realm. In the First World War, President Woodrow Wilson sent U.S. troops into the heart of the balance of power in Europe and then attempted to commit the United States to enforce the peace, albeit on the assumption that the peace would not need much enforcing. Moral suasion would replace physical coercion, or so Wilson and the Wilsonians anticipated. Once totalitarian powers dashed those hopes in the 1930s, the officials and intellectuals who had stewarded America's rise in previous decades forthrightly aligned with Anglo-French preeminence. Then, once totalitarians conquered much of Europe and East Asia, destroying France and weakening Britain, U.S. foreign policy elites overwhelmingly decided to cast off old restraints and seek maximum power for the United States. Not without reason have some scholars interpreted this outcome as the logical and perhaps inevitable conclusion of decades of American conduct.

Yet it took the most improbable of events—the German military's rapid and absolute victory over its superior French counterpart—for the United States to contemplate and pursue global supremacy, to make itself the armed policeman of the world. Had Hitler not made a massive gamble by ordering an invasion of France, had Allied leaders anticipated that Germany might launch an offensive through the Ardennes Forest, had the Wehrmacht been slightly slowed in its advance to the Meuse River, had French generals not sent their best troops and tanks to the wrong spot, then Germany would not have overrun France and might never have come close to dominating Europe.[6] Without the credible prospect of an ascendant Axis, the United States might well have played a circumscribed role in the war and the world to come. U.S. policymakers would have had insufficient cause to abandon their traditional extrahemispheric formula of peaceful engagement by Americans and power balancing by Asians and Europeans. They applied this formula during the opening months of the war, prior to the fall of France. They likely would have continued to do so if French defenses had held. It remains possible, of course, that the United States would have entered the war nonetheless, perhaps in roughly the way it did. Even so, the United States may well have declined to police the postwar world, a costly and morally dubious under-taking that could have been left to Britain and France if it needed to be per-formed at all. Alternatively, the United States might have expanded its postwar security perimeter in the Far East but played more of a supporting role in Europe and the rest of Asia. Only the specter of a Nazi Europe—with France flattened and Britain potentially next—created a sense of crisis capable of breaking the old consensus and forging a new one. Axis world leadership, leading to a hemispherically "isolated" United States, compelled elites to envi-sion U.S. military dominance and opened the political space to achieve it.

As it turned out, France did fall. The United States eyed a hemispheric existence, if only for a matter of months. And with all the vehemence with which prior generations vowed to avoid entangling alliances and faraway wars, a new class of leaders insisted that it was precisely America's reluctance to commit and apply military power that courted disaster. In a world tor-mented by rampaging great powers, their prescription looked responsible and humane. At the time, however, many planners of U.S. dominance also under-stood themselves to be making a tragic choice. In order to stop existing ag-gressors and prevent future ones, they risked putting the United States in the position of an aggressor itself. Some planners, like Isaiah Bowman, won-dered aloud how to distinguish U.S. ambitions from Nazi ones. Others were troubled that the United States was inheriting the basic role of the British Empire; Arthur Sweetser, for example, warned that global policing by the United States, in tandem with Britain, constituted a bid for "Anglo-Saxon domination" that would provoke the rest of the world. Those who made the decision for primacy appreciated why American statecraft had operated dif-ferently for so long. They understood U.S. military supremacy to be fraught with moral compromise and strategic risk.

SINCE THEN, Americans have lost sight both of the specific circumstances that elicited the decision for primacy and the weighty trade-offs that primacy entails. Primacy has come to seem obvious, not contestable; thrust upon the United States, not ambitiously chosen by it. This predicament is rooted in the story Americans have told themselves about their global ascendance in World War II. The story says that the United States turned away from selfish isola-tionism in order to take the lead in world affairs. By developing the pejorative concept of isolationism, and applying it to all advocates of limits on military intervention, American officials and intellectuals found a way to make global supremacy sound unimpeachable. With isolationism as its foil, primacy became the only basis through which the United States could participate in the world. Anything less would be an abdication, tantamount to inactivity, absence, and head-in-the-sand disregard for the fate of the world. In other words, the only way to practice internationalism, to constrain and transcend power politics, was to dominate power politics. The United States forged global supremacy by erasing this fundamental contradiction from view.

As the decades advanced, primacy's privileged status in American politics was reinforced by several factors that primacy itself helped to bring into being. One was a succession of external threats, starting with Soviet-backed communism, to the now expansive global interests of the United States.[7] Another was what President Dwight D. Eisenhower called the "military-industrial complex": domestic interests dependent on, and perpetuating, large-scale mobilization.[8] Perhaps these factors suffice to explain the endurance of America's commitment to armed supremacy for eight decades and counting after the fall of France triggered its conception. Yet perhaps they do not. The existence of foreign threats might have given rise to the criticism that it was America's excessive definition of its interests, and its provocative actions in their pursuit, that produced unnecessary adversaries. Moreover, few other world-shaping initiatives—even those supported by entrenched interests—have generated so little intellectual scrutiny and political opposition as has the global dominance of the United States. American supremacy has been sustained, virtually without challenge, by a policymaking elite and a collective imagination that holds supremacy to be the only viable course and rejects those who disagree as beyond the pale.

The bugaboo of isolationism, and the equation of internationalism with armed supremacy, stifled political debate from 1945 onward. As a result, politicians may disagree over discrete episodes—whether to intervene in one place or another—but they take for granted the structure of power that enables the question in the first place. Every U.S. president since Franklin D. Roosevelt has warned against the peril of "isolationism," despite the paucity of voices advocating a return to hemispheric limits on military commitments.[9] "Isolationism is the road to war," Roosevelt's successor, Harry S. Truman, stated as the Cold War began.[10] "Nothing today can present more danger to us than a retreat to the folly of isolationism," his successor, Eisenhower, affirmed.[11]

And so on.[12] "To be called an isolationist in the context of the Cold War was," the historian Michael Hunt writes, "nearly as bad as being called a communist."[13] More striking, perhaps, is the continuance of the anti-isolationist chorus, and the bipartisan consensus for global military dominance, after the collapse of the Soviet Union. As U.S. planners anticipated in 1941, seeking to order the world by force has caused the United States to mete out continual violence, akin to policing the frontier by empires past. Many Americans now object that the United States pursues "endless war." The moniker is a doubly apt description for conflict that lacks both a terminus and a purpose. In the early twenty-first century, largely free from conquering rivals, global supremacy has left the United States with awesome destructive power and little prospect of peace.

IN 1945, the moment later deemed the "triumph of internationalism," Quincy Wright did not speak triumphantly. He deserved to if anyone did. Since the First World War, no American academic had been more trenchant and prolific, inspired as many careers, and advised policy elites as widely on the subject of internationalism as a basis for world peace.[14] And in the Second World War, no one attempted to stay as loyal to the ideals of prewar internationalism while simultaneously espousing the new anti-isolationism. Yet when the U.N. Charter came into being, Wright was sober. In his judgment, the U.N. was better than isolationism but by no means realized Woodrow Wilson's vision of creating an "opinion, permeating the public of every important nation, prepared to subordinate immediate national interests to world law." Power politics, produced by clashing interests of separate states, was not about to be replaced by a superior organization animated by the good of the whole. Instead, Wright admitted, "power politics is today the basis of the world's political organization."[15] The new institution did incorporate several different kinds of bodies, but the most important one, the Security Council, constituted a "world empire" run by the most powerful nations.[16]

Wright still refused to reduce internationalism to the projection of American power. But if he illustrated how prewar internationalists had sought something other than U.S. global supremacy, he leveled no criticisms of the new world role adopted by his colleagues. Rather than confront American power, Wright emphasized world opinion. The way forward, he wrote, was to begin again to cultivate a global public disposed to put the welfare of humankind first. The United Nations could evolve into a world state only on the foundation of a "world state of mind," however long that took.[17] Until then, states could not trust their security to international law and organization, so they had to look out for themselves. Placing faith in a "still inchoate world opinion not yet aware of itself," Wright divorced his residual prewar internationalism from his prescriptions for U.S. foreign policy. In the late 1940s, as he helped to pen the Preliminary Draft of a World Constitution, Wright supported the Truman Doctrine, a landmark in the advent of the Cold War that pledged U.S. support for nations resisting communism.[18] "It is regrettable," he wrote, "that we must play the game of power politics until the United Nations is strong enough."[19] Little separated Wright's outlook from that of Hans Morgenthau and other first-generation "realists" who created the academic field of international relations and championed power politics until the distant day when world federation might arrive.[20]

In 1966, four years before his death, Wright saw American B-52s over Vietnam and no world constitution on the horizon. He was ready to reckon with U.S. supremacy. He wrote to Walter Lippmann, himself dismayed by the indiscriminate use of American power, that "the trouble with the American people is that they do not recognize the difference between 'imperialism' and 'internationalism.'" In the 1940s the country "jumped from 'isolationism' to 'imperialism,'" acquiring a taste for unilateral intervention everywhere in order to remake the world in the image of the United States. Wright recognized the same impulse in the imperialism of Rudyard Kipling's Britain. No longer willing to assume the best of U.S. policymakers, he specified exactly what they needed to do: "We should renounce unilateral intervention in both Europe and Asia"; accept Ho Chi Minh's victory in a unified Vietnam; and bring both Germanys, both Koreas, and Communist China into the United Nations. "Such are the policies," after all, "to which we committed ourselves in the San Francisco Charter."[21]

Were they? Although newly critical of American supremacy, Wright continued to think within the ideology that underpinned it. In World War II, Americans told themselves they were casting off isolationism and committing, through the U.N. Charter, to build a just and durable order. Far from openly espousing imperialism, foreign policy elites generated a surfeit of terms to evoke the scale of imperial power while sidestepping its moral undertones: the American Century, Pax Democratica, the Grand Area, world leadership.

Their favorite formula called on Americans to graduate from isolationism into precisely the internationalism in which Wright still invested his hopes. The American people did not necessarily fail to appreciate what this kind of internationalism meant. It was Wright who misunderstood. He did not see that so long as the phantom of isolationism is held to be the most grievous sin, all is permitted.

NOTES

SOURCES

ACKNOWLEDGMENTS

INDEX

NOTES

ABBREVIATIONS

AB Adolf Berle Papers, Franklin D. Roosevelt Presidential Library and
Museum

AJT Arnold J. Toynbee Papers, Weston Library, Bodleian Libraries, University of
Oxford

AS Arthur Sweetser Papers, Manuscript Division, Library of Congress

AW Arnold Wolfers Papers, Sterling Memorial Library, Yale University

CDA Committee to Defend America by Aiding the Allies Papers, Seeley G. Mudd
Manuscript Library, Princeton University

CFRP Council on Foreign Relations Papers, Seeley G. Mudd Manuscript Library,
Princeton University

CFRWPS Studies of American Interests in the War and the Peace, Council on Foreign
Relations Library

CW Charles Webster Papers, Archives Division, London School of Economics

EB Edwin Borchard Papers, Sterling Memorial Library, Yale University

EME Edward Mead Earle Papers, Seeley G. Mudd Manuscript Library, Princeton
University

ER Elihu Root Papers, Manuscript Division, Library of Congress

FFF Fight for Freedom Papers, Seeley G. Mudd Manuscript Library, Princeton
University

FRUS *Foreign Relations of the United States*

HFA Hamilton Fish Armstrong Papers, Seeley G. Mudd Manuscript Library,
Princeton University

HH Harry Hopkins Papers, Franklin D. Roosevelt Presidential Library and
Museum

HN Harley Notter Files, National Archives and Records Administration

HRL Henry R. Luce Papers, Manuscript Division, Library of Congress

JFD John Foster Dulles Papers, Seeley G. Mudd Manuscript Library, Princeton
University

JS James Shotwell Papers, Rare Book and Manuscript Library, Columbia
University

LP   Leo Pasvolsky Files, National Archives and Records Administration
ND   Norman H. Davis Papers, Manuscript Division, Library of Congress
PJ   Philip Jessup Papers, Manuscript Division, Library of Congress
PPF   President's Personal File, Franklin D. Roosevelt Presidential Library and
        Museum
PSF   President's Secretary's File, Franklin D. Roosevelt Presidential Library and
        Museum
QW   Quincy Wright Papers, Special Collections Research Center, University of
        Chicago
RLB   Raymond Leslie Buell Papers, Manuscript Division, Library of Congress
SW   Sumner Welles Papers, Franklin D. Roosevelt Presidential Library and Museum
WL   Walter Lippmann Papers, Sterling Memorial Library, Yale University
WS   Whitney Shepardson Papers, Franklin D. Roosevelt Presidential Library and
        Museum
WWF   Woodrow Wilson Foundation Papers, Seeley G. Mudd Manuscript Library,
        Princeton University
YIIS   Yale Institute for International Studies Papers, Sterling Memorial Library, Yale
        University

INTRODUCTION

1. Harry S. Truman, "Address before a Joint Session of Congress on Universal Military Training," October 23, 1945, http://trumanlibrary.org/publicpapers/viewpapers.php ?pid=183.

2. Melvyn Leffler, *A Preponderance of Power: National Security, the Truman Administration, and the Cold War* (Stanford, CA: Stanford University Press, 1992).

3. Henry R. Luce, "The American Century," *Life,* February 17, 1941, 64.

4. Gerald Ford, "Remarks and a Question-and-Answer Session in La Crosse," March 27, 1976, in *Public Papers of the Presidents of the United States: Gerald R. Ford, 1976–1977* (Washington, DC: Government Printing Office, 1979), 839.

5. Gerald Ford, "Remarks at a Briefing for Representatives of Military Organizations on Defense and Foreign Policy," in *Public Papers of the Presidents of the United States: Gerald R. Ford, 1976–1977,* 247.

6. "The traditional isolationist / internationalist duality in American foreign policy," in the historian Elizabeth Borgwardt's words, remains rife in popular political discourse and interdisciplinary scholarship alike. A voluminous academic literature casts U.S. foreign relations either as isolationist before becoming internationalist or as constantly oscillating between the two poles, assumed to be embodied in opposing constellations of actors. Elizabeth Borgwardt, *A New Deal for the World: America's Vision for Human Rights* (Cambridge, MA: Harvard University Press, 2005), 63; and see Andrew Johnstone, "Isolationism and Internationalism in American Foreign Relations," *Journal of Transatlantic Studies* 9, no. 1 (2011): 7–20.

    Works that approach World War II in this vein—by positing a traditional "isolationism" against which they define the internationalism under study—include Townsend Hoopes and Douglas Brinkley, *FDR and the Creation of the U.N.* (New

Haven, CT: Yale University Press, 1997); Inderjeet Parmar, *Foundations of the American Century: The Ford, Carnegie, and Rockefeller Foundations in the Rise of American Power* (New York: Columbia University Press, 2012), ch. 3; Daniel Plesch, *America, Hitler and the UN: How the Allies Won World War II and Forged a Peace* (London: I. B. Tauris, 2011); Stephen Schlesinger, *Act of Creation: The Founding of the United Nations* (Boulder, CO: Westview, 2003); and David Schmitz, *The Triumph of Internationalism: Franklin D. Roosevelt and a World in Crisis, 1933–1941* (Washington, DC: Potomac Books, 2007).

Some scholars of wartime internationalism recognize that the category of *isolationism* oversimplifies or distorts the views of those who opposed America's entry into the war or its assumption of military supremacy in the postwar period. Even so, they still take advocates of intervention and supremacy to be the exemplars of the internationalism they chronicle. Isolationists, however renamed, continue to be positioned as noninternationalists. The narrative result is similar to that of the orthodox account: a group of internationalists is said to have battled their detractors for decades before emerging victorious in World War II. As Hilde Eliassen Restad writes, "the literature still reproduces the dichotomy of isolationism / internationalism by substituting separateness or aloofness for isolationism—or, in other cases, authors still use the term isolationism." Hilde Eliassen Restad, *American Exceptionalism: An Idea That Made a Nation and Remade the World* (London: Routledge, 2015), 67–68. Notable examples from the past few decades are Andrew Johnstone, *Against Immediate Evil: American Internationalists and the Four Freedoms on the Eve of World War II* (Ithaca, NY: Cornell University Press, 2014); Andrew Johnstone, *Dilemmas of Internationalism: The American Association for the United Nations and U.S. Foreign Policy, 1941–1948* (Burlington, VT: Ashgate, 2009); and Warren Kuehl and Lynne Dunn, *Keeping the Covenant: American Internationalists and the League of Nations, 1920–1939* (Kent, OH: Kent State University Press, 1997).

Two earlier sets of historiography established the analytical framework that allowed the triumph of internationalism in 1945 to look like the fulfillment of a preexisting agenda. The first, produced during and after World War II, made little secret of its effort to extol "internationalism" and discredit "isolationism." In addition to the works discussed in Chapter 5, see Walter Johnson, *The Battle against Isolation* (Chicago: University of Chicago Press, 1944); William Langer and S. Everett Gleason, *The Challenge to Isolation, 1937–1940* (New York: Harper, 1952); and William Langer and S. Everett Gleason, *The Undeclared War, 1940–1941* (New York: Harper, 1953). In literature of the 1960s and 1970s, the oeuvre of Robert Divine is exemplary. The title of his masterpiece *Second Chance: The Triumph of Internationalism in America during World War II* (New York: Atheneum, 1967) indicates how Divine, despite the richness of his analysis, reproduced the teleological narrative propagated by wartime anti-isolationists. See also Mark Lincoln Chadwin, *The Warhawks: American Interventionists before Pearl Harbor* (New York: W. W. Norton, 1970); Robert Divine, *The Illusion of Neutrality* (Chicago: University of Chicago Press, 1962); Robert Divine, *The Reluctant Belligerent: American Entry into World War II* (New York: Wiley, 1965); and Harold Josephson, *James T. Shotwell and the Rise of Internationalism in America* (Rutherford, NJ: Fairleigh Dickinson University Press, 1974).

7. In debating why "internationalism" defeated "isolationism" in World War II after the reverse ostensibly occurred in World War I, scholars assume the stability of the

categories across the wars. Divine claims that it was the mobilization of elite activists that largely made the difference, Jeffrey Legro points to the lessons of another world war, and Borgwardt privileges the legacy of New Deal institution building. The debate misses that self-identified internationalists before World War II opposed, or sought to make unnecessary, the pursuit of global supremacy by the United States or any other power, until the concept of internationalism changed to become nearly synonymous with global supremacy. Divine, *Second Chance*, 4–5; Jeffrey Legro, *Rethinking the World: Great Power Strategies and International Order* (Ithaca, NY: Cornell University Press, 2005), ch. 3; Jeffrey Legro, "Whence American Internationalism," *International Organization* 54, no. 2 (April 2000): 253–89; and Borgwardt, *A New Deal for the World*, 6.

8. Some of the most perceptive accounts of the U.S. rise to global power in World War II treat isolationism as an actually existing political position, whose decline they seek to explain, rather than as a concept used almost exclusively by one side in a political debate to the effect of misrepresenting and disparaging those it named: Borgwardt, *A New Deal for the World*, 152; Frank Ninkovich, *The Global Republic: America's Inadvertent Rise to World Power* (Chicago: University of Chicago Press, 2014), 141, 146, 166; James T. Sparrow, *Warfare State: World War II Americans and the Age of Big Government* (New York: Oxford University Press, 2011), 10, 26, 76, 94; and John A. Thompson, *A Sense of Power: The Roots of America's Global Role* (Ithaca, NY: Cornell University Press, 2015), 132–36, 162, 168, 180–81, 184.

Likewise, in narratives of opponents of extrahemispheric political-military entanglements, historians tend to characterize such actors as isolationists, a labeling that subverts their interpretive aim of showing that so-called isolationists possessed more sophisticated and diverse views than the moniker implies. For example, despite seeking to rehabilitate "isolationists" of the 1930s for developing thorough analyses of the crises in Europe and Asia, Manfred Jonas simultaneously pathologizes isolationism as a psychological deficiency. He writes that isolationism entailed an "inordinate fear of war" and is "permanently attractive . . . produc[ing] at least a nostalgic yearning for it whenever world events become too unpleasant to contemplate with equanimity." Manfred Jonas, *Isolationism in America, 1935–1941* (Ithaca, NY: Cornell University Press, 1966), 3, 23, 260, 275. Also see Wayne Cole, *Roosevelt and the Isolationists, 1932–1945* (Lincoln: University of Nebraska Press, 1983); John Milton Cooper, *The Vanity of Power: American Isolationism and the First World War, 1914–1917* (Westport, CT: Greenwood, 1969); Divine, *The Illusion of Neutrality;* Christopher McKnight Nichols, *Promise and Peril: America at the Dawn of a Global Age* (Cambridge, MA: Harvard University Press, 2011); and Ralph Stone, *The Irreconcilables: The Fight Against the League of Nations* (Lexington, KY: University Press of Kentucky, 1970).

Some scholars replace "isolationism" with more determinate and productive categories of analysis. George C. Herring and Walter McDougall refer to "unilateralism," a proclivity they trace back to the American founding. Justus Doenecke addresses "anti-interventionism" in his studies of antiwar Americans in the lead-up to Pearl Harbor. Robert David Johnson recasts would-be isolationist senators from 1913 to 1935 as anti-imperialist "peace progressives," although he detects "isolationism" among some members of the group. All these accounts, however, tell the history of isolationism (or its replacement concept) as the story of the ideas and actors branded as isolationist by their contemporary opponents, not of how the opponents performed the branding. Whether scholars have applied "isolationism" to history or denied that it applies, they have neglected the concept's formation and operation in history. Justus Doenecke, *In Danger Undaunted: The Anti-Interventionist Movement of 1940–1941 as Revealed in the Papers of the America First Committee* (Stanford, CA: Hoover Institution Press, 1990); Justus Doenecke, *Storm on the Horizon: The Challenge to American Intervention, 1939–1941* (Lanham, MD: Rowman and Littlefield, 2000); George C. Herring, *From Colony to Superpower: U.S. Foreign Relations Since 1776* (Oxford: Oxford University Press, 2008); Robert David Johnson, *The Peace Progressives and American Foreign Relations* (Cambridge, MA: Harvard University Press, 1995); and Walter McDougall, *Promised Land, Crusader State: The American Encounter with the World Since 1776* (Boston: Houghton Mifflin, 1997), ch. 2.

9. On rare occasions, prominent noninterventionists affiliated themselves with "isolation" or "isolationism," but they did so either selectively, in order to favor isolation in political-military affairs only while rejecting the label overall, or sarcastically. For example, Senator William Borah wrote in 1934 that "in all matters political, in all commitments of any nature or kind, which encroach in the slightest upon the free and unembarrassed action of our people, or which circumscribe their discretion and judgment, we have been free, we have been independent, we have been isolationists." This line came at the end of a long passage in which Borah emphasized that on the whole his foreign policy vision "is not isolation," contrary to his critics. In matters of trade, commerce, finance, humanitarian disaster, and the pursuit of peace and amity, he wrote, "we have not been isolationists, and never will be." Elsewhere Borah rejected the label outright, stating that "there is no such thing as an isolationist." William E. Borah, "American Foreign Policy in a Nationalistic World," *Foreign Affairs* 12, no. 2 (January 1934): xi; and quoted in Charles W. Toth, "Isolationism and the Emergence of Borah: An Appeal to the American Tradition," *Western Political Quarterly* 14, no. 2 (1961): 555.

Missouri representative William Elmer used the sarcastic self-descriptor in a speech in Congress in 1943. "You may call me an isolationist if you please," he said, "if that term means adhering to and practicing the principles enunciated by our founding fathers and under which we have operated a successful Government for 150 years." Self-identifying as a "nationalist" as opposed to an "internationalist or interventionist," he went on to dismiss the concept of isolationism: "As derisively defined by those who seek advantage, I declare there are no isolationists in this country, and no political party of consequence has ever declared for isolationism." 89 Cong. Rec. A3341 (June 30, 1943).

10. See Brooke Blower, "From Isolationism to Neutrality: A New Framework for Understanding American Political Culture, 1919–1941," *Diplomatic History* 38, no. 2 (April 2014): 345–76; Bear F. Braumoeller, "The Myth of American Isolationism," *Foreign Policy Analysis* 6 (2010): 349–71; Herring, *From Colony to Superpower*, 1; and William Appleman Williams, "The Legend of Isolationism in the 1920's," *Science and Society* 18, no. 1 (Winter 1954): 1–20.

11. Langer and Gleason, *The Challenge to Isolation;* Langer and Gleason, *The Undeclared War.*

12. This book endeavors to show how, why, and to what effect *isolationism* was formulated and *internationalism* changed its meaning. Whereas existing accounts of the subject apply concepts to history, this one explains the operation of concepts *in* history. In so doing, it makes a start at taking up the call of the historian Willibald Steinmetz to

perform "micro-diachronic analyses" that explain conceptual change in specific moments and places. The twentieth century, which generated countless concepts for political combat, is ripe for the sort of treatment that the theorist Reinhart Koselleck gave to the onset of modernity in Europe. Willibald Steinmetz, "Some Thoughts on a History of Twentieth-Century German Basic Concepts," *Contributions to the History of Concepts* 7, no. 2 (Winter 2012): 87–100. See Reinhart Koselleck, *Futures Past: On the Semantics of Historical Time,* trans. Keith Tribe (New York: Columbia University Press, 2004); Reinhart Koselleck, *The Practice of Conceptual History: Timing History, Spacing Concepts,* trans. Todd Samuel Presner and others (Stanford, CA: Stanford University Press, 2002); and Willibald Steinmetz, ed., *Political Languages in the Age of Extremes* (Oxford: Oxford University Press, 2011).

In examining the invention of *isolationism,* this book builds on a landmark article by the historian Brooke Blower, who dates the coinage of the term to the 1930s and replaces the *internationalism / isolationism* dualism in the interwar years with a complex set of positions on neutrality. Blower nonetheless provides what the political scientist Ole Waever calls a conceptual analysis, which seeks to employ the signifiers that most accurately represent what they signify. A conceptual history, by contrast, explains how historical actors constructed concepts and what those concepts produced. Blower, "From Isolationism to Neutrality," 345–76; and Ole Waever, "Détente between Conceptual Analysis and Conceptual History," in *Transitions: In Honour of Kjell Goldmann,* ed. Jan Hallenberg, Bertil Nygren, and Alexa Robertson (Stockholm: Department of Political Science, Stockholm University, 2003), 85–107. An analysis of isolationist name-calling in political debate since the 1990s is David Dunn, "Isolationism Revisited: Seven Persistent Myths in the Contemporary American Foreign Policy Debate," *Review of International Studies* 31, no. 2 (April 2005): 237–61.

13. The urtext of the "revisionist" school of U.S. diplomatic history, foundational partly because it leaves open whether capitalism or ideology drove U.S. expansion, is William Appleman Williams, *The Tragedy of American Diplomacy* (Cleveland: World Publishing Company, 1959). Among the many works in this vein are John Fousek, *To Lead the Free World: American Nationalism and the Cultural Roots of the Cold War* (Chapel Hill, NC: University of North Carolina Press, 2000); Lloyd C. Gardner, *A Covenant with Power: America and World Order from Wilson to Reagan* (London: Macmillan, 1984); Walter L. Hixson, *The Myth of American Diplomacy: National Identity and U.S. Foreign Policy* (New Haven, CT: Yale University Press, 2008); Walter LaFeber, *America, Russia, and the Cold War, 1945–1966* (New York: Wiley, 1967); Thomas J. McCormick, *America's Half-Century: United States Foreign Policy in the Cold War* (Baltimore: Johns Hopkins University Press, 1989); Emily S. Rosenberg, *Spreading the American Dream: American Economic and Cultural Expansion, 1890–1945* (New York: Hill and Wang, 1982); and Anders Stephanson, *Manifest Destiny: American Expansion and the Empire of Right* (New York: Hill and Wang, 1995).

14. Even some accounts that dismiss isolationism as a myth unintentionally rely on the concept of isolationism because they simply invert the story. Anything nonisolationist, which is everything, becomes a will to power. William Appleman Williams himself, in denying that U.S. foreign policy was isolationist in the 1920s, interpreted policymakers of the decade as "the most vigorous interventionists" instead. Much as Williams integrated the 1920s into a narrative of relentless American expansion, so the revisionist scholarship that followed him has often conjured a static U.S. desire to dominate the

world. The turn to global political-military supremacy becomes less a decision than the culmination of America's time-honored quest to open the world to capitalist production and exchange. Williams, "The Legend of Isolationism in the 1920's," 3.

A case in point is Patrick Hearden's account of postwar planning within the State Department, the most comprehensive and meticulous treatment of the subject. Following up his *Roosevelt Confronts Hitler: America's Entry into World War II* (DeKalb: Northern Illinois University Press, 1987), Hearden argues that the overriding objective of planners was the reconstruction of a "liberal capitalist world system" that would absorb American surpluses, preventing the need for excessive centralized planning or deficit spending. Although the book's empirical wealth often overwhelms its interpretive aims, Hearden's "architects of globalism" read as though they are implementing old blueprints rather than conceiving new ones. In the lone chapter set prior to Pearl Harbor, Hearden foregrounds the Roosevelt administration's attempts to pressure Great Britain to remove postwar barriers to trade, as though this effort was tantamount to pursuing political-military globalism. Yet at the beginning of 1940, armed globalism struck postwar planners as implausible and undesirable. Over the next two years, the postwar area that they envisioned the United States defending would dramatically shrink before it expanded. Patrick Hearden, *Architects of Globalism: Building a New World Order during World War II* (Fayetteville, AR: University of Arkansas Press, 2002), xiv and ch. 1.

The geographer Neil Smith also offers a significant account of U.S. postwar planning in the Council on Foreign Relations and the State Department. In his penetrating Marxist analysis of America's "antigeographical ideology," however, U.S. economic and territorial expansion is an unceasing, taken-for-granted backdrop rather than an object of explanation. Smith thus renders postwar planning in World War II as one point on a straight line across "moments of U.S. global ambition" from 1898 through 2001. "The period," he writes teleologically, "is the American Century, which I take to have been announced in 1898, even if it was not recognized and named until decades later." Neil Smith, *American Empire: Roosevelt's Geographer and the Prelude to Globalization* (Berkeley: University of California Press, 2003), xiii, xvii, and chs. 10–14.

15. Michael Hunt, *The American Ascendancy: How the United States Gained and Wielded Global Dominance* (Chapel Hill, NC: University of North Carolina Press, 2007), 81.

16. Moreover, since the 1990s, the field of U.S. diplomatic history has shifted to emphasize how non-American actors have related to U.S. power. Quietly this transnational and international turn, coupled with an evaporating job market, has tended to move historians away from inquiring into the domestic sources of U.S. global power, however impressively it has delivered new and overdue insights. The turn away from explaining the constitution of U.S. power was prefigured as early as 1969, from within the revisionist camp, when Thomas J. McCormick called on scholars to "get beyond historiographical squabbling over the motivations of America's economic expansion to some realistic assessment of its consequences." Thomas J. McCormick, "The State of American Diplomatic History," in *The State of American History*, ed. Herbert J. Bass (Chicago: Quadrangle, 1970), 139. For a critique of the transnational and international turn, see Daniel Bessner and Fredrik Logevall, "Recentering the United States in the Historiography of American Foreign Relations," *Texas National Security Review* 3, no. 2 (Spring 2020), https://tnsr.org/2020/04/recentering-the-united-states-in-the-historiography-of-american-foreign-relations.

The historians Mary Dudziak, Barbara Keys, and Samuel Moyn have written partial counterexamples that explore how discourses of wartime and human rights served to legitimate U.S. interventions abroad. But these works largely presuppose U.S. global power itself, neglecting to explain why American officials, intellectuals, and activists apparently assumed that U.S. military dominance should be preserved and extended. Mary Dudziak, *War Time: An Idea, Its History, Its Consequences* (New York: Oxford University Press, 2012); Barbara Keys, *Reclaiming American Virtue: The Human Rights Revolution of the 1970s* (Cambridge, MA: Harvard University Press, 2014); and Samuel Moyn, *The Last Utopia: Human Rights in History* (Cambridge, MA: Harvard University Press, 2010).

17. Robert E. Gallman, "Economic Growth and Structural Change in the Long Nineteenth Century," in *The Cambridge Economic History of the United States,* vol. 2, *The Long Nineteenth Century,* ed. Stanley L. Engerman and Robert E. Gallman (Cambridge: Cambridge University Press, 2000), 3; and Angus Maddison, "Historical Statistics of the World Economy: 1–2008 AD," Groningen Growth and Development Centre, University of Groningen, Netherlands, 2010, https://www.rug.nl/ggdc /historicaldevelopment/maddison/releases/maddison-database-2010.

18. This book builds on the work of historians Andrew Preston, Anders Stephanson, and John A. Thompson, who in articles and chapters have outlined the transformation of the U.S. concept of national security in 1940 and 1941. This book extends their research and analysis in several ways. It examines a breadth of officials and intellectuals who devoted themselves to thinking about and planning the postwar world prior to Pearl Harbor. It foregrounds ideas of internationalism as an explanatory context and a source of legitimation. It also interprets the wartime embrace of global military supremacy as breaking more sharply from the Wilsonian past than does Thompson. Andrew Preston, "Monsters Everywhere: A Genealogy of National Security," *Diplomatic History* 38, no. 3 (June 2014): 477–500; Anders Stephanson, "Liberty or Death: The Cold War as US Ideology," in *Reviewing the Cold War: Approaches, Interpretations, Theory,* ed. Odd Arne Westad (London: Frank Cass, 2000), ch. 4; Anders Stephanson, "Fourteen Notes on the Very Concept of the Cold War," in *Rethinking Geopolitics,* ed. Gearóid Ó Tuathail and Simon Dalby (London: Routledge, 1998), 62–85; John A. Thompson, "Another Look at the Downfall of 'Fortress America,'" *Journal of American Studies* 26, no. 3 (December 1992): 393–408; John A. Thompson, "Conceptions of National Security and American Entry into World War II," *Diplomacy and Statecraft* 16, no. 4 (December 2005): 671–97; and John A. Thompson, *A Sense of Power: The Roots of America's Global Role* (Ithaca, NY: Cornell University Press, 2015).

The 1940–1941 moment figures as a turning point in several wide-ranging studies, including Legro, *Rethinking the World,* ch. 3; Ninkovich, *The Global Republic,* ch. 6; Michael Sherry, *In the Shadow of War: The United States since the 1930s* (New Haven, CT: Yale University Press, 1995), chs. 1–2; and Douglas Stuart, *Creating the National Security State: A History of the Law That Transformed America* (Princeton, NJ: Princeton University Press, 2008), ch. 1.

19. This book uses *global dominance, leadership, preeminence, primacy,* and *supremacy* more or less interchangeably. *Leadership* was used most often by U.S. officials and intellectuals during World War II, but because Americans had long claimed to lead the world while avoiding armed entanglements, the other terms better capture America's novel political-military role. *Empire,* despite its popularity among critics of U.S. foreign

policy, is less useful in this context because it is typically defined by the relationship between a metropolitan center and its periphery, whereas global supremacy concerns the relationship between the United States and other states. Supremacy entails both more and less than empire. Further, when World War II began, the United States already possessed a considerable colonial empire, accumulated since its purchase of Alaska in 1867. As historian Carl Becker observed in 1944, "Since the United States has acquired Alaska, Puerto Rico, the Hawaiian Islands and the Philippines . . . it has, by every common test, the right to be recognized as an empire, as one of the great imperial powers." Nevertheless, *empire* also connotes power and leadership on a grand scale, and Chapter 3 will show that many U.S. officials and intellectuals conceived of the postwar United States as the inheritor of the world role of the Roman and British empires and planned for the United States to combine with portions of the British Empire. Carl Becker, *How New Will the Better World Be? A Discussion of Post-war Reconstruction* (New York: Alfred A. Knopf, 1944), 88. Two compelling analyses of the United States as an empire are Daniel Immerwahr, *How to Hide an Empire: A History of the Greater United States* (New York: Farrar, Straus and Giroux, 2019); and Paul A. Kramer, "Power and Connection: Imperial Histories of the United States in the World," *American Historical Review* 116, no. 5 (December 2011): 1348–91.

20. On axioms in foreign policy, see Ernest R. May, "The Nature of Foreign Policy: The Calculated and the Axiomatic," *Daedalus* 91, no. 4 (Fall 1962): 653–67.

21. On U.S. policymakers' belief prior to World War II that U.S. security did not depend on the balance of power in Europe and Asia, see Robert Osgood, *Ideals and Self-Interest in America's Foreign Relations: The Great Transformation of the Twentieth Century* (Chicago: University of Chicago Press, 1953); and John A. Thompson, "The Geopolitical Vision: The Myth of an Outmatched USA," in *Uncertain Empire: American History and the Idea of the Cold War,* ed. Joel Isaac and Duncan Bell (New York: Oxford University Press, 2012), 91–114.

22. For the classic account of the structure and formation of the "power elite," conceived as the circle of leaders of economic, political, and military institutions who make decisions insulated from popular pressure, see C. Wright Mills, *The Power Elite* (New York: Oxford University Press, 1956). Adaptations and reconsiderations of Mills include G. William Domhoff, "Mills's *The Power Elite* 50 Years Later," *Contemporary Sociology* 35, no. 6 (November 2006): 547–50; G. William Domhoff, *The Power Elite and the State: How Policy Is Made in America* (New York: A. De Gruyter, 1990); and Daniel Geary, *Radical Ambition: C. Wright Mills, the Left, and American Social Thought* (Berkeley: University of California Press, 2009). Although it reads post-1940 anti-isolationism back to the early twentieth century, a portrait of an "establishment" specific to foreign policy is Godfrey Hodgson, "The Foreign Policy Establishment," in *Ruling America: A History of Wealth and Power in a Democracy,* ed. Steve Fraser and Gary Gerstle (Cambridge, MA: Harvard University Press, 2005), 215–49.

23. James T. Sparrow, *Warfare State: World War II Americans and the Age of Big Government* (New York: Oxford University Press, 2011), esp. 5–6.

24. On the formation of the U.S. foreign policy elite before World War II, see Tomoko Akami, *Internationalizing the Pacific: The United States, Japan and the Institute of Pacific Relations in War and Peace, 1919–1945* (New York: Routledge, 2002); Daniel Bessner, *Democracy in Exile: Hans Speier and the Rise of the Defense Intellectual* (Ithaca, NY:

Cornell University Press, 2018), chs. 1–3; Benjamin Coates, *Legalist Empire: International Law, Civilization, and U.S. Foreign Relations in the Early Twentieth Century* (New York: Oxford University Press, 2016); Katherine Epstein, *Torpedo: Inventing the Military-Industrial Complex in the United States and Great Britain* (Cambridge, MA: Harvard University Press, 2014); Hodgson, "The Foreign Policy Establishment"; Alfred McCoy and Francisco Scarano, eds., *Colonial Crucible: Empire in the Making of the Modern American State* (Madison, WI: University of Wisconsin Press, 2009); Parmar, *Foundations of the American Century,* chs. 1–3; Paulo Ramos, "The Role of the Yale Institute for International Studies in the Construction of United States National Security Ideology, 1935–1951" (PhD diss., University of Manchester, 2003); Katharina Rietzler, "From Peace Advocacy to International Relations Research: The Transformation of Transatlantic Philanthropic Networks, 1900–1930," in *Shaping the Transnational Sphere: Experts, Networks and Issues from the 1840s to the 1930s,* ed. Davide Rodogno, Bernhard Struck, and Jakob Vogel (New York: Berghahn Books, 2014), ch. 8; Emily S. Rosenberg, *Financial Missionaries to the World: The Politics and Culture of Dollar Diplomacy, 1900–1930* (Durham, NC: Duke University Press, 2003); Susan Schulten, *The Geographical Imagination in America, 1880–1950* (Chicago: Chicago University Press, 2001); Hatsue Shinohara, *US International Lawyers in the Interwar Years: A Forgotten Crusade* (Cambridge: Cambridge University Press, 2012); and Robert Vitalis, *White World Order, Black Power Politics: The Birth of American International Relations* (Ithaca, NY: Cornell University Press, 2015).

25. On the CFR's postwar planning in World War II, see Luke Fletcher, "Confusion and Convergence: The Nazi Challenge to World Order and the CFR Response, 1940–1941," *International Politics* 55, no. 6 (November 2018): 888–903; Inderjeet Parmar, *Think Tanks and Power in Foreign Policy: A Comparative Study of the Role and Influence of the Council on Foreign Relations and the Royal Institute of International Affairs, 1939–1945* (New York: Palgrave Macmillan, 2004), ch. 5; Carlo Santoro, *Diffidence and Ambition: The Intellectual Sources of U.S. Foreign Policy* (Boulder, CO: Westview, 1991); Robert D. Schulzinger, *The Wise Men of Foreign Affairs: The History of the Council on Foreign Relations* (New York: Columbia University Press, 1984), ch. 3; Laurence Shoup and William Minter, *Imperial Brain Trust: The Council on Foreign Relations and United States Foreign Policy* (New York: Monthly Review Press, 1977), ch. 4; and Smith, *American Empire,* chs. 10–14. On the CFR's formation and early decades, see Peter Grose, *Continuing the Inquiry: The Council on Foreign Relations from 1921 to 1996* (New York: Council on Foreign Relations, 1996); Schulzinger, *The Wise Men of Foreign Affairs;* Whitney H. Shepardson, *Early History of the Council on Foreign Relations* (Stamford, CT: Overbrook, 1960); Shoup and Minter, *Imperial Brain Trust,* chs. 1–3; and Michael Wala, *Winning the Peace: The Council on Foreign Relations and American Foreign Policy in the Early Cold War* (Providence, RI: Berghahn Books, 1994).

26. On postwar planning in the State Department, see Hearden, *Architects of Globalism;* Aiyaz Husain, *Mapping the End of Empire: American and British Strategic Visions in the Postwar World* (Cambridge, MA: Harvard University Press, 2014); Smith, *American Empire,* chs. 10–14; Christopher O'Sullivan, *Sumner Welles, Postwar Planning, and the Quest for a New World Order, 1937–1943* (New York: Columbia University Press, 2002); and Benjamin Welles, *Sumner Welles: FDR's Global Strategist: A Biography* (New York: St. Martin's, 1997).

27. Beginning with the war mobilization in 1942, the government strengthened its capacity to set current and future objectives. The process culminated in 1947, when the administration of President Harry S. Truman established the Policy Planning Staff within the State Department and Congress passed the National Security Act. The latter integrated the armed forces into the new Department of Defense and set up the Central Intelligence Agency and the National Security Agency. See Michael J. Hogan, *A Cross of Iron: Harry S. Truman and the Origins of the National Security State* (Cambridge: Cambridge University Press, 1998), ch. 2; Wilson Miscamble, *George F. Kennan and the Making of American Foreign Policy, 1947–1950* (Princeton, NJ: Princeton University Press, 1992), ch. 1; and Stuart, *Creating the National Security State.*

28. Political Group, Memorandum of Discussions, No. P-A14, August 26, 1941, CFRWPS.

29. Claiming that the United States "chose to bind itself to multilateral institutions that would manifestly limit its historic obsession with unfettered freedom of action" is Borgwardt, *A New Deal for the World*, 10. For a critique of nostalgia for the liberal international order supposedly created around 1945, see Patrick Porter, *The False Promise of Liberal Order: Nostalgia, Delusion and the Rise of Trump* (Cambridge: Polity, 2020); and Stephen Wertheim, "Paeans to the Postwar Order Won't Save Us," *War on the Rocks*, August 6, 2018, https://warontherocks.com/2018/08/paeans-to-the-postwar -order-wont-save-us/.

30. See, among many, Jason A. Edwards and David Weiss, eds., *The Rhetoric of American Exceptionalism: Critical Essays* (Jefferson, NC: McFarland and Company, 2011); Fabian Hilfrich, *Debating American Exceptionalism: Empire and Democracy in the Wake of the Spanish-American War* (New York: Palgrave Macmillan, 2012); Michael Ignatieff, ed., *American Exceptionalism and Human Rights* (Princeton, NJ: Princeton University Press, 2005); Deborah Madsen, *American Exceptionalism* (Jackson, MS: University Press of Mississippi, 1998); Restad, *American Exceptionalism;* and Stephanson, *Manifest Destiny.*

31. G. John Ikenberry, "Power and Liberal Order: America's Postwar World Order in Transition," *International Relations of the Asia-Pacific* 5, no. 2 (August 2005): 150.

1. INTERNATIONALISM BEFORE "ISOLATIONISM," 1776–1940

1. Edwin Borchard, "The Legal Evolution of Peace," *American Law Review* 45, no. 5 (September–October 1911): 717.

2. Edwin Borchard, "The Impracticability of 'Enforcing' Peace," *Yale Law Journal* 55, no. 5 (August 1946): 969.

3. Borchard, "The Impracticability of 'Enforcing' Peace," 969.

4. Justus Doenecke, "Edwin M. Borchard, John Bassett Moore, and Opposition to American Intervention in World War II," *Journal of Libertarian Studies* 6, no. 1 (Winter 1982): 7.

5. Edwin Borchard to Philip C. Jessup, October 13, 1941, Box I:4, PJ.

6. Harold Josephson, *James T. Shotwell and the Rise of Internationalism in America* (Rutherford, NJ: Fairleigh Dickinson University Press, 1974). See also Katharina Rietzler, "The Wars as History: Writing the Economic and Social History of the First World War," *Diplomatic History* 38, no. 4 (September 2014): 826–39.

7. James Shotwell, "Peace in the International Pod: Dissimilarities among Nations," *Outlook and Independent* 154, no. 11 (March 12, 1930): 435, Box 274, JS.

8. For surveys of internationalist ideas and activities rooted in nineteenth-century Europe, see Mark Mazower, *Governing the World: The History of an Idea* (New York: Penguin, 2012); Glenda Sluga, *Internationalism in the Age of Nationalism* (Philadelphia: University of Pennsylvania Press, 2013); and Glenda Sluga and Patricia Clavin, eds., *Internationalisms: A Twentieth-Century History* (Cambridge: Cambridge University Press, 2017).

9. James Shotwell, "Peace in the International Pod," Box 274, JS, 409.

10. On exceptionalism (or manifest destiny) as a national ideology, as opposed to a falsifiable assertion of American uniqueness, see Deborah Madsen, *American Exceptionalism* (Jackson, MS: University Press of Mississippi, 1998); Daniel Rodgers, "Exceptionalism," in *Imagined Histories: American Historians Interpret the Past,* ed. Anthony Molho and Gordon S. Wood (Princeton, NJ: Princeton University Press, 1998), 21–40; and Anders Stephanson, *Manifest Destiny: American Expansion and the Empire of Right* (New York: Hill and Wang, 1995).

11. George Washington, *An Address to the People of the United States* (New Castle, DE: Samuel and John Adams, 1796), 18.

12. Alexander Hamilton, "The Utility of the Union in Respect to Commercial Relations and a Navy," Federalist Paper no. 11, 1788, in *The Federalist Papers,* ed. Lawrence Goldman (New York: Oxford University Press, 2008), 60.

13. David C. Hendrickson, *Peace Pact: The Lost World of the American Founding* (Lawrence, KS: University Press of Kansas, 2003); and David C. Hendrickson, *Union, Nation, or Empire: The American Debate over International Relations, 1789–1941* (Lawrence, KS: University Press of Kansas, 2009).

14. Washington, *An Address to the People of the United States,* 18–19. See also Felix Gilbert, *To the Farewell Address: Ideas of Early American Foreign Policy* (Princeton, NJ: Princeton University Press, 1961); and Jeffrey J. Malanson, *Addressing America: George Washington's Farewell and the Making of National Culture, Politics, and Diplomacy, 1796–1852* (Kent, OH: Kent State University Press, 2015).

15. The literature is voluminous, but see Thomas R. Hietala, *Manifest Design: American Exceptionalism and Empire,* rev. ed. (Ithaca, NY: Cornell University Press, 2003); Daniel Immerwahr, *How to Hide an Empire: A History of the Greater United States* (New York: Farrar, Straus and Giroux, 2019), chs. 1–2; Matthew Karp, *This Vast Southern Empire: Slaveholders at the Helm of American Foreign Policy* (Cambridge, MA: Harvard University Press, 2016); Patricia N. Limerick, *The Legacy of Conquest: The Unbroken Past of the American West* (New York: W. W. Norton, 1987); D. W. Meinig, *The Shaping of America: A Geographical Perspective on 500 Years of History,* 4 vols. (New Haven, CT: Yale University Press, 1986–2004); Walter Nugent, *Habits of Empire: A History of American Expansion* (New York: Alfred A. Knopf, 2008); and Robert W. Tucker and David C. Hendrickson, *Empire of Liberty: The Statecraft of Thomas Jefferson* (New York: Oxford University Press, 1990).

16. See Caitlin Fitz, *Our Sister Republics: The United States in an Age of American Revolutions* (New York: Liveright, 2016); Ernest R. May, *The Making of the Monroe Doctrine* (Cambridge, MA: Belknap Press of Harvard University Press, 1975); Gretchen

Murphy, *Hemispheric Imaginings: The Monroe Doctrine and Narratives of U.S. Empire* (Durham, NC: Duke University Press, 2005); and Jay Sexton, *The Monroe Doctrine: Empire and Nation in Nineteenth-Century America* (New York: Hill and Wang, 2011).

17. James Monroe, "Message to Congress, December 2, 1823," in John Bassett Moore, *The Monroe Doctrine: Its Origin and Meaning* (New York: Evening Post Publishing, 1895).

18. See Martin Ceadel, *The Origins of War Prevention: The British Peace Movement and International Relations, 1730–1854* (Oxford: Clarendon Press, 1996), chs. 6–7; and Merle Curti, *The American Peace Crusade, 1815–1860* (Durham, NC: Duke University Press, 1929).

19. Stephen Wertheim, "Reading the International Mind: International Public Opinion in Early Twentieth Century Anglo-American Thought," in *The Decisionist Imagination: Sovereignty, Social Science and Democracy in the 20th Century*, ed. Daniel Bessner and Nicolas Guilhot (New York: Berghahn Books, 2019), 27–36. See also Theodore Lewis Glasser and Charles Salmon, eds., *Public Opinion and the Communication of Consent* (New York: Guilford Press, 1995); Carsten Holbraad, *The Concert of Europe: A Study in German and British International Theory, 1815–1914* (London: Longman, 1970); and Mazower, *Governing the World*, chs. 1–2.

20. The phrase "people-democracy" is from "learned blacksmith" Elihu Burritt, founder of the League of Universal Brotherhood and a leader of the mid-nineteenth-century peace movement; see Elihu Burritt, *People-Diplomacy, or The Mission of Friendly International Addresses between England and France* (London: W. and F. G. Cash, 1852). See also Martin Ceadel, *Semi-detached Idealists: The British Peace Movement and International Relations, 1854–1945* (Oxford: Oxford University Press, 2000).

21. For example, Francis Lieber, *Fragments of Political Science on Nationalism and Inter-Nationalism* (New York: Scribner and Company, 1868); E. Gryzanovski, "On the International Workingmen's Association: Its Origin, Doctrines, and Ethics," *The North American Review* 114, no. 235 (April 1872): 328; and "The Means of Lessening the Chances of War," *Advocate of Peace* 5, no. 9 (September 1874): 69. Possibly the earliest mention of "internationalism" in the U.S. Congress came on June 10, 1874, when Kentucky representative Elisha Standiford dispelled accusations that the forces of "communism and internationalism" were behind efforts to incorporate a national iron-molders' union. 2 Cong. Rec. 4796 (June 9, 1874).

22. The classic analysis along these lines is F. H. Hinsley, *Power and the Pursuit of Peace: Theory and Practice in the History of Relations between States* (Cambridge: Cambridge University Press, 1963).

23. William Ladd, *An Essay on a Congress of Nations for the Adjustment of International Disputes without Resort to Arms* (Boston: Whipple and Damrell, 1840), iv. See also Mark W. Janis, *America and the Law of Nations, 1776–1939* (New York: Oxford University Press, 2010), ch. 4; and Georg Schwarzenberger, *William Ladd: An Examination of an American Proposal for an International Equity Tribunal* (London: New Commonwealth Institute, 1935).

24. On the U.S. colonial empire, see Laura Briggs, *Reproducing Empire: Race, Sex, Science, and U.S. Imperialism in Puerto Rico* (Berkeley: University of California, 2002); Christina Duffy Burnett, "Untied States: American Expansion and Territorial Deannexation," *University of Chicago Law Review* 72, no. 3 (Summer 2005): 797–879;

Julian Go, *American Empire and the Politics of Meaning: Elite Political Cultures in the Philippines and Puerto Rico during U.S. Colonialism* (Durham, NC: Duke University Press, 2008); Kristin Hoganson, *Fighting for American Manhood: How Gender Policies Provoked the Spanish-American and Philippine-American Wars* (New Haven, CT: Yale University Press, 1998); Immerwahr, *How to Hide an Empire*, chs. 4–15; Paul A. Kramer, *The Blood of Government: Race, Empire, the United States, and the Philippines* (Chapel Hill, NC: University of North Carolina Press, 2006); Paul A. Kramer, "Power and Connection: Imperial Histories of the United States in the World," *American Historical Review* 116, no. 5 (2011): 1348–91; Alfred W. McCoy, *Policing America's Empire: The United States, the Philippines, and the Rise of the Surveillance State* (Madison, WI: University of Wisconsin Press, 2009); and Mary A. Renda, *Taking Haiti: Military Occupation and the Culture of U.S. Imperialism, 1915–1940* (Chapel Hill, NC: University of North Carolina Press, 2001).

25. Frank Ninkovich, *Global Dawn: The Cultural Foundation of American Internationalism, 1865–1890* (Cambridge, MA: Harvard University Press, 2009); and Daniel T. Rodgers, *Atlantic Crossings: Social Politics in a Progressive Age* (Cambridge, MA: Harvard University Press, 1998).

26. Frank Ninkovich, "Theodore Roosevelt: Civilization as Ideology," *Diplomatic History* 10, no. 3 (July 1986): 221–45; William N. Tilchin, *Theodore Roosevelt and the British Empire: A Study in Presidential Statecraft* (New York: St. Martin's, 1997); and Stephen Wertheim, "Reluctant Liberator: Theodore Roosevelt's Philosophy of Self-Government and Preparation for Philippine Independence," *Presidential Studies Quarterly* 39, no. 3 (September 2009): 494–518.

27. On domestic opposition to U.S. colonialism, see Robert Beisner, *Twelve against Empire: The Anti-imperialists, 1898–1900* (New York: McGraw-Hill, 1968); Michael Cullinane, *Liberty and American Anti-imperialism, 1898–1909* (New York: Palgrave Macmillan, 2012); Stephen Kinzer, *The True Flag: Theodore Roosevelt, Mark Twain, and the Birth of American Empire* (New York: Henry Holt and Company, 2017); and Wertheim, "Reluctant Liberator," 508–14.

28. Emily S. Rosenberg, *Financial Missionaries to the World: The Politics and Culture of Dollar Diplomacy, 1900–1930* (Cambridge, MA: Harvard University Press, 1999).

29. *The International American Conference: Reports of Committees and Discussions Thereon*, vol. 1 (Washington, DC: Government Publishing Office, 1890), 40. On the Pan-American system, see Benjamin Coates, "The Pan-American Lobbyist: William Eleroy Curtis and U.S. Empire, 1884–99," *Diplomatic History* 38, no. 1 (January 2014): 22–48; Charles Jones, *American Civilization* (London: Institute for the Study of the Americas, 2007); Arnulf Becker Lorca, *Mestizo International Law: A Global Intellectual History, 1842–1933* (Cambridge: Cambridge University Press, 2014); Juan Pablo Scarfi, *The Hidden History of International Law in the Americas: Empire and Legal Networks* (New York: Oxford University Press, 2017); and Juan Pablo Scarfi, "In the Name of the Americas: The Pan-American Redefinition of the Monroe Doctrine and the Emerging Language of American International Law in the Western Hemisphere, 1898–1933," *Diplomatic History* 40, no. 2 (April 2016): 189–218.

30. On the professionalization of international law in Europe, see Martti Koskenniemi, *The Gentle Civilizer of Nations: The Rise and Fall of International Law, 1870–1960* (Cambridge: Cambridge University Press, 2001).

31. Benjamin Coates, *Legalist Empire: International Law, Civilization, and U.S. Foreign Relations in the Early Twentieth Century* (New York: Oxford University Press, 2016).

32. Francis Anthony Boyle, *Foundations of World Order: The Legalist Approach to International Relations, 1898–1922* (Durham, NC: Duke University Press, 1999), 25–36, 123–24; Arthur Eyffinger, *The 1899 Hague Peace Conference: "The Parliament of Man, the Federation of the World"* (The Hague: Kluwer Law International, 2000); Arthur Eyffinger, *The 1907 Hague Peace Conference: "The Conscience of the Civilized World"* (The Hague: Judicap, 2007); and Warren Kuehl, *Seeking World Order: The United States and International Organization to 1920* (Nashville, TN: Vanderbilt University Press, 1969), 30–31, 101–6, 113–14, 138–42.

33. Theodore Roosevelt, "Sound Nationalism and Sound Internationalism," August 4, 1918, in *Roosevelt in the Kansas City Star: War-Time Editorials* (Boston: Houghton Mifflin, 1921), 191.

34. In 1914, for instance, Theodore Roosevelt envisioned that by pledging to enforce the rulings of an international court, the great powers could take "the first necessary step" toward "the organization of the international force, precisely as in civil life the posse comitatus precedes the creation of an efficient constabulary." Theodore Roosevelt to Susan Dexter Dalton Cooley, December 2, 1914, in Elting E. Morison, ed., *The Letters of Theodore Roosevelt,* vol. 8, *The Days of Armageddon, 1914–1919* (Cambridge, MA: Harvard University Press, 1954), 853. See also Hidemi Suganami, *The Domestic Analogy and World Order Proposals* (Cambridge: Cambridge University Press, 1989).

35. Nicholas Murray Butler, *The International Mind: An Argument for the Judicial Settlement of International Disputes* (New York: Charles Scribner's Sons, 1912). Also see Steven W. Witt, "International Mind Alcoves: The Carnegie Endowment for International Peace, Libraries, and the Struggle for Global Public Opinion, 1917–54," *Library and Information History* 30, no. 4 (November 2014): 273–90.

36. Butler himself used "the international mind" as a synonym for "international public opinion" but clarified that the international mind operated when the world's "strong, brave, enlightened men" could "stand with patience and self-control in a post of high responsibility when a strong current of *public opinion* goes sweeping by, careless of consequences and unrestrained in its expression of feeling." He illustrates that "public opinion" was often a paternalistic concept and cannot be read literally. Even in its paternalistic guises, however, it assumed the existence of harmony among nations, if only the right people would interpret public opinion. Butler, *The International Mind,* 98–99, 102–3, emphasis added. See Wertheim, "Reading the International Mind," 27–36.

37. On the turn to international organization, see David Kennedy, "The Move to Institutions," *Cardozo Law Review* 8, no. 5 (April 1987): 841–988; Kuehl, *Seeking World Order;* and Mazower, *Governing the World,* ch. 5. The term *international anarchy* appears to have been coined in World War I by British internationalist Goldsworthy Lowes Dickinson. See Jeanne Morefield, "The Never-Satisfied Idealism of Goldsworthy Lowes Dickinson," in *British International Thinkers from Hobbes to Namier,* ed. Ian Hall and Lisa Hill (New York: Palgrave Macmillan, 2009); and Brian Schmidt, *The Political Discourse of Anarchy: A Disciplinary History of International Relations* (Albany: State University of New York Press, 1998).

38. Elihu Root to George Gibbons, December 8, 1916, Box 136, ER.

39. On the Inquiry, see Lawrence E. Gelfand, *The Inquiry: American Preparations for Peace, 1917–1919* (New Haven, CT: Yale University Press, 1963); and Nicole Phelps, *U.S.-Habsburg Relations from 1815 to the Paris Peace Conference: Sovereignty Transformed* (New York: Cambridge University Press, 2013), ch. 6.

40. Woodrow Wilson, "An Address to the Senate," January 22, 1917, in Arthur S. Link, ed., *The Papers of Woodrow Wilson*, vol. 40, *November 20, 1916–January 23, 1917* (Princeton, NJ: Princeton University Press, 1983), 536, 539.

41. Woodrow Wilson, "A Memorial Day Address," May 30, 1916, in Arthur S. Link, ed., *The Papers of Woodrow Wilson*, vol. 37, *May 9–August 7, 1916* (Princeton, NJ: Princeton University Press, 1981), 126.

42. William Howard Taft, "League to Enforce Peace," June 17, 1915, in David Burton, gen ed., *The Collected Works of William Howard Taft*, vol. 7, *Taft Papers on League of Nations*, ed. Frank X. Gerrity (Athens, OH: Ohio University Press, 2003), 3–4.

43. On the LEP's legalism versus Wilson's organicism, see Coates, *Legalist Empire*, ch. 7; David Patterson, "The United States and the Origins of the World Court," *Political Science Quarterly* 91, no. 2 (July 1976): 279–95; John A. Thompson, "Woodrow Wilson and a World Governed by Evolving Law," *Journal of Policy History* 20, no. 1 (January 2008): 113–25; and Stephen Wertheim, "The League That Wasn't: American Designs for a Legalist-Sanctionist League of Nations and the Intellectual Origins of International Organization, 1914–1920," *Diplomatic History* 35, no. 5 (November 2011): 797–836.

44. George Kennan, *American Diplomacy* (Chicago: University of Chicago Press, 1951), 95.

45. Elihu Root, Address on the Outlook for International Law, December 28, 1915, Box 221, ER.

46. Woodrow Wilson, "An Address to the Third Plenary Session of the Peace Conference," February 14, 1919, in Arthur S. Link, ed., *The Papers of Woodrow Wilson*, vol. 55, *February 8–March 16, 1919* (Princeton, NJ: Princeton University Press, 1987), 175.

47. Because it was viewed as an alternative to armed force more than a vehicle for armed force, the League of Nations commanded popularity despite the flaws of the theory of collective security elaborated in Inis Claude, *Swords into Plowshares: The Problems and Progress of International Organization* (New York: Random House, 1964), 223–38.

48. 58 Cong. Rec. 4014 (August 20, 1919).

49. William Howard Taft, "Proposals of the League to Enforce Peace," June 17, 1915, in *Taft Papers on League of Nations*, 51.

50. Quincy Wright to Raymond Leslie Buell, April 5, 1932, Box 19, QW.

51. Phillips Payson O'Brien, *British and American Naval Power: Politics and Policy, 1900–1936* (Westport, CT: Praeger, 1998), chs. 5–6; and Adam Tooze, *The Deluge: The Great War, America and the Remaking of the Global Order, 1916–1931* (New York: Viking, 2014), 12–13.

52. John A. Thompson, "The Geopolitical Vision: The Myth of an Outmatched USA," in *Uncertain Empire: American History and the Idea of the Cold War*, ed. Joel Isaac and Duncan Bell (New York: Oxford University Press, 2012), 91–114. However, leading

Republicans were more supportive than Wilson of making a postwar security guarantee specifically to France. Lloyd Ambrosius, "Wilson, the Republicans, and French Security after World War I," *Journal of American History* 59, no. 2 (September 1972): 341–52.

53. For example, John Milton Cooper writes that "the isolationists . . . preferred to call themselves 'irreconcilables,'" yet he proceeds to deem League opponents isolationists. John Milton Cooper, *Breaking the Heart of the World: Woodrow Wilson and the Fight for the League of Nations* (Cambridge: Cambridge University Press, 2001), 5.

54. In 1919 and 1920, U.S. newspapers frequently referenced "isolation" but scarcely "isolationist" or "isolationism." Neither the *–ist* nor the *–ism* appeared in the *Atlanta Constitution, Boston Globe, Chicago Tribune, New York Tribune,* or *Washington Post.* In the *New York Times,* "isolationist" appeared three times, once pertaining to women's suffrage rather than foreign policy and another in a quotation of a London editorial. "Isolationism" did not appear. All statistics according to a search of the ProQuest Historical Newspapers database conducted on May 31, 2017. "Bergerism and the Treaty," *New York Times,* December 22, 1919; Virginia Herrick Fox, "Test of Suffrage," *New York Times,* October 31, 1920; and "Predicts Party Split if Republicans Win," *New York Times,* November 1, 1920.

55. Michael Weatherson and Hal Bochin, *Hiram Johnson: Political Revivalist* (Lanham, MD: University Press of America, 1995), 88. An extended comparison of the Holy Alliance and the League of Nations is "The Doctrine or the League," *North American Review* 210, no. 765 (August 1919): 145–54. On the mandates system, see Susan Pedersen, *The Guardians: The League of Nations and the Crisis of Empire* (New York: Oxford University Press, 2015).

56. However, some political leaders, like Senator Henry Cabot Lodge, rejected internationalism as such. "We must be now and ever for Americanism and nationalism, and against internationalism," Lodge declared at the 1920 Republican convention. Henry Cabot Lodge, "Address of the Temporary Chairman," June 8, 1920, in *Official Report of the Proceedings of the Seventeenth Republican National Convention* (New York: The Tenny Press, 1920), 32.

57. 57 Cong. Rec. 4414 (February 27, 1919).

58. Kuehl, *Seeking World Order,* 329–30.

59. William Borah, *Closing Speech of Hon. William Borah on the League of Nations in the Senate of the United States,* November 19, 1919 (Washington, DC: Government Publishing Office, 1919), 8–9.

60. "The Doctrine or the League," 153.

61. Michael Hogan, *Informal Entente: The Private Structure of Cooperation in Anglo-American Economic Diplomacy, 1918–1928* (Columbia, MO: University of Missouri Press, 1977); and Melvyn Leffler, *The Elusive Quest: America's Pursuit of European Stability and French Security, 1919–1933* (Chapel Hill, NC: University of North Carolina Press, 1979).

62. Patricia Clavin, *Securing the World Economy: The Reinvention of the League of Nations, 1920–1946* (Oxford: Oxford University Press, 2013); Hatsue Shinohara, *US International Lawyers in the Interwar Years: A Forgotten Crusade* (Cambridge: Cambridge

University Press, 2012), ch. 2; and Ludovic Tournès, "La Philanthropie Américaine, La Société des Nations et la Coproduction d'un Ordre International (1919–1946)," *Relations Internationales* 151, no. 3 (2012): 25–36.

63. Erik Goldstein and John Maurer, eds., *The Washington Conference, 1921–22: Naval Rivalry, East Asian Stability and the Road to Pearl Harbor* (Portland, OR: Frank Cass, 1994); and Tooze, *The Deluge,* ch. 21.

64. Robert H. Ferrell, *Peace in Their Time: The Origins of the Kellogg-Briand Pact* (New Haven, CT: Yale University Press, 1952); Daniel Gorman, *The Emergence of International Society in the 1920s* (Cambridge: Cambridge University Press, 2012), chs. 8–9; Oona Hathaway and Scott Shapiro, *The Internationalists: How a Radical Plan to Outlaw War Remade the World* (New York: Simon & Schuster, 2017), ch. 5; Josephson, *James T. Shotwell and the Rise of Internationalism,* ch. 7; Harold Josephson, "Outlawing War: Internationalism and the Pact of Paris," *Diplomatic History* 3, no. 4 (October 1979): 377–90; and Shinohara, *US International Lawyers in the Interwar Years,* ch. 3.

65. Frank Kellogg, "Nobel Prize Acceptance and Banquet Speech," December 10, 1929, in Frederick W. Haberman, ed., *Nobel Lectures: Peace,* vol. 2, *1926–1950* (River Edge, NJ: World Scientific, 1972), 81.

66. Charles DeBenedetti, "Borah and the Kellogg-Briand Pact," *Pacific Northwest Quarterly* 63, no. 1 (January 1972): 22–29; and John Chalmers Vinson, *William E. Borah and the Outlawry of War* (Athens, GA: University of Georgia Press, 1957).

67. Robert David Johnson, *The Peace Progressives and American Foreign Relations* (Cambridge, MA: Harvard University Press, 1995).

68. In 1928 Buell created a sensation by publishing an exposé of labor practices in colonial Africa. Raymond Leslie Buell, *The Native Problem in Africa* (New York: Macmillan, 1928).

69. Raymond Leslie Buell, "The Future of American Imperialism," *Yale Review* 15 (October 1925): 29.

70. James Shotwell, "Taking Stock of Peace and War," *Scribner's Magazine* 90, no. 1 (July 1931): 5–6, Box 276, JS.

71. *Year Book, 1938* (Washington, DC: Carnegie Endowment for International Peace, 1938), 44.

72. Daniel M. Smith, "Authoritarianism and American Policy Makers in Two World Wars," *Pacific Historical Review* 43, no. 3 (August 1974): 303–23; and David Steigerwald, *Wilsonian Idealism in America* (Ithaca, NY: Cornell University Press, 1994), 58.

73. Les K. Adler and Thomas G. Paterson, "Red Fascism: The Merger of Nazi Germany and Soviet Russia in the American Image of Totalitarianism, 1930's–1950's," *American Historical Review* 75, no. 4 (April 1970): 1046–64; Benjamin Alpers, *Dictators, Democracy, and American Public Culture: Envisioning the Totalitarian Enemy, 1920s–1950s* (Chapel Hill, NC: University of North Carolina Press, 2003), ch. 5; and Thomas R. Maddux, "Red Fascism, Brown Bolshevism: The American Image of Totalitarianism in the 1930s," *Historian* 40, no. 1 (November 1977): 85–103.

74. Anne Morrow Lindbergh, *The Wave of the Future: A Confession of Faith* (New York: Harcourt Brace, 1940). See also Ira Katznelson, *Fear Itself: The New Deal and the Origins of Our Time* (New York: W.W. Norton, 2013), ch. 1.

75. Quincy Wright, ed., *Public Opinion and World-Politics* (Chicago: University of Chicago Press, 1933).

76. Edward Mead Earle, "American Military Policy and National Security," *Political Science Quarterly* 53, no. 1 (March 1938): 3. On the irreconcilability of Nazism and existing international law, see Virginia L. Gott, "The National Socialist Theory of International Law," *American Journal of International Law* 32, no. 4 (October 1938): 704–18; John Herz, "The National Socialist Doctrine of International Law and the Problems of International Organization," *Political Science Quarterly* 54, no. 4 (December 1939): 536–54; and Lawrence Preuss, "Bolshevist and National Socialist Doctrines of International Law," *American Political Science Review* 29, no. 4 (August 1935): 594–609. American observers formed less uniform assessments of the compatibility of Soviet communism and international law; Timothy A. Taracouzio emphasizes "the fundamentally different conceptions of international law held by non-Communists and Communists." See Timothy A. Taracouzio, *The Soviet Union and International Law: A Study Based on the Legislation, Treaties and Foreign Relations of the Union of Socialist Soviet Republics* (New York: Macmillan Company, 1935), 351.

77. Donald Birn, *The League of Nations Union, 1918–1945* (New York: Clarendon Press, 1981), 198.

78. George Egerton, "Collective Security as Political Myth: Liberal Internationalism and the League of Nations in Politics and History," *International History Review* 5, no. 4 (November 1983): 502–3. Among the earliest American books examining "collective security" are Raymond Leslie Buell, *American Neutrality and Collective Security* (Geneva: Geneva Research Center, 1935); and Philip C. Jessup, *The United States and the Stabilization of Peace: A Study of Collective Security* (New York: Council on Foreign Relations, 1935).

79. Arthur Sweetser to Norman H. Davis, October 21, 1935, Box 62, ND.

80. Arthur Sweetser to Norman H. Davis, October 8, 1935, Box 62, ND.

81. James Shotwell, "Peace Enforcement: Which Way to Lasting Peace?," CBS Radio, Broadcast no. 11, April 6, 1940, Box 275, JS.

82. Edwin Borchard to Hiram Johnson, September 26, 1939, Box 4, EB.

83. Secretary of State Henry Stimson viewed the Kellogg-Briand Pact, and his own Stimson Doctrine, in these terms. Shinohara, *US International Lawyers in the Interwar Years*, chs. 3–5; and Henry Stimson, "The Pact of Paris: Three Years of Development," *Foreign Affairs* 11, no. 1, special supplement (October 1932): vii–xv.

84. Arthur Sweetser to Franklin D. Roosevelt, April 9, 1938, PPF 506. In 1939 a League commission chaired by Stanley Bruce, the former prime minister of Australia, fielded a proposal to develop economic and social competencies of the League. The nonpolitical forms of international organization promoted by the Bruce Report became popular among American League advocates both as an alternative to international political organization and in its own right. See Clavin, *Securing the World Economy*, ch. 8; Martin David Dubin, "Toward the Bruce Report: The Economic and Social Program of the League of Nations in the Avenol Era," in *The League of Nations in Retrospect / La Société des Nations: Rétrospective* (Berlin: W. de Gruyter, 1983), 42–72; and David Ekbladh, "American Asylum: The United States and the

Campaign to Transplant the Technical League, 1939–1940," *Diplomatic History* 39, no. 4 (September 2015): 629–60.

85. James Shotwell, *On the Rim of the Abyss* (New York: Macmillan, 1936); and Quincy Wright to Arnold Toynbee, March 26, 1934, Addenda I, Box 26, QW.

86. The term *world order* significantly increased in usage in the 1930s. During World War I, Americans spoke mainly of "peace." Only a handful of publications featured *world order* in their titles, often in reference to the Christian church. See, for example, William Herbert Perry Faunce, *Christian Principles Essential to a New World Order* (New York: Association Press, 1919); and Robert Wells Rogers, *The Basis of a World Order* (Boston: Gorham, 1918).

87. Charles DeBenedetti, *The Peace Reform in American History* (Bloomington, IN: Indiana University Press, 1980), 122–33.

88. Robert Divine, *The Illusion of Neutrality* (Chicago: University of Chicago Press, 1962); and Manfred Jonas, *Isolationism in America, 1935–1941* (Ithaca, NY: Cornell University Press, 1966), chs. 2, 5.

89. 70 Cong. Rec. 4009 (February 22, 1929).

90. For contemporaneous explorations of "isolation" (which avoided inquiring into the very recent origins of "isolationism"), see "Seminar on Isolation, Name and Thing," *Huntington Library Quarterly* 8, no. 1 (November 1944): 7–33; and Albert Weinberg, "The Historical Meaning of the American Doctrine of Isolation," *American Political Science Review* 34, no. 3 (June 1, 1940): 539–47. On the roots of the term *isolation* in eighteen-century English diplomatic discourse, see Gilbert, *To the Farewell Address,* 19–43.

91. The term *isolationism* first appeared in 1923 in the *American Political Science Review,* the *Chicago Daily Tribune,* and *Foreign Affairs;* in 1925 in the *New York Times;* and in 1927 in the *American Journal of International Law,* according to searches of JSTOR and ProQuest databases conducted on May 31, 2017. "Independence," *Chicago Daily Tribune,* July 4, 1923; Pittman Potter, "The Nature of American Foreign Policy," *American Journal of International Law* 21, no. 1 (January 1927): 74; "Self-Contained," *New York Times,* February 1, 1925; Henry R. Spencer, "International Politics and History," *American Political Science Review* 17, no. 3 (August 1923): 398; and Alfred Zimmern, "Nationalism and Internationalism," *Foreign Affairs* 1, no. 4 (June 1923): 115. The term *isolationist* followed a similar trajectory, although its first uses in the 1920s and 1930s often slightly preceded those of *isolationism.*

92. *Isolationism* first appeared in floor speeches in the House and Senate in 79 Cong. Rec. 4778 (April 1, 1935) (statement of Rep. Treadway) and 79 Cong. Rec. 7904 (May 21, 1935) (statement of Sen. Tydings), respectively, according to a search of the HeinOnline U.S. Congressional Documents Library conducted on October 8, 2017.

93. J. Fred Rippy, review of *American Foreign Policy, Formulation and Practice: Selected Readings* by Wilson Leon Godshall, *American Historical Review* 43, no. 4 (July 1938): 884. According to a search of JSTOR conducted on October 8, 2017, the *American Historical Review* first printed *isolationism* in 1930 but in reference to Canadian policy vis-à-vis the British Commonwealth: Carl Wittke, review of *The Dominions and Diplomacy: The Canadian Contribution* by A. Gordon Dewey, *American Historical Review* 35, no. 3 (April 1930): 620.

94. Walter Lippmann, "An Estimate of American Public Opinion about Foreign Affairs," *New York Herald Tribune,* March 23, 1939, 21.

95. Edwin Borchard to John Bassett Moore, September 25, 1941, Box 10, EB.

96. 83 Cong. Rec. A1065 (March 17, 1938).

97. Robert Sherwood, "Plan for Union," *Life,* October 7, 1940, 102; and "Isolation," *Chicago Daily Tribune,* June 25, 1933.

98. Jonas, *Isolationism in America,* 48–51.

99. 81 Cong. Rec. 2257 (March 15, 1937).

100. Thomas F. Woodlock, "Hermit Economy," *Wall Street Journal,* March 18, 1932, 2; and 83 Cong. Rec. A1065 (March 17, 1938).

101. For example, in his classic statement of modernization theory, Daniel Lerner writes of "the isolated and illiterate peasants and tribesmen who compose the bulk of the world's population"; see Daniel Lerner, *The Passing of Traditional Society: Modernizing the Middle East* (Glencoe, IL: Free Press, 1958), 411. On the image of traditional peoples in U.S. discourses of development and modernization, see David Ekbladh, *The Great American Mission: Modernization and the Construction of an American World Order* (Princeton, NJ: Princeton University Press, 2010); Daniel Immerwahr, *Thinking Small: The United States and the Lure of Community Development* (Cambridge, MA: Harvard University Press, 2015); and Michael Latham, *Modernization as Ideology: American Social Science and "Nation Building" in the Kennedy Era* (Chapel Hill, NC: University of North Carolina Press, 2000), esp. ch. 1.

102. "Independence," *Chicago Daily Tribune,* July 4, 1923.

103. Edwin Borchard to Harry F. Ward, June 30, 1938, Box 1, EB.

104. Charles Beard, *A Foreign Policy for America* (New York: Alfred A. Knopf, 1940), 89, 108.

105. Jerome Frank, *Save America First: How to Make Our Democracy Work* (New York: Harper, 1939), v, 27–37.

106. 86 Cong. Rec. A3468 (May 31, 1940).

107. Vandenberg did, however, write privately that he wished for "all of the isolation which modern circumstances will permit." Arthur H. Vandenberg, Jr., ed., *The Private Papers of Senator Vandenberg* (Boston: Houghton Mifflin, 1952), 4.

108. Beard, *A Foreign Policy for America,* ch. 4.

109. David Darrah, "U.S. Interests Come First, Says Envoy Kennedy," *Chicago Daily Tribune,* March 19, 1938; and Arthur Sears Henning, "Hull Outlines Foreign Policy Based on Peace," *Chicago Daily Tribune,* March 18, 1938.

110. On returning to London from Munich, British prime minister Neville Chamberlain announced that the "method of consultation" employed in the Munich talks would be "adopted to deal with any other questions that may concern our two countries." Hamilton Fish Armstrong, "Armistice at Munich," *Foreign Affairs* 17, no. 2 (January 1939): 197–290, which provides a vivid, contemporaneous account of the Munich crisis.

111. *Fortune* polls in October and December 1939, cited in Steven Casey, *Cautious Crusade: Franklin D. Roosevelt, American Public Opinion, and the War against Nazi Germany* (New York: Oxford University Press, 2001), 28.

112. Walter Lippmann, "The American Destiny," *Life,* June 5, 1939, 73.

113. Sumner Welles, Speech at the New York Bar Association, January 27, 1939, Box 194, SW.

114. Many League of Nations advocates prior to 1941 faulted the League for failing both to provide armed sanctions and to accommodate "peaceful change." See, for example, Frederick Sherwood Dunn, *Peaceful Change: A Study of International Procedures* (New York: Council on Foreign Relations, 1937); and Pitman Potter, *Collective Security and Peaceful Change: The Relations of Order and Progress in International Society* (Chicago: University of Chicago Press, 1937).

115. Franklin D. Roosevelt to Roger B. Merriman, February 15, 1939, Merriman Family Papers, Massachusetts Historical Society, http://www.masshist.org/database/viewer.php ?item_ id=1842&pid=3. On Lothian in America, see David Reynolds, "Lord Lothian and Anglo-American Relations, 1939–1940," *Transactions of the American Philosophical Society* 73, no. 2 (1983): 1–65.

116. Priscilla Roberts, "'The Council Has Been Your Creation': Hamilton Fish Armstrong, Paradigm of the American Foreign Policy Establishment?," *Journal of American Studies* 35, no. 1 (April 2001): 67.

117. George Messersmith, Memorandum of Conversation, September 12, 1939, Box 78, HFA.

118. Carlo Maria Santoro, *Diffidence and Ambition: The Intellectual Sources of U.S. Foreign Policy* (Boulder, CO: Westview, 1991), 49.

119. Messersmith, Memorandum of Conversation, September 12, 1939, Box 78, HFA.

120. Hamilton Fish Armstrong to Harley Notter, November 15, 1948, Box 50, HFA. See also Harley Notter, *Postwar Foreign Policy Preparation, 1939–1945* (Washington, DC: U.S. Department of State, 1949), 54.

121. See, in particular, Daniel Bessner, *Democracy in Exile: Hans Speier and the Rise of the Defense Intellectual* (Ithaca, NY: Cornell University Press, 2018), chs. 1–3; Inderjeet Parmar, *Foundations of the American Century: The Ford, Carnegie, and Rockefeller Foundations in the Rise of American Power* (New York: Columbia University Press, 2012), chs. 2–3; Katharina Rietzler, "From Peace Advocacy to International Relations Research: The Transformation of Transatlantic Philanthropic Networks, 1900–1930," in *Shaping the Transnational Sphere: Experts, Networks and Issues from the 1840s to the 1930s,* ed. Davide Rodogno, Bernhard Struck, and Jakob Vogel (New York: Berghahn Books, 2014), ch. 8; and Robert Vitalis, *White World Order, Black Power Politics: The Birth of American International Relations* (Ithaca, NY: Cornell University Press, 2015).

122. A Peace Aims Group was added in 1941. On Bowman, see Neil Smith, *American Empire: Roosevelt's Geographer and the Prelude to Globalization* (Berkeley: University of California Press, 2003).

123. On Davis's interwar activities promoting disarmament, see Thomas Casey Irvin, "Norman H. Davis and the Quest for Arms Control, 1931–1938" (PhD diss., Ohio State University, 1963).

124. Parmar argues that U.S. foundations formed in the interwar period in order to promote their conviction that "the American elite was fit to lead the world." In his telling, these organizations never wavered in their attempt to counter the hegemony of "isolationism" and replace it with "globalism." Parmar, *Foundations of the American Century,* 67, 79. In a similar vein is Laurence Shoup and William Minter, *Imperial Brain Trust: The Council*

on Foreign Relations and United States Foreign Policy (New York: Monthly Review Press, 1977), chs. 1–3.

125. Tournès, "La Philanthropie Américaine."

126. For an overview, see Parmar, *Foundations of the American Century*, 83–87. On the Foreign Policy Association, see David Allen, "Every Citizen a Statesman: Building a Democracy for Foreign Policy in the American Century" (PhD diss., Columbia University, 2019) ; and Warren Kuehl and Lynne Dunn, *Keeping the Covenant: American Internationalists and the League of Nations, 1920–1939* (Kent, OH: Kent State University Press, 1997). On the Institute of Pacific Relations, see Tomoko Akami, *Internationalizing the Pacific: The United States, Japan and the Institute of Pacific Relations in War and Peace, 1919–1945* (New York: Routledge, 2002); John King Fairbank, "William L. Holland and the IPR in Historical Perspective," *Pacific Affairs* 52, no. 4 (Winter 1979–1980): 587–90; Paul F. Hooper, *Elusive Destiny: The Internationalist Movement in Modern Hawaii* (Honolulu: University of Hawai'i Press, 1980); and Priscilla Roberts, "The Institute of Pacific Relations: Pan-Pacific and Pan-Asian Visions of International Order," *International Politics* 55, no. 6 (November 2018): 836–51.

127. Nicholas Murray Butler, *Across the Busy Years: Recollections and Reflections* (New York: Charles Scribner's Sons, 1939), 105.

128. On both institutes, see Robert Vitalis, review of "Present at the Creation: Edward Mead Earle and the Depression-Era Origins of Security Studies" by David Ekbladh, *H-Diplo ISSF* 14 (June 15, 2012), http://issforum.org/articlereviews/14-present-creation-earle. On Earle's Princeton seminar, see David Ekbladh, "Present at the Creation: Edward Mead Earle and the Depression-Era Origins of Security Studies," *International Security* 36, no. 3 (Winter 2011–2012): 107–41. On the Yale Institute, see Paulo Ramos, "The Role of the Yale Institute for International Studies in the Construction of United States National Security Ideology, 1935–1951" (PhD diss., University of Manchester, 2003).

129. Anders Stephanson, *George Kennan and the Art of Foreign Policy* (Cambridge, MA: Harvard University Press, 1989), 332.

130. George T. Davis, *A Navy Second to None: The Development of Modern American Naval Policy* (New York: Harcourt, 1940), 430–32. See also A. Whitney Griswold, *The Far Eastern Policy of the United States* (New York: Harcourt, 1938); and A. Whitney Griswold, "The Influence of History upon Sea Power: A Comment on American Naval Policy," *Journal of the American Military Institute* 4, no. 1 (Spring 1940): 1–7.

131. Edward Mead Earle, "The Future of Foreign Policy," *New Republic,* November 1939, 92.

132. Political Group, "American Attitudes towards the War and the Peace, May 1940," Memorandum, No. P-B5, May 17, 1940, CFRWPS.

133. Almost nothing has been written about the State Department committee except for an article that argues that the committee prefigured postwar planning after Pearl Harbor. Yet although members contemplated some ideas that resemble subsequent proposals— an international air force, the economic integration of Europe—the committee matters precisely because it shows how differently officials conceived the world role of the United States prior to the fall of France than they did afterward. See J. Simon Rofe, "Pre-war Post-war Planning: The Phoney War, the Roosevelt Administration, and the

Case of the Advisory Committee on Problems of Foreign Relations," *Diplomacy and Statecraft* 23, no. 2 (2012): 254–79.

134. Adolf Berle, "Organization of Peace," Memorandum, January 3, 1940, Box 108, HN.

135. "The Political Subcommittee's Consideration of Three Memoranda Relating to a Possible World Order," Memorandum, n.d., Box 108, HN (summarizing Breckinridge Long, "Considerations of Political and Economic Nature," Memorandum, January 31, 1940, Box 108, HN).

136. At the outset, planner Leo Pasvolsky explicitly stated his "assumption that a victory on the part of Great Britain and France would be followed by a determined and enlightened attempt on their part to rebuild the whole of Europe along peaceful lines." Or, he added, there might not be a "decisive victory for either side." Leo Pasvolsky, "Bases of an International Economic Program in Connection with a Possible Conference of Neutrals," Preliminary Memorandum, January 29, 1940, Box 108, HN.

137. Economic and Financial Group, Memorandum of Discussions, No. E-A3, April 6, 1940, CFRWPS.

138. Adolf Berle, diary, January 29, 1940, Box 211, AB.

139. Hugh Wilson, "World Order," Memorandum, January 22, 1940, Box 108, HN.

140. Adolf Berle, diary, September 4 and 13, 1939, Box 211, AB.

141. David Reynolds, *From Munich to Pearl Harbor: Roosevelt's America and the Origins of the Second World War* (Chicago: Ivan R. Dee, 2001), 75.

142. "Suggested Agenda for Conference of Neutral States," January 18, 1940, Box 108, HN; and Hugh Wilson, "Memorandum concerning Mediation," January 20, 1940, Box 108, HN.

143. "Circular Instruction to Certain American Diplomatic Representatives," April 2, 1940, Box 108, HN; and "The Political Subcommittee's Consideration of Three Memoranda."

144. On the Welles mission, see Christopher O'Sullivan, *Sumner Welles, Postwar Planning, and the Quest for a New World Order, 1937–1943* (New York: Columbia University Press, 2002), ch. 3; and J. Simon Rofe, *Franklin Roosevelt's Foreign Policy and the Welles Mission* (New York: Palgrave Macmillan, 2007).

145. J. Fred Essary, "Welles' Mission to Europe Confined to One Question," *Baltimore Sun*, March 1, 1940; and Franklin Delano Roosevelt, quoted in Rofe, *Franklin Roosevelt's Foreign Policy*, 78, 88.

146. Notter, *Postwar Foreign Policy*, 24.

147. Adolf Berle, "Organization of Peace," Memorandum, January 3, 1940, Box 108, HN.

148. Hugh Wilson, "Conversations in Mr. Welles' Office, April 19 and 26," Memorandum, May 1, 1940, Box 108, HN; and Rofe, "Pre-war Post-war Planning," 267.

149. Armaments Group, "Possible Outcomes of the European War in Relation to the Armaments Problem," Memorandum, No. A-B1, April 5, 1940, CFRWPS, emphasis in the original.

150. Armaments Group, "A Survey of Significant Disarmament Proposals Prior to the World War," Memorandum, No. A-B2, May 1, 1940, CFRWPS. Similarly, the CFR Political Group spent the Phoney War studying the experience of the League and related bodies like the world court. Political Group, Memorandum of Discussions, No. P-A1,

February 26, 1940, CFRWPS; Political Group, "Relations with the Neutral States at the Peace Conference of Paris," Memorandum, No. P-B1, March 29, 1940, CFRWPS; Walter Langsam, Political Group, "History of the Campaign to Bring About American Entry into the World Court, as a Possible Object Lesson in Procedure," Memorandum, No. P-B3, February 22, 1940, CFRWPS.

151. On the establishment and objectives of CSOP, see Josephson, *James T. Shotwell and the Rise of Internationalism,* ch. 13; and Smith Simpson, "The Commission to Study the Organization of Peace," *American Political Science Review* 35, no. 2 (April 1941): 317–24.

152. John Foster Dulles to Quincy Wright, December 19, 1939, Addenda I, Box 13, QW. For other members, see Philip Jessup to Quincy Wright, December 13, 1939, Box 5, QW; and Arnold Wolfers to Quincy Wright, December 12, 1939, Box 5, QW.

153. James Shotwell to Quincy Wright, April 1, 1940, Box 5, QW.

154. Quincy Wright to Clyde Eagleton, October 10, 1940, Box 5, QW. On Wright's similar views in the spring, see Quincy Wright to James Shotwell, April 9, 1940, Box 5, QW; and Quincy Wright, "Proposals Respecting Political International Organization," March 25, 1940, Box 5, QW.

155. Quincy Wright, "Second Draft of Statement," June 22, 1940, Box 5, QW.

156. William Langer to Charles Webster, April 6, 1940, Section 1/9, CW.

157. Economic and Financial Group, Memorandum of Discussions, No. E-A4, May 11, 1940, CFRWPS.

158. Economic and Financial Group, Memorandum of Discussions, No. E-A2, March 9, 1940, CFRWPS.

159. Economic and Financial Group, Memorandum of Discussions, No. E-A3.

160. Hugh Wilson, "World Order," Memorandum, January 22, 1940, Box 108, HN.

161. Rofe, "Pre-war Post-war Planning," 255.

162. Hugh Wilson, Memorandum of Meeting, March 31, 1940, Box 191, SW.

163. William Langer to Charles Webster, April 6, 1940, Section 1/9, CW.

164. "Tin Cans and Peace," *Uncensored,* February 24, 1940, Box 5, QW.

165. Frank Simonds, "Shall We Join the Next War?" *Saturday Evening Post,* August 17, 1935, 72.

166. Edwin Borchard to John Herman Randall, March 22, 1940, Box 13, EB; Divine, *The Illusion of Neutrality,* 7; and "To Seek War Curb Again: Ludlow Will Reintroduce Plan Calling for Popular Vote," *New York Times,* November 29, 1936. On the Ludlow Amendment, see Arthur Scherr, "Louis Ludlow's War Referendum of 1938: A Reappraisal," *Mid-America* 76 (Spring–Summer 1994): 133–55; and Arthur Scherr, "Presidential Power, the Panay Incident, and the Defeat of the Ludlow Amendment," *International History Review* 32, no. 3 (September 2010): 455–500.

2. WORLD WAR FOR WORLD ORDER, MAY–DECEMBER 1940

1. Adolf Berle, diary, May 16, 1940, Box 211, AB.

2. Adolf Berle, diary, May 17, 1940, Box 211, AB.

3. Adolf Berle, diary, May 21, 1940, Box 211, AB.

4. David Reynolds, *From Munich to Pearl Harbor: Roosevelt's America and the Origins of the Second World War* (Chicago: Ivan R. Dee, 2001), 78; and Mark A. Stoler, *Allies and Adversaries: The Joint Chiefs of Staff, the Grand Alliance, and U.S. Strategy in World War II* (Chapel Hill, NC: University of North Carolina Press, 2000), 25.

5. Foreign Research and Press Service, "Problems of Defence," United States Memoranda and Economic Notes, No. 25, July 31, 1940, Section 10/4, CW.

6. Charles Seymour, "Aid for the Allies," address over WICC and NBC Radio, June 22, 1940, Box 36, CDA.

7. "Minutes of Meeting of the Advisory Committee on Problems of Foreign Relations," May 31, 1940, Box 108, HN.

8. See, for example, Mark Lincoln Chadwin, *The Warhawks: American Interventionists before Pearl Harbor* (New York: W. W. Norton, 1970); Robert Divine, *Second Chance: The Triumph of Internationalism in America during World War II* (New York: Atheneum, 1967); William Langer and S. Everett Gleason, *The Challenge to Isolation, 1937–1940* (New York: Harper and Row, 1952); and David Schmitz, *The Triumph of Internationalism: Franklin D. Roosevelt and a World in Crisis, 1933–1941* (Washington, DC: Potomac Books, 2007).

9. Patrick Hearden, *Architects of Globalism: Building a New World Order during World War II* (Fayetteville, AR: University of Arkansas Press, 2002); and Thomas J. McCormick, *America's Half-Century: United States Foreign Policy in the Cold War and After,* 2nd ed. (Baltimore: Johns Hopkins University Press, 1995).

10. William Allen White, Speech to the Union League Club, November 20, 1940, Box 38, CDA.

11. "Statement of Program," July 8, 1940, Box 9, CDA.

12. For present purposes, *interventionism* encompasses two distinct positions: that the United States should aid Britain in order to assure its survival and that the United States should formally enter the war. Advocates of both positions considered a Nazi-led world to be unacceptable and came to favor postwar U.S. global supremacy.

13. Quincy Wright to Frank Lorimer, October 3, 1940, Box 5, QW.

14. Committee to Defend America by Aiding the Allies, press release, August 7, 1940, Box 36, CDA.

15. Foreign Research and Press Service, "Hemisphere Defence."

16. Walter Lippmann, "The Accessary Plan of American Defense," *New York Herald Tribune,* May 14, 1940.

17. For one of the most sophisticated yet still speculative scenarios of a German attack on North America, see Eugene Staley, "The Myth of the Continents," *Foreign Affairs* 19, no. 3 (April 1941): 481–94.

18. John A. Thompson, "Conceptions of National Security and American Entry into World War II," *Diplomacy and Statecraft* 16, no. 4 (December 2005): 671–97.

19. Raymond Leslie Buell, Foreign Affairs Weekly Memorandum, May 22, 1940, Box 18, RLB.

20. See especially Franklin D. Roosevelt, "Fireside Chat 16: On the 'Arsenal of Democracy,'" December 29, 1940, University of Virginia Miller Center, https://millercenter.org/the-presidency/presidential-speeches/december-29-1940-fireside-chat-16-arsenal-democracy; and Franklin D. Roosevelt, "Fireside Chat 17: On An Unlimited National Emergency," May 27, 1941, University of Virginia Miller Center, https://millercenter.org/the-presidency/presidential-speeches/may-27-1941-fireside-chat-17-unlimited-national-emergency.

21. Thomas Jefferson, "Inaugural Address, March 4, 1801," in *The Inaugural Addresses of President Thomas Jefferson, 1801 and 1805,* ed. Noble E. Cunningham (Columbia, MO: University of Missouri Press, 2001), 5.

22. Stoler, *Allies and Adversaries,* 32.

23. Walter Lippmann, "The Economic Consequences of a German Victory," *Life,* July 22, 1940, 65–71.

24. For example, "America's Duty," *Christian Science Monitor,* July 5, 1941; Hanson Baldwin, *United We Stand! Defense of the Western Hemisphere* (New York: Whittlesey House, 1941), 120–28; and Philip La Follette, Statement to the Senate Foreign Relations Committee, in U.S. Senate, *To Promote the Defense of the United States: Hearings Before the Committee on Foreign Relations,* 77th Cong., 1st sess. (February 3, 1941), 264–65. On the diversity of noninterventionist arguments, see Justus Doenecke, *Storm on the Horizon: The Challenge to American Intervention, 1939–1941* (Lanham, MD: Rowman and Littlefield, 2000), ch. 9.

25. Examples include Stuart Chase, *The New Western Front* (New York: Harcourt, Brace, 1939); and Graeme K. Howard, *America and a New World Order* (New York: Charles Scribner's Sons, 1940).

26. "Closed World or Open World?" February 17, 1941, *Sarasota (FL) Herald-Tribune.* An important interventionist argument emphasizing the danger of the closure of European markets is Douglas Miller, *You Can't Do Business with Hitler* (Boston: Little, Brown, 1941).

27. Thomas J. Watson, "After the War—What?" *International Conciliation* 20 (September 1940): 329.

28. *Hearings before the Senate Committee on Foreign Relations,* 77th Cong., 1st Sess, 275, Part 3 (February 11, 1941), 877; and Roosevelt, "Fireside Chat 17."

29. David G. Haglund, "George C. Marshall and the Question of Military Aid to England, May–June 1940," *Journal of Contemporary History* 15, no. 4 (October 1980): 745–60; Stoler, *Allies and Adversaries,* 24–29; and Mark A. Stoler, "From Continentalism to Globalism: General Stanley D. Embick, the Joint Strategic Survey Committee, and the Military View of American National Policy during the Second World War," *Diplomatic History* 6, no. 3 (Summer 1982): 303–21.

30. Political Group, Memorandum of Discussions, No. P-A3, June 28, 1940, CFRWPS.

31. Armaments Group, Memorandum of Discussions, No. A-A3, June 28, 1940, CFRWPS; Armaments Group, Memorandum of Discussions, No. A-A4, July 25, 1940, CFRWPS; Economic and Financial Group, Memorandum of Discussions, No. E-A7, July 26, 1940, CFRWPS; Political Group, Memorandum of Discussions, No. P-A3; and Political Group, "An Examination of Western Hemisphere Affinities," Memorandum, No. P-B8, October 5, 1940, CFRWPS.

32. Economic and Financial Group, Memorandum of Discussions, No. E-A4, May 11, 1940, CFRWPS; and Economic and Financial Group, Memorandum of Discussions, No. E-A7.

33. Armaments Group, Memorandum of Discussions, No. A-A4.

34. Economic and Financial Group, Memorandum of Discussions, No. E-A7.

35. Economic and Financial Group, "A Pan-American Trade Bloc," Preliminary Memorandum, No. E-B12, June 7, 1940, CFRWPS.

36. Economic and Financial Group, Memorandum of Discussions, No. E-A7.

37. Isaiah Bowman, "Guiding Principles for the Preparation of Memoranda," May 20, 1940, Box 298, CFRP.

38. Commission to Study the Organization of Peace, "Second Draft of Statement," June 22, 1940, Box 5, QW. See also Quincy Wright, "Proposals Respecting Political International Organization," March 25, 1940, Box 5, QW.

39. Adolf Berle, diary, June 12, 1940, Box 211, AB.

40. David Ekbladh, "American Asylum: The United States and the Campaign to Transplant the Technical League, 1939–1940," *Diplomatic History* 39, no. 4 (September 2015): 629–60.

41. "Editorial in Louisville Courier-Journal," November 17, 1940, Box 55, FFF; Henry Breckinridge, Address in Berwyn, PA, October 18, 1940, Box 36, CDA; and "Sailing To Byzantium," *Washington Post,* June 16, 1940, B8.

42. Franklin D. Roosevelt, "June 10, 1940: 'Stab in the Back' Speech," University of Virginia Miller Center, https://millercenter.org/the-presidency/presidential-speeches /june-10-1940-stab-back-speech.

43. Walter Lippmann, "Our Duty to America," *New York Herald Tribune,* May 11, 1940.

44. Walter Lippmann, "America and the World," *Life,* June 3, 1940, 102–6.

45. Sumner Welles, Address at the Eighth American Scientific Congress Held in Washington, May 16, 1940, Box 194, SW.

46. Lippmann, "America and the World."

47. Raymond Leslie Buell, Foreign Affairs Weekly Memorandum, May 22, 1940.

48. Raymond Leslie Buell, Foreign Affairs Weekly Memorandum, June 26, 1940, Box 18, RLB.

49. Political Group, "An Examination of Western Hemisphere Affinities," Memorandum, No. P-B8.

50. Chadwin, *The Warhawks,* 47–48.

51. Emiliano Alessandri, "The Atlantic Community as Christendom: Some Reflections on Christian Atlanticism in America, circa 1900–1950," in *Defining the Atlantic Community: Culture, Intellectuals, and Policies in the Mid-Twentieth Century,* ed. Marco Mariano (New York: Taylor and Francis, 2010), 65; and Mark Edwards, "'God Has Chosen Us': Re-membering Christian Realism, Rescuing Christendom, and the Contest of Responsibilities during the Cold War," *Diplomatic History* 33, no. 1 (January 2009): 67–94.

52. Political Group, Memorandum of Discussions, No. P-A3. See also Political Group, "An Examination of Western Hemisphere Affinities," Memorandum, No. P-B8.

53. "Decisions by Mr. White," July 2, 1940, Box 10, CDA.

54. See, for example, John F. Kennedy, *Why England Slept* (New York: W. Funk, 1940); Raymond Leslie Buell, Foreign Affairs Weekly Memorandum, June 20, 1940, Box 18, RLB; and Charles Seymour, "Aid for the Allies," address over WICC and NBC Radio, June 22, 1940, Box 36, CDA.

55. Walter Lippmann, "The Triple Alliance and American Defense," *New York Herald Tribune,* October 1, 1940. See also Walter Lippmann, "Resistance and Appeasement," *New York Herald Tribune,* June 4, 1940.

56. Armaments Group, Memorandum of Discussions, No. A-A3.

57. Sherman A. Miles, Speech in Charlottesville, June 14, 1940, Box 18, RLB.

58. Edward Mead Earle, "Political and Military Strategy for the United States," *Proceedings of the Academy of Political Science* 19, no. 2 (January 1941): 1–9; and John A. Thompson, "Another Look at the Downfall of 'Fortress America,'" *Journal of American Studies* 26, no. 3 (December 1992): 393–408.

59. Charles Beard, *A Foreign Policy for America* (New York: Alfred A. Knopf, 1940), 13, 136.

60. Foreign Research and Press Service, "Hemisphere Defence," United States Memoranda and Economic Notes, No. 20, July 3, 1940, Section 10/4, CW.

61. On the now forgotten cartel idea, see Adolf Berle, diary, June–July 1940, Box 212, AB; and Arthur Whitaker, *The Western Hemisphere Idea: Its Rise and Decline* (Ithaca, NY: Cornell University Press, 1954), 148–49, 157.

62. Foreign Research and Press Service, "Hemisphere Defence."

63. Reynolds, *From Munich to Pearl Harbor,* 84–87.

64. Foreign Research and Press Service, "The Pact between the Axis and Japan," United States Memoranda and Economic Notes, No. 38, October 31, 1940, Section 10/4, CW.

65. See, for example, Reynolds, *From Munich to Pearl Harbor,* ch. 5.

66. On the America First Committee, see Wayne Cole, *America First: The Battle Against Intervention, 1940–1941* (Madison, WI: University of Wisconsin Press, 1953); and Justus Doenecke, *In Danger Undaunted: The Anti-Interventionist Movement of 1940–1941 as Revealed in the Papers of the America First Committee* (Stanford, CA: Hoover Institution Press, 1990).

67. Territorial Group, Memorandum of Discussions, No. T-A7, October 5, 1940, CFRWPS.

68. Economic and Financial Group, "The War and United States Foreign Policy: Needs of Future United States Foreign Policy," Preliminary Memorandum, No. E-B19, October 19, 1940, CFRWPS.

69. Economic and Financial Group, Memorandum of Discussions, No. E-A8, September 6, 1940, CFRWPS.

70. Economic and Financial Group, Memorandum of Discussions, No. E-A9, October 4, 1940, CFRWPS.

71. Territorial Group, Memorandum of Discussions, No. T-A14, June 17, 1941, CFRWPS.

72. Economic and Financial Group, "The War and United States Foreign Policy: Needs of Future United States Foreign Policy," Preliminary Memorandum, No. E-B19.

73. Economic and Financial Group, "The Future Position of Germany and the United States in World Trade," Memorandum, No. E-B18, August 1, 1940, CFRWPS.

74. Economic and Financial Group, "The Future Position of Germany and the United States in World Trade: Foreign Trade Needs of a German-Dominated Europe," Supplement I, Memorandum, No. E-B18, September 6, 1940, CFRWPS; and Economic and Financial Group, "The War and United States Foreign Policy: A Comparison of the Trade Position of a German-Dominated Europe and a Western Hemisphere–British Empire–Far East Trade Bloc," Supplement I, Memorandum, No. E-B19, October 19, 1940, CFRWPS.

75. Economic and Financial Group, "The Future Position of Germany and the United States in World Trade: Foreign Trade Needs of a German-Dominated Europe," Supplement I, Memorandum, No. E-B18.

76. Economic and Financial Group, "The Future Position of Germany and the United States in World Trade: A Western Hemisphere-Pacific Area Economic Bloc," Supplement II, Memorandum, No. E-B18, September 6, 1940, CFRWPS.

77. Economic and Financial Group, "The Future Position of Germany and the United States in World Trade," Supplement II, Memorandum, No. E-B18; and Economic and Financial Group, "The War and United States Foreign Policy: A Comparison of the Trade Position of a German-Dominated Europe and a Western Hemisphere–British Empire–Far East Trade Bloc," Supplement I, Memorandum, No. E-B19.

78. Economic and Financial Group, "The War and United States Foreign Policy: A Comparison of the Trade Position of a German-Dominated Europe and a Western Hemisphere–British Empire–Far East Trade Bloc," Supplement I, Memorandum, No. E-B19.

79. Economic and Financial Group, Memorandum of Discussions, No. E-A9.

80. Economic and Financial Group, Memorandum of Discussions, No. E-A10, October 16, 1940, CFRWPS.

81. Economic and Financial Group, "The War and United States Foreign Policy: Needs of Future United States Foreign Policy," Preliminary Memorandum, No. E-B19.

82. Arguing that the geopolitical foundations of British preeminence were destroyed from 1940 to 1942 is John Darwin, *The Empire Project: The Rise and Fall of the British World-System, 1830–1970* (Cambridge: Cambridge University Press, 2009), ch. 11.

83. Economic and Financial Group, "The War and United States Foreign Policy: Needs of Future United States Foreign Policy," Preliminary Memorandum, No. E-B19.

84. Economic and Financial Group, "The War and United States Foreign Policy: Needs of Future United States Foreign Policy," Preliminary Memorandum, No. E-B19.

85. Territorial Group, Agenda for the Seventh Meeting, October 5, 1940, Box 298, CFRP.

86. Economic and Financial Group, "The War and United States Foreign Policy: Needs of Future United States Foreign Policy," Preliminary Memorandum, No. E-B19.

87. Economic and Financial Group, "The War and United States Foreign Policy: Needs of Future United States Foreign Policy," Memorandum, No. E-B24, November 23, 1940, CFRWPS; and Economic and Financial Group, Memorandum of Discussions, No. E-A11, November 23, 1940, CFRWPS.

88. Economic and Financial Group, Memorandum of Discussions, No. E-A9.

89. Economic and Financial Group, "The War and United States Foreign Policy: Needs of Future United States Foreign Policy," Preliminary Memorandum, No. E-B19.

90. Economic and Financial Group, "The War and United States Foreign Policy: Needs of Future United States Foreign Policy," Preliminary Memorandum, No. E-B19.

91. Economic and Financial Group, Memorandum of Discussions, No. E-A10.

92. Political Group, "The Political Feasibility of the Proposals Advanced in Memorandum E-B19: Needs of Future United States Foreign Policy," Preliminary Memorandum, No. P-B13, November 10, 1940, CFRWPS.

93. Political Group, Memorandum of Discussions, No. P-A4, September 27, 1940, CFRWPS.

94. Political Group, "The Political Feasibility of the Proposals Advanced in Memorandum E-B19," Preliminary Memorandum, No. P-B13; and Political Group, "Memorandum on the Creation of Two Democratic Blocs in the Post-war Non-German World," Memorandum, No. P-B14, November 24, 1940, CFRWPS.

95. Political Group, "Memorandum on the Creation of Two Democratic Blocs in the Post-war Non-German World," Memorandum, No. P-B14.

96. Economic and Financial Group, "The War and United States Foreign Policy: Needs of Future United States Foreign Policy," Preliminary Memorandum, No. E-B19.

97. "Gallup and Fortune Polls," *Public Opinion Quarterly* 5, no. 2 (June 1941): 326. For public opinion polls throughout the period, see Hadley Cantril, *Public Opinion, 1935–1946* (Princeton, NJ: Princeton University Press, 1951); and George Gallup, *The Gallup Poll: Public Opinion, 1935–1971*, vol. 1 (Wilmington, DE: Scholarly Resources, 1972).

98. "New Deal Leads America to War, Says Gen. Wood," *Chicago Daily Tribune,* October 5, 1940.

99. Franklin D. Roosevelt, "Address on Hemisphere Defense, Dayton, Ohio," October 12, 1940, American Presidency Project, https://www.presidency.ucsb.edu/documents /address-hemisphere-defense-dayton-ohio.

100. Walter Lippmann, "Seapower: Weapon of Freedom," *Life,* October 28, 1940, 45, 111.

101. Adolf Berle, diary, August 27, 1940, Box 212, AB; and Franklin D. Roosevelt to Frank Syre (draft by Sumner Welles), December 30, 1940, Box 150, SW.

102. "Outline of Policy," CDA Executive Committee Minutes, September 9, 1940, Box 10, CDA.

103. "Prince Konoye's Statement," *Sydney Morning Herald,* October 7, 1940.

104. Sumner Welles, Address before the Foreign Affairs Council, Cleveland, September 28, 1940, Box 194, SW.

105. Walter Lippmann, "On a New Order in the World," *New York Herald Tribune,* October 10, 1940.

106. Franklin D. Roosevelt, "Address on Armistice Day, Arlington National Cemetery," November 11, 1940, American Presidency Project, https://www.presidency.ucsb.edu /documents/address-armistice-day-arlington-national-cemetery-0. See also Donald White, "History and American Internationalism: The Formulation from the Past after World War II," *Pacific Historical Review* 58, no. 2 (May 1989): 145–72.

107. Lippmann, "On a New Order in the World," 26.

108. Walter Lippmann, "Sleepwalking in Washington," *New York Herald Tribune,* October 5, 1940.

109. Lippmann, "Seapower: Weapon of Freedom," 45, 110–12; and Walter Lippmann, "The Reasoned Courage of the British," *New York Herald Tribune,* September 17, 1940. On the linkage of sea power and liberty in the British imperial imaginary, see David Armitage, *The Ideological Origins of the British Empire* (Cambridge: Cambridge University Press, 2000), esp. 100–24.

110. Louis Morton, "Germany First: The Basic Concept of Allied Strategy in World War II," in *Command Decisions,* ed. Kent Roberts Greenfield (Washington, DC: U.S. Department of the Army, 1960), 35.

111. Reynolds, *From Munich to Pearl Harbor,* 91–92; and Stoler, *Allies and Adversaries,* 29–34.

112. Harold Stark, "Memorandum for the Secretary," Op-12-CTB, Box 4, PSF; it can also be found at Franklin D. Roosevelt Presidential Library and Museum, http://docs .fdrlibrary.marist.edu/psf/box4/a48b01.html.

113. Stark, "Memorandum for the Secretary," emphasis in the original.

114. Adolf Berle, diary, September 2, 1940, Box 212, AB.

115. International Consultative Group of Geneva, "Causes of the Peace Failure, 1919–1939," *International Conciliation* 20 (October 1940): 366.

116. International Consultative Group of Geneva, "Causes of the Peace Failure," 358, 368.

117. Adolf Berle, diary, October 11, 1940, Box 212, AB.

118. Francis P. Miller, quoted in Chadwin, *The Warhawks,* 146.

119. Miller, quoted in Chadwin, *The Warhawks,* 76; and Francis P. Miller, *Man from the Valley: Memoirs of a 20th Century Virginian* (Chapel Hill, NC: University of North Carolina Press, 1971), 96.

3. THE AMERICO-BRITISH NEW ORDER OF 1941

1. Henry R. Luce, "The American Century," *Life,* February 17, 1941, 63.

2. Pertinent uses of "philosophy of life" include Moritz Bonn, "The New World Order," *Annals of the American Academy of Political and Social Science* 216 (July 1941): 165; Vera Micheles Dean, "Can Democracy Win the Peace?" *Survey Graphic,* June 1941, 342; Hans Kohn, "The Totalitarian Philosophy of War," in "Symposium on the Totalitarian State," special issue, *Proceedings of the American Philosophical Society* 82, no. 1

(February 23, 1940): 63; and Walter Lippmann, "Education vs. Western Civilization," *American Scholar* 10, no. 2 (Spring 1941): 190.

3. Michael G. Carew, *The Power to Persuade: FDR, the Newsmagazines, and Going to War, 1939–1941* (Lanham, MD: University Press of America, 2005), 53.

4. Mark Lincoln Chadwin, *The Warhawks: American Interventionists before Pearl Harbor* (New York: W. W. Norton, 1970), 41.

5. Henry R. Luce, quoted in Alan Brinkley, *The Publisher: Henry Luce and His American Century* (New York: Alfred A. Knopf, 2010), 264.

6. Responses to Luce fill boxes 107 and 108, HRL. See also Stephen J. Whitfield, "The American Century of Henry R. Luce," *Revue LISA/LISA E-Journal*, January 1, 2004, https://journals.openedition.org/lisa/917?lang=en.

7. Robert E. Herzstein, *Henry R. Luce: A Political Portrait of the Man Who Created the American Century* (New York: Charles Scribner's Sons, 1994), 179.

8. Luce, "The American Century," 63–64.

9. For both the poll numbers and how they were presented in real time, see the recurring feature "Gallup and Fortune Polls," *Public Opinion Quarterly* 5, nos. 1–4 (1941).

10. Luce, "The American Century," 63.

11. Luce, "The American Century," 63–64, emphasis in the original.

12. Political Group, Memorandum of Discussions, No. P-A6, March 7, 1941, CFRWPS.

13. Political Group, Memorandum of Discussions, No. P-A6.

14. Eliot has yet to attract a biographer, but see the amusing two-part profile of the "acknowledged grand old man of the military-expert industry" in John Bainbridge, "Profiles: Business behind the Lines: Major George Fielding Eliot," *New Yorker*, September 5, 1942, 20–28, and September 12, 1942, 22–29.

15. Political Group, Memorandum of Discussions, No. P-A6.

16. Political Group, Memorandum of Discussions, No. P-A5, February 19, 1941, CFRWPS.

17. In most historical accounts, "the policies of the Four Freedoms, the Atlantic Charter and the UN," as Dan Plesch phrases it, are reduced to a teleological progression and a single package. Plesch, for instance, argues that the postwar United Nations Organization grew out of the Allies' wartime U.N. Declaration, which in turn "built on Roosevelt's 'Four Freedoms' speech of January 1941 and the Atlantic Charter he and Churchill had issued that August." Likewise, Elizabeth Borgwardt links the Atlantic Charter to the principle of "multilateral institutions," claiming that the charter "prefigured the rule-of-law orientation of the Nuremberg Charter, the collective security articulated in the United Nations Charter, and even the free-trade ideology of the Bretton Woods charters that established the World Bank and the International Monetary Fund." David Reynolds sums up the consensus view: "The Four Freedoms, the Atlantic Charter, and the UN Declaration became benchmarks for a new international order." Dan Plesch, *America, Hitler and the UN: How the Allies Won World War II and Forged a Peace* (London: I. B. Tauris, 2011), 2, 9; Elizabeth Borgwardt, *A New Deal for the World: America's Vision for Human Rights* (Cambridge, MA:

Harvard University Press, 2005), 5; and David Reynolds, *From World War to Cold War: Churchill, Roosevelt, and the International History of the 1940s* (Oxford: Oxford University Press, 2016), 328.

18. In a major work in political science, G. John Ikenberry argues that the United States crafted a highly institutionalized postwar order in which it accepted restraints on the exercise of its power in order to cement and prolong its superior position. His argument rests in part on his assumption that the United States was by nature a "reluctant superpower": because it did not seek to dominate others, it readily assented to institutional constraints. By contrast, this book reveals that American officials and planners valued the projection of overwhelming armed power above the creation of a universal political organization. As a result, they initially ruled out the latter altogether. And as Chapter 4 chronicles, they changed course only by stripping what became the U.N. Charter of the most binding collective security provisions of the League of Nations Covenant. G. John Ikenberry, *After Victory: Institutions, Strategic Restraint, and the Rebuilding of Order after Major Wars* (Princeton, NJ: Princeton University Press, 2001), 201–12.

19. Harold Vinacke, "What Shall America Defend?," *Yale Review* 30, no. 3 (March 1941): 499, 506, 510.

20. Vinacke, "What Shall America Defend?," 506, 518.

21. For other public expressions of globalism by figures of Vinacke's stature, see Percy Bidwell and Arthur Upgren, "A Trade Policy for National Defense," *Foreign Affairs* 19, no. 2 (January 1941): 282–96; Francis P. Miller, "The Atlantic Area," *Foreign Affairs* 19, no. 4 (July 1941): 727–28; and Edgar Ansel Mowrer, *The World or the Western Hemisphere* (Charlottesville, VA: Institute of Pubic Affairs, 1941).

22. Harley Notter, *Postwar Foreign Policy Preparation, 1939–1945* (Washington, DC: U.S. Department of State, 1949), 41–42.

23. Isaiah Bowman to Louise Wright, March 5, 1942, Box 21, WWF.

24. Examples from 1941 and 1942 include *Bibliography on Postwar Planning* (Washington, DC: Construction and Civic Development Department, Chamber of Commerce of the United States of America, 1942); Fawn M. Brodie, *Peace Aims and Post-war Reconstruction: An Annotated Bibliography (Preliminary)* (Princeton, NJ: American Committee for International Studies, 1941); George B. Galloway, *A Survey of Institutional Research on American Postwar Problems* (New York: Twentieth Century Fund, 1941); *Guides for Post-war Planning* (Washington, DC: National Planning Association, 1941); Letha F. McCance, *Post-war Planning: A Bibliography* (Washington, DC: National Resources Planning Board, 1942); and *Research and Postwar Planning: Bibliography,* vol. 1 (New York: Section for Information on Studies in Postwar Reconstruction, Inter-Allied Information Center, 1942).

25. See, for example, Alan Brinkley, "The Concept of an American Century," in *The American Century in Europe,* ed. Laurence Moore and Maurizio Vaudagna (Ithaca, NY: Cornell University Press, 2002), 7–21; Herzstein, *Henry R. Luce;* and David Reynolds, *From Munich to Pearl Harbor: Roosevelt's America and the Origins of the Second World War* (Chicago: Ivan R. Dee, 2001).

26. Reynolds, *From Munich to Pearl Harbor,* ch. 5.

27. Franklin D. Roosevelt, "State of the Union Address," January 6, 1942, American Presidency Project, https://www.presidency.ucsb.edu/documents/state-the-union -address-1.

28. Edwin Borchard to John Bassett Moore, January 13, 1941, Box 10, EB.

29. Anders Stephanson, "Cold War Degree Zero," in *Uncertain Empire: American History and the Idea of the Cold War,* ed. Duncan Bell and Joel Isaac (New York: Oxford University Press, 2012), 46. See Franklin D. Roosevelt, "Fireside Chat," December 24, 1943, American Presidency Project, https://www.presidency.ucsb.edu/documents /fireside-chat.

30. Raymond Leslie Buell, Foreign Affairs Weekly Memorandum, May 29, 1941, Box 19, RLB.

31. Quincy Wright, "The Transfer of Destroyers to Great Britain," *American Journal of International Law* 34, no. 4 (October 1940): 680–89; and Wright, "The Lend-Lease Bill and International Law," *American Journal of International Law* 35, no. 2 (April 1941): 305–14.

32. Edwin Borchard to John Bassett Moore, January 3, 1941, Box 10, EB.

33. Walter Lippmann, "Hitler's New American Policy," *New York Herald Tribune,* June 17, 1941.

34. Michael S. Sherry, *In the Shadow of War: The United States since the 1930s* (New Haven, CT: Yale University Press, 1995), 47.

35. Henry Wallace, "Democracy's Road Ahead in the World Crisis" (radio address before the National Farm Institute, Des Moines, IA, February 22, 1941), in *Proceedings of the National Farm Institute* (Des Moines, IA: National Farm Institute, 1941), 125.

36. Henry Wallace, "Our Second Chance," April 8, 1941, in *Prefaces to Peace* (New York: Simon and Schuster / Doubleday / Doran / Reynal and Hitchcock / Columbia University Press, 1943), 364.

37. Max Lerner, "American Leadership in a Harsh Age," *Annals of the American Academy of Political and Social Science* 216 (July 1941): 117.

38. Otto Tod Mallery, "Economic Union and Enduring Peace," *Annals of the American Academy of Political and Social Science* 216 (July 1941): 125.

39. "The U.S. and Foreign Trade," *Fortune Round Table* 6 (April 1940), Box 21, RLB (original Round Table held January 12–14, 1940).

40. "Peace Aims," *Fortune Round Table* 8 (April 1941), Box 21, RLB (original Round Table held February 14–16, 1940).

41. "The Launching of the International Recreation Association," *Recreation* 50, no. 1 (January 1957): 11–14.

42. Wallace, "Democracy's Road Ahead in the World Crisis," 125.

43. Dean, "Can Democracy Win the Peace?" See also Vera Micheles Dean, "Toward a New World Order," *Foreign Policy Report,* May 15, 1941, 50–68.

44. Raymond Leslie Buell to Time Inc. Post-War Committee, "Americo-British Power in the Post-war World," January 13, 1942, Box 25, RLB.

45. Vera Micheles Dean, *The Struggle for World Order* (New York: Foreign Policy Association, 1941).

46. Robert A. Taft, "Aid to Britain—Short of War" (statement on Lend-Lease agreement, Washington, DC, February 26, 1941), in Clarence E. Wunderlin, ed., *The Papers of Robert A. Taft*, vol. 2, *1939–1942* (Kent, OH: Kent State University Press, 2001), 230.

47. *To Promote the Defense of the United States: Hearings before the Senate Committee on Foreign Relations*, 77th Cong., 1st Sess. (February 4, 1941), (statement of Charles Beard), 311.

48. Wayne Cole, *Roosevelt and the Isolationists, 1932–45* (Lincoln, NE: University of Nebraska Press, 1983), 417–20.

49. Justus Doenecke, *Storm on the Horizon: The Challenge to American Intervention, 1939–1941* (Lanham, MD: Rowman and Littlefield, 2000), chs. 6–8; and John A. Thompson, "Conceptions of National Security and American Entry into World War II," *Diplomacy and Statecraft* 16, no. 4 (December 2005): 671–97.

50. Walter Lippmann, "The American Role," *New York Herald Tribune*, January 12, 1941.

51. Woodrow Wilson, "Address on Memorial Day, Arlington, VA," May 30, 1916, in Arthur S. Link, ed., *The Papers of Woodrow Wilson*, vol. 37, *May 9–August 7, 1916* (Princeton, NJ: Princeton University Press, 1981), 126.

52. Luce, "The American Century," 63.

53. Fight for Freedom Committee, press release, April 20, 1941, Box 56, FFF.

54. Fight for Freedom Committee, "Listen!," press release, May 12, 1941, Box 56, FFF.

55. Theodore P. Wright to Francis P. Miller, September 13, 1941, Box 74, HFA.

56. Martha Dalrymple to Raymond Leslie Buell, n.d. [between May and December 1940], Box 17, RLB.

57. Commission to Study the Organization of Peace, Memorandum on Plans for Commission, January 11, 1941, Box 5, QW.

58. Commission to Study the Organization of Peace, "Outline of Program," June 7, 1941, Box 5, QW. CSOP used almost the same wording as did the CFR planners in their recommendation for the State Department; see Political Group, "Basic American Interests," Memorandum, No. P-B23, July 10, 1941, CFRWPS.

59. Roger S. Greene to Clyde Eagleton, October 23, 1941, Box 5, QW.

60. Political Group, Memorandum of Discussions, No. P-A10, May 22, 1941, CFRWPS.

61. For example, expressing confidence that Americans were learning to face up to international responsibilities, Washington congressman John Coffee surveyed American history and concluded that "the isolationism so characteristic of America for its first century and a quarter is not a predominant factor in our national concept today." 87 Cong. Rec. A164 (January 16, 1941).

62. 87 Cong. Rec. A3310 (July 9, 1941) (statement of Rear Adm. Adolphus).

63. Walter Lippmann, "The Atlantic and America," *Life*, April 7, 1941, 91.

64. "Turning Point," *Time*, May 20, 1940, 19.

65. 87 Cong. Rec. 8630 (November 7, 1941).

66. Wallace, "Our Second Chance," 363.

67. Cong. Rec. A895 (February 28, 1941). "Isolationism" was often analyzed in psycho-logical terms, nowhere more directly than in "The Psychology of Isolationism" by the neurologist Foster Kennedy. Kennedy relayed the case of an elderly lady who "showed me a picture of herself shaking hands with [noninterventionist] Senator [Burton] Wheeler; and, with no insight at all, went on to explain how all her life she'd been so afraid of things." Foster Kennedy, "The Psychology of Isolationism," *Virginia Medical Monthly* 69 (April 1942): 179.

68. Adolf Berle, diary, July 31, 1941, Box 213, AB.

69. See James Belich, *Replenishing the Earth: The Settler Revolution and the Rise of the Anglo-World, 1783–1939* (Oxford: Oxford University Press, 2009); Duncan Bell, *The Idea of Greater Britain: Empire and the Future of World Order, 1860–1900* (Princeton, NJ: Princeton University Press, 2007); and Duncan Bell, *Reordering the World: Essays on Liberalism and Empire* (Princeton, NJ: Princeton University Press, 2016).

70. For the exception of Andrew Carnegie, see Duncan Bell, "Before the Democratic Peace: Racial Utopianism, Empire and the Abolition of War," *European Journal of International Relations* 20, no. 3 (September 2014): 647–70.

71. Whitney Shepardson, "America and the War," Address to Chatham House, July 15, 1941, Box 3, WS.

72. Clarence Streit, *Union Now with Britain* (New York: Harper, 1941). On Streit and his reception in America, see Or Rosenboim, *The Emergence of Globalism: Visions of World Order in Britain and the United States, 1939–1950* (Princeton, NJ: Princeton University Press, 2017), 114–21; and Wesley T. Wooley, *Alternatives to Anarchy: American Supranationalism since World War II* (Bloomington, IN: Indiana University Press, 1988), 89–100.

73. Meeting Minutes, Committee on Reconstruction, Chatham House, July 7, 1941, Box 3, WS.

74. See Shepardson's *Round Table* writings in Box 9, WS. On the Round Table movement and its leader, Lionel Curtis, see Andrea Bosco and Alex May, eds., *The Round Table: The Empire/Commonwealth and British Foreign Policy* (London: Lothian Foundation Press, 1997); John Kendle, *The Round Table Movement and Imperial Union* (Toronto: Toronto University Press, 1975); Deborah Lavin, *From Empire to International Commonwealth: A Biography of Lionel Curtis* (Oxford: Clarendon Press, 1995); Alex May, "The Round Table, 1910–66" (DPhil diss., University of Oxford, 1995); and Walter Nimocks, *Milner's Young Men: The "Kindergarten" in Edwardian Imperial Affairs* (Durham, NC: Duke University Press, 1968).

75. David Bruce, *OSS against the Reich: World War Two Diaries* (Kent, OH: Kent State University Press, 1992), 22.

76. Minutes of Meeting, Steering Committee, War and Peace Studies Project, January 25, 1941, Box 74, HFA.

77. Territorial Group, Memorandum of Discussions, No. T-A8, November 2, 1940, CFRWPS.

78. Political Group, Memorandum of Discussions, No. P-A13, August 11, 1941, CFRWPS.

79. Michael Todd Bennett, "Anglophilia on Film: Creating an Atmosphere for Alliance, 1935–1941," in *The American Experience in World War II,* ed. Walter Hixon (New York: Routledge, 2003), 22–40; and Nicholas Cull, *Selling War: The British Propaganda against American "Neutrality" in World War II* (New York: Oxford University Press, 1995).

80. Minutes of the Meeting of the American Committee for International Studies, Social Science Research Council, New York City, February 21, 1941, Box 1, EME.

81. *Document: Conference on North Atlantic Relations* (Princeton, NJ: American Committee for International Studies, 1941).

82. Economic and Financial Group, Memorandum of Discussions, No. E-A13, February 15, 1941, CFRWPS.

83. Political Group, "Memorandum on the Creation of Two Democratic Blocs in the Post-war Non-German World," Memorandum, No. P-B14, November 24, 1940, CFRWPS.

84. Political Group, Memorandum of Discussions, No. P-A5.

85. See Daniel Immerwahr, *How to Hide an Empire: A History of the Greater United States* (New York: Farrar, Straus and Giroux, 2019), chs. 10–12.

86. See Robert D. Schulzinger, *The Wise Men of Foreign Affairs: The History of the Council on Foreign Relations* (New York: Columbia University Press, 1984), 78–79. For the quite different views of Owen Lattimore, a CFR planner, see Or Rosenboim, "Geopolitics and Global Democracy in Owen Lattimore's Political Thought," *International History Review* 36, no. 4 (2014): 745–76.

87. See Les K. Adler and Thomas G. Paterson, "Red Fascism: The Merger of Nazi Germany and Soviet Russia in the American Image of Totalitarianism, 1930's–1950's," *American Historical Review* 75, no. 4 (April 1970): 1046–64; and Stephanson, "Cold War Degree Zero."

88. The Free World Association was located in the same building as the Woodrow Wilson Foundation in New York, and not by coincidence: the group was established in June 1941 by Clark Eichelberger and other interwar advocates of the League of Nations turned interventionists in World War II. Andrew Johnstone, *Dilemmas of Internationalism: The American Association for the United Nations and U.S. Foreign Policy, 1941–1948* (Burlington, VT: Ashgate, 2009), 25.

89. "Editorial," *Free World* 1, no. 2 (October 1941): 7–8.

90. Franklin D. Roosevelt to Frank Syre (draft by Sumner Welles), December 30, 1940, Box 150, SW; the passage is repeated in Franklin D. Roosevelt to Joseph Grew, January 21, 1941, in *FRUS: Diplomatic Papers, 1940,* vol. 4, *The Far East,* 7.

91. John Darwin, *The Empire Project: The Rise and Fall of the British World-System, 1830–1970* (Cambridge: Cambridge University Press, 2009), 1–6.

92. Political Group, Memorandum of Discussions, No. P-A5.

93. Francis P. Miller, Political Group, "Note on a Program of Joint Action for the American and British Governments," Memorandum, No. P-B18, May 2, 1941, CFRWPS; and Political Group, Memorandum of Discussions, No. P-A7, March 25, 1941, CFRWPS.

94. Raymond Leslie Buell to Time Inc. Post-War Committee, "Americo-British Power in the Post-war World," January 13, 1942, Box 25, RLB.

95. Quoted in R. M. Douglas, *The Labour Party, Nationalism and Internationalism, 1939–1951* (London: Routledge, 2004), 107.

96. "Union Now with America?" *The Economist,* May 17, 1941, 650.

97. Patrick Hearden, *Architects of Globalism: Building a New World Order during World War II* (Fayetteville, AR: University of Arkansas Press, 2002), ch. 2; and Warren Kimball, "Lend-Lease and the Open Door: The Temptation of British Opulence, 1937–1942," *Political Science Quarterly* 86, no. 2 (June 1971): 232–59.

98. Warren Kimball, *The Juggler: Franklin Roosevelt as Wartime Statesman* (Princeton, NJ: Princeton University Press, 1991), ch. 7; and William Roger Louis, *Imperialism at Bay: The United States and the Decolonization of the British Empire, 1941–1945* (New York: Oxford University Press, 1978).

99. Political Group, Memorandum of Discussions, No. P-A5.

100. Political Group, Memorandum of Discussions, No. P-A6.

101. Political Group, "The Political Considerations of American-British Partnership," Memorandum, No. P-B20, June 4, 1941, CFRWPS.

102. Hamilton Fish Armstrong to Grayson Kirk, June 19, 1941, Box 72, HFA.

103. Political Group, Memorandum of Discussions, No. P-A8, April 10, 1941, CFRWPS.

104. Political Group, Memorandum of Discussions, No. P-A10; Political Group, "Basic American Interests," Memorandum, No. P-B23.

105. Political Group, Memorandum of Discussions, No. P-A5.

106. Economic and Financial Group, "The War and United States Foreign Policy: Needs of Future United States Foreign Policy," Preliminary Memorandum, No. E-B19, October 19, 1940, CFRWPS.

107. Armaments Group, Memorandum of Discussions, No. A-A11, June 4, 1941, CFRWPS.

108. Territorial Group, Memorandum of Discussions, No. T-A13, May 15, 1941, CFRWPS.

109. Armaments Group, Memorandum of Discussions, No. A-A4, July 25, 1940, CFRWPS.

110. Political Group, Memorandum of Discussions, No. P-A5.

111. Robert David Johnson, *The Peace Progressives and American Foreign Relations* (Cambridge, MA: Harvard University Press, 1995), chs. 6–8.

112. George Fielding Eliot, Political Group, "The Island of Great Britain as a Factor in the Strategy of American Defense," Memorandum, No. P-B19, May 16, 1941, CFRWPS.

113. Economic and Financial Group, Memorandum of Discussions, No. E-A13. See also Ernst Haas, "The Balance of Power: Prescription, Concept or Propaganda?' *World Politics* 5, no. 4 (July 1953): 444.

114. Armaments Group, Memorandum of Discussions, No. A-A14, September 10, 1941, CFRWPS.

115. See Andrew J. Bacevich, *Diplomat in Khaki: Major General Frank Ross McCoy and American Foreign Policy, 1898–1949* (Lawrence, KS: University Press of Kansas, 1989).

116. Armaments Group, Memorandum of Discussions, No. A-A14; and Armaments Group, Memorandum of Discussions, No. A-A15, October 1, 1941, CFRWPS. On British imperial policing, see Priya Satia, *Spies in Arabia: The Great War and the Cultural Foundations of Britain's Covert Empire in the Middle East* (Oxford: Oxford University Press, 2008); and Priya Satia, "The Defense of Inhumanity: Air Control and the British Idea of Arabia," *American Historical Review* 111, no. 1 (2006): 16–51.

117. Armaments Group, Memorandum of Discussions, No. A-A15.

118. Political Group, Memorandum of Discussions, No. P-A9, May 1, 1941, CFRWPS.

119. Hamilton Fish Armstrong to Grayson Kirk, June 19, 1941, Box 72, HFA.

120. John Lewis Gaddis, *Strategies of Containment: A Critical Appraisal of American National Security Policy during the Cold War,* 2nd ed. (New York: Oxford University Press, 2005); and Robert S. Litwak, *Rogue States and U.S. Foreign Policy: Containment after the Cold War* (Baltimore: Woodrow Wilson Center, 2000).

121. Political Group, Memorandum of Discussions, No. P-A5.

122. Armaments Group, Memorandum of Discussions, No. A-A11.

123. Miller, Political Group, "Note on a Program of Joint Action for the American and British Governments," Memorandum, No. P-B18; Armaments Group, Memorandum of Discussions, No. A-A11; and Armaments Group, Memorandum of Discussions, No. A-A14.

124. Armaments Group, Memorandum of Discussions, No. A-A11.

125. Report of the Twenty-Third Special Meeting, Research Sub-Committee on International Organisation, British Foreign Research and Press Service, Balliol College, Oxford, June 20, 1941, Box 3, WS.

126. Territorial Group, Memorandum of Discussions, No. T-A13.

127. Roosevelt, "State of the Union Address."

128. Miller, Political Group, "Note on a Program of Joint Action for the American and British Governments," Memorandum, No. P-B18; Political Group, "The Political Considerations of American-British Partnership," Memorandum, No. P-B20; Political Group, "Basic American Interests," Memorandum, No. P-B23; and Political Group, "Institutional Arrangements for Postwar American-British Cooperation," Memorandum, No. P-B28, September 17, 1941, CFRWPS.

129. Political Group, "The Political Considerations of American-British Partnership," Memorandum, No. P-B20.

130. See Patricia Clavin, *Securing the World Economy: The Reinvention of the League of Nations, 1920–1946* (Oxford: Oxford University Press, 2013), esp. 262–304; and David Ekbladh, "American Asylum: The United States and the Campaign to Transplant the Technical League, 1939–1940," *Diplomatic History* 39, no. 4 (September 2015): 629–60.

131. Duncan Bell, "Beyond the Sovereign State: Isopolitan Citizenship, Race and Anglo-American Union," *Political Studies* 62, no. 2 (June 2014): 423.

132. Political Group, Memorandum of Discussions, No. P-A11, June 9, 1941, CFRWPS.

133. Political Group, "The Political Considerations of American-British Partnership," Memorandum, No. P-B20.

134. Political Group, "Institutional Arrangements for Postwar American-British Coopera-
    tion," Memorandum, No. P-B28.

135. See Ananda Burra, "Petitioning the Mandates: Anticolonial and Antiracist Publics in
    International Law" (PhD diss., University of Michigan, 2017); Mark Mazower,
    "Minorities and the League of Nations in Interwar Europe," *Daedalus* 126, no. 2
    (Spring 1997): 47–63; Susan Pedersen, *The Guardians: The League of Nations and the
    Crisis of Empire* (New York: Oxford University Press, 2015); and Natasha Wheatley,
    "Mandatory Interpretation: Legal Hermeneutics and the New International Order in
    Arab and Jewish Petitions to the League of Nations," *Past and Present* 227, no. 1
    (May 2015): 205–48.

136. Political Group, "Basic American Interests," Memorandum, No. P-B23. For an
    overview of the functional League of Nations bodies, see Martin David Dubin,
    "Transgovernmental Processes and the League of Nations," *International Organization*
    24, no. 2 (Spring 1970): 288–318; and Patricia Clavin and Jens-Wilhelm Wessel,
    "Transnationalism and the League of Nations: Understanding the Work of Its
    Economic and Financial Organisation," *Contemporary European History* 14, no. 4
    (November 2005): 465–92.

137. Political Group, "Basic American Interests," Memorandum, No. P-B23.

138. C. P. Stacey, "The Canadian-American Permanent Joint Board on Defence, 1940–
    1945," *International Journal* 9, no. 2 (Spring 1954): 107–24.

139. Edgar P. Dean, Political Group, "Canadian War Problems and the Role of the United
    States," Memorandum, No. P-B17, April 14, 1941, CFRWPS.

140. Political Group, "An Examination of Western Hemisphere Affinities," Memorandum,
    No. P-B8, October 5, 1940, CFRWPS.

141. Miller, Political Group, "Note on a Program of Joint Action for the American and
    British Governments," Memorandum, No. P-B18.

142. Miller, Political Group, "Note on a Program of Joint Action for the American and
    British Governments," Memorandum, No. P-B18; and Political Group, Memorandum
    of Discussions, No. P-A11.

143. Miller, Political Group, "Note on a Program of Joint Action for the American and
    British Governments," Memorandum, No. P-B18.

144. Political Group, Memorandum of Discussions, No. P-A8.

145. Political Group, "Institutional Arrangements for Postwar American-British Coopera-
    tion," Memorandum, No. P-B28.

146. Raymond Leslie Buell to Time Inc. Post-War Committee, "Proposed First Project,"
    December 23, 1941, Box 25, RLB.

147. Walter Lippmann, "The British-American Connection," *New York Herald Tribune*,
    February 4, 1941; Walter Lippmann, "The Atlantic and America," *Life*, April 7, 1941,
    85–92. For invocations of the Monroe Doctrine against Britain, see Jay Sexton, *The
    Monroe Doctrine: Empire and Nation in Nineteenth-Century America* (New York: Hill
    and Wang, 2011), 11, 63, 90–98, 112, 133–40, 193, 202–5.

148. Walter Lippmann, "The Reasoned Courage of the British," *New York Herald Tribune*,
    September 17, 1940.

149. Raymond Leslie Buell, "Relations with Britain," supplement to *Fortune,* May 1942, 5.

150. Buell to Time Inc. Post-War Committee, "Americo-British Power."

151. Buell, "Relations with Britain," 7.

152. Fill Calhoun, "How Isolationist Is the Midwest?" *Life,* December 1, 1941, 20.

153. Charles K. Webster, diary, April 10, 1941, Section 29/9, CW. For details on Webster's trip to America and planning in Britain, see P. A. Reynolds and E. J. Hughes, *The Historian as Diplomat: Charles Kingsley Webster and the United Nations, 1939–1946* (London: Martin Robertson, 1976), ch. 2.

154. Charles K. Webster, diary, April 9 and 14, 1941, Section 29/9, CW.

155. See Leo Pasvolsky to Sumner Welles, April 11, 1941, Box 54, HN; Leo Pasvolsky to Cordell Hull, "Proposal for the Organization of Work for the Formulation of Post-war Foreign Policies," September 12, 1941, Box 54, HN; and Cordell Hull to Franklin D. Roosevelt, December 22, 1941, Box 54, HN.

156. Hamilton Fish Armstrong to Norman H. Davis, August 18, 1941, Box 78, HFA; Leo Pasvolsky to Cordell Hull, "Proposal." The CFR planners in Donovan's group included historian William Langer and political scientist Walter Sharp. On Donovan's bid to plan the peace, see John Hedley, "The Evolution of Intelligence Analysis in the U.S. Intelligence Community," in *Analyzing Intelligence: National Security Practitioners' Perspectives,* 2nd ed., ed. James Bruce and Roger George (Washington, DC: Georgetown University Press, 2014), 23–24; Barry M. Katz, *Foreign Intelligence: Research and Analysis in the Office of Strategic Services, 1942–1945* (Cambridge, MA: Harvard University Press, 1989), 2–18; and Thomas F. Troy, *Donovan and the CIA: A History of the Establishment of the Central Intelligence Agency* (Frederick, MD: Aletheia Books, 1981), chs. 4–5.

157. Donald G. Stevens, "Organizing for Economic Defense: Henry Wallace and the Board of Economic Warfare's Policy Initiatives, 1942," *Presidential Studies Quarterly* 26, no. 4 (Fall 1996): 1126–39.

158. Henry Wallace to Hamilton Fish Armstrong, April 9, 1941, Box 64, HFA.

159. Wallace, "Our Second Chance," 363–64; and Henry Wallace, "The Century of the Common Man," May 8, 1942, in *Prefaces to Peace,* 369–75.

160. The strong points ranged from the Western Hemisphere (Newfoundland; Guantanamo, Cuba, to Puerto Rico; Panama; Natal to Pernambuco, Brazil); to Europe (the British Isles; Gibraltar); Africa (Dakar to Freetown; Cape Town); the Middle East (Suez; Aden); and the Asia Pacific (Port Darwin, Singapore, Hawaii, Dutch Harbor).

161. Hamilton Fish Armstrong, "Notes on the Conversation of May 3d [1941]," Box 64, HFA.

162. Economic and Financial Group, Memorandum of Discussions, No. E-A16, May 17, 1941, CFRWPS.

163. Adolf Berle, diary, July 19, 1941, Box 213, AB.

164. See, for example, Townsend Hoopes and Douglas Brinkley, *FDR and the Creation of the U.N.* (New Haven, CT: Yale University Press, 1997), 40; Paul Kennedy, *The Parliament of Man: The Past, Present, and Future of the United Nations* (New York: Random House, 2006), 25; and Plesch, *America, Hitler and the UN,* 24–27.

165. U.S. Department of State, Memorandum of Conversation, August 11, 1941, 11:00 a.m. meeting, Box 151, SW.

166. U.S. Department of State, Memorandum of Conversation, "British-American Cooperation," August 11, 1941, afternoon meeting, Box 151, SW.

167. See Mark Reeves, "The Broad, Toiling Masses in All the Continents: Anticolonial Activists and the Atlantic Charter" (MA thesis, Western Kentucky University, 2014); Penny Von Eschen, *Race against Empire: Black Americans and Anticolonialism, 1937–1957* (Ithaca, NY: Cornell University Press, 1997), 25–28; and Fredrik Logevall, *Embers of War: The Fall of an Empire and the Making of America's Vietnam* (New York: Random House, 2012), 48–50.

168. Elizabeth Borgwardt makes a strong claim for an anticolonial Atlantic Charter, teleologically writing that the charter offered "aspirational outlines of objectives, classically 'thin' sets of general principles," which in turn included "self-determination." Elizabeth Borgwardt, "'When You State a Moral Principle, You Are Stuck With It': The 1941 Atlantic Charter as a Human Rights Instrument," *Virginia Journal of International Law* 46, no. 3 (Spring 2006): 503, 505.

169. Frank Knox, "World Peace Must Be Enforced: We Should Prevent the Rise of New Hitlers," address to the American Bar Association, Indianapolis, October 1, 1941, in *Vital Speeches of the Day* 8, no. 1 (November 15, 1941): 18.

4. INSTRUMENTAL INTERNATIONALISM, 1941–1943

1. Arguing that realism in the practice and academic field of international relations came "out of Europe" or is "un-American," in Martti Koskenniemi's and Anders Stephanson's respective words, are Daniel Bessner, *Democracy in Exile: Hans Speier and the Rise of the Defense Intellectual* (Ithaca, NY: Cornell University Press, 2018); Udi Greenberg, *The Weimar Century: German Émigrés and the Ideological Foundations of the Cold War* (Princeton, NJ: Princeton University Press, 2014); Nicolas Guilhot, *After the Enlightenment: Political Realism and International Relations in the Mid-twentieth Century* (Cambridge: Cambridge University Press, 2017); Martti Koskenniemi, *The Gentle Civilizer of Nations: The Rise and Fall of International Law, 1870–1960* (Cambridge: Cambridge University Press, 2001), 413–94; Felix Rösch, ed., *Émigré Scholars and the Genesis of International Relations: A European Discipline in America?* (New York: Palgrave Macmillan, 2014); and Anders Stephanson, "Kennan: Realism as Desire," in *The Invention of International Relations Theory: Realism, the Rockefeller Foundation, and the 1954 Conference on Theory,* ed. Nicolas Guilhot (New York: Columbia University Press, 2011), 162–81.

2. Edward Mead Earle, *Against This Torrent* (Princeton, NJ: Princeton University Press, 1941), 39; and Edward Mead Earle, "National Defense and Political Science," *Political Science Quarterly* 55, no. 4 (December 1940): 490.

3. Yale Institute for International Studies to Rockefeller Foundation, "Report for the Year 1940–41," Box 4, YIIS.

4. Nicholas J. Spykman, *America's Strategy in World Politics: The United States and the Balance of Power* (New Brunswick, NJ: Transaction, 2007), 18, 124, 463, 465–70.

5. Earle, *Against This Torrent,* 33–36; and Spykman, *America's Strategy in World Politics,* 472.

6. Spykman, *America's Strategy in World Politics*, 64, 121.

7. Quincy Wright to Edward Mead Earle, August 19, 1940, Box 19, QW.

8. Edward Mead Earle, "Power Politics and American World Policy," *Political Science Quarterly* 58, no. 1 (March 1943): 104.

9. Arnold Wolfers, "Anglo-American Post-war Coöperation and the Interests of Europe," *American Political Science Review* 36, no. 6 (August 1942): 666, Box 21, AW.

10. In 1944 and 1945, Earle consulted for the State Department's Division of International Security and Organization. Yale Institute members David Rowe and Grayson Kirk served as American representatives to the Dumbarton Oaks and San Francisco conferences that set up the U.N. See Box 25, EME; Yale Institute for International Studies to Rockefeller Foundation, "Report for the Year 1944–45," Box 4, YIIS; and Ryan Irwin, "One World? Rethinking America's Margins, 1935–1945," in *Foreign Policy at the Periphery: The Shifting Margins of US International Relations since World War II,* ed. Bevan Sewell and Maria Ryan (Lexington, KY: University Press of Kentucky, 2016), 152–71.

11. George Egerton, *Great Britain and the Creation of the League of Nations: Strategy, Politics, and International Organization, 1914–1919* (Chapel Hill, NC: University of North Carolina Press, 1978), 92–94; and Peter Yearwood, *Guarantee of Peace: The League of Nations in British Policy, 1914–1925* (Oxford: Oxford University Press, 2009), 123.

12. Interpreting the U.N. as a device for maintaining order and peace among states are Elizabeth Borgwardt, *A New Deal for the World: America's Vision for Human Rights* (Cambridge, MA: Harvard University Press, 2005); Robert Hildebrand, *Dumbarton Oaks: The Origins of the United Nations and the Search for Postwar Security* (Chapel Hill, NC: University of North Carolina Press, 1990); Townsend Hoopes and Douglas Brinkley, *FDR and the Creation of the U.N.* (New Haven, CT: Yale University Press, 1997); Daniel Plesch, *America, Hitler and the UN: How the Allies Won World War II and Forged a Peace* (London: I. B. Tauris, 2011); and Stephen Schlesinger, *Act of Creation: The Founding of the United Nations* (Boulder, CO: Westview, 2003). Arguing instead that U.S. elites sought primarily to promote capitalism and counterrevolution are Patrick Hearden, *Architects of Globalism: Building a New World Order during World War II* (Fayetteville, AR: University of Arkansas Press, 2002), 175–200; and Gabriel Kolko, *The Politics of War: The World and United States Foreign Policy, 1943–1945* (New York: Random House, 1968), ch. 18.

13. A prominent exchange between the two schools is Robert Keohane and Lisa L. Martin, "The Promise of Institutionalist Theory," *International Security* 20, no. 1 (Summer 1995): 39–51; and John Mearsheimer, "The False Promise of International Institutions," *International Security* 19, no. 3 (Winter 1994–1995): 5–49.

14. For a critique within the field that recovers the approaches of political scientists in the mid-twentieth century and proposes research on the relationship between international organization and domestic politics, see Lisa L. Martin and Beth A. Simmons, "Theories and Empirical Studies of International Institutions," *International Organization* 52, no. 4 (Autumn 1998): 729–57.

15. Political Group, Memorandum of Discussions, No. P-A5, February 19, 1941, CFRWPS.

16. Political Group, Memorandum of Discussions, No. P-A6, March 7, 1941, CFRWPS.

17. Political Group, Memorandum of Discussions, No. P-A10, May 22, 1941, CFRWPS.

18. Wendell Willkie, *One World* (New York: Simon and Schuster, 1943).

19. Territorial Group, Memorandum of Discussions, No. T-A14, June 17, 1941, CFRWPS.

20. Economic and Financial Group, "Methods of Economic Collaboration: Introductory—The Role of the Grand Area in American Economic Policy," Memorandum, No. E-B34, July 24, 1941, CFRWPS.

21. Economic and Financial Group, Memorandum of Discussions, No. E-A17, June 14, 1941, CFRWPS.

22. Territorial Group, Memorandum of Discussions, No. T-A14. See also Economic and Financial Group, Memorandum of Discussions, No. E-A16, May 17, 1941, CFRWPS.

23. Eric Helleiner, *Forgotten Foundations of Bretton Woods: International Development and the Making of the Postwar Order* (Ithaca, NY: Cornell University Press, 2014), 124–25.

24. Lynn Edminster, "Foreign Trade and the World Crisis," *Department of State Bulletin* 4, no. 100 (May 24, 1941): 625.

25. Economic and Financial Group, Memorandum of Discussions, No. E-A17.

26. Economic and Financial Group, Memorandum of Discussions, No. E-A15, April 12, 1941, CFRWPS.

27. Helleiner, *Forgotten Foundations of Bretton Woods,* 124–27.

28. On the connection between the War and Peace Studies project and the creation of the International Monetary Fund and the World Bank, see G. William Domhoff, *The Power Elite and the State: How Policy Is Made in America* (New York: A. De Gruyter, 1990), ch. 6; and Laurence Shoup and William Minter, *Imperial Brain Trust: The Council on Foreign Relations and United States Foreign Policy* (New York: Monthly Review Press, 1977), 166–69.

29. Economic and Financial Group, Memorandum of Discussions, No. E-A16.

30. Economic and Financial Group, Memorandum of Discussions, No. E-A22, September 20, 1941, CFRWPS.

31. Economic and Financial Group, Memorandum of Discussions, No. E-A22.

32. Hearden, *Architects of Globalism;* Thomas J. McCormick, *America's Half-Century: United States Foreign Policy in the Cold War and After,* 2nd ed. (Baltimore: Johns Hopkins University Press, 1995), esp. 28–33; and Laurence Shoup and William Minter, *Imperial Brain Trust.*

33. Economic and Financial Group, Memorandum of Discussions, No. E-A16.

34. See, for example, Economic and Financial Group, Memorandum of Discussions, No. E-A16; and Territorial Group, Memoranda of Discussions, No. T-A14.

35. Territorial Group, Memoranda of Discussions, No. T-A14.

36. Economic and Financial Group, Memorandum of Discussions, No. E-A16.

37. Territorial Group, Memoranda of Discussions, No. T-A12, April 21, 1941, CFRWPS.

38. Political Group, Memoranda of Discussions, No. P-A12, June 25, 1941, CFRWPS.

39. Political Group, Memorandum of Discussions, No. P-A5.

40. Division of Special Research, "Problems of Study Regarding Post-war Political Reconstruction," Division of Special Research, July 12, 1941, Box 11, NF.

41. Sumner Welles, "An Association of Nations," address at the dedication of the Norwegian Legation, July 22, 1941, Box 195, SW.

42. Adolf Berle, diary, July 23, 1941, Box 213, AB.

43. Arthur Sweetser, Political Group, "Approaches to Postwar International Organization," Memorandum, No. P-B30, September 17, 1941, CFRWPS.

44. Sweetser, Political Group, "Approaches to Postwar International Organization," Memorandum, No. P-B30, emphasis in the original.

45. Political Group, Memoranda of Discussions, No. P-A12.

46. Francis P. Miller to Hamilton Fish Armstrong, October 2, 1941, Box 74, HFA.

47. Territorial Group, Memorandum of Discussions, No. T-A18, October 8, 1941, CFRWPS.

48. Report of the Twenty-Fourth Special Meeting, Research Sub-Committee on International Organisation, British Foreign Research and Press Service, Balliol College, Oxford, July 18, 1941, Box 3, WS.

49. "Johnson Says Alliance Forged by Peace Aims," *Los Angeles Times,* August 20, 1941.

50. Robert A. Taft, "Radio Broadcast to the Citizens of Ohio," August 29, 1941, in Clarence E. Wunderlin Jr., ed., *The Papers of Robert A. Taft,* vol. 2, *1939–1942,* 284.

51. 87 Cong. Rec. A4363 (September 25, 1941).

52. John Foster Dulles, "Long Range Peace Objectives Including an Analysis of the Roosevelt-Churchill Eight Point Declaration," Commission to Study the Bases of a Just and Durable Peace, Federal Council of Churches, September 18, 1941, Box 282, JFD.

53. John Foster Dulles to John McNeill, October 1, 1941, quoted in Ronald W. Pruessen, *John Foster Dulles: The Road to Power* (New York: Free Press, 1982), 210–11.

54. Walter Lippmann, "The Beginning of the Road," *New York Herald Tribune,* September 11, 1941.

55. Political Group, Memorandum of Discussions, No. P-A14, August 26, 1941, CFRWPS.

56. Political Group, "A Comparative Analysis of the Wilsonian and Roosevelt-Churchill Peace Programs," Memorandum, No. P-B32, December 3, 1941, CFRWPS, emphasis in the original.

57. Political Group, Memorandum of Discussions, No. P-A14.

58. Political Group, Memorandum of Discussions, No. P-A14.

59. William Paton to Arnold J. Toynbee, September 26, 1941, Box 119, AJT.

60. Arthur Sweetser to the Board of Directors of the Woodrow Wilson Foundation, October 7, 1941, Box 5, WWF. See also the proceedings from a conference of League of Nations supporters held September 2–13, 1941: *World Organization: A Balance Sheet of the First Great Experiment* (Washington, DC: American Council on Public Affairs, 1942).

61. Armaments Group, Memorandum of Discussions, No. A-A16, October 22, 1941, CFRWPS. See also Grayson Kirk, "International Policing (A Survey of Recent Proposals)," Draft Memorandum, September 27, 1941, Box 72, HFA.

62. Economic and Financial Group, Memoranda of Discussions, No. E-A21, October 11, 1941, CFRWPS.

63. Political Group, Memoranda of Discussions, No. P-A16, October 15, 1941, CFRWPS.

64. Freda Kirchwey, "Luce Thinking," *The Nation*, March 1, 1941, 229.

65. Thomas, "How to Fight for Democracy," 59.

66. "A War for Sea Power," *Christian Century*, April 16, 1941, 520–21.

67. Norman Thomas, "How to Fight for Democracy," *Annals of the American Academy of Political and Social Science* 216 (July 1941): 58.

68. Freda Kirchwey, "Luce Thinking," 230.

69. Max Lerner, "American Leadership in a Harsh Age," *Annals of the American Academy of Political and Social Science* 216 (July 1941): 123.

70. Political Group, Memorandum of Discussions, No. P-A15, September 17, 1941, CFRWPS; and Armaments Group, Memorandum of Discussions, No. A-A14, September 10, 1941, CFRWPS.

71. American Institute of Public Opinion Poll, August 26, 1941, in Hadley Cantril, *Public Opinion, 1935–1946* (Princeton, NJ: Princeton University Press, 1951), 1083.

72. Another 10 percent of respondents "said they could name a provision but didn't give any answer." American Institute of Public Opinion Poll, August 26, 1941, and American Institute of Public Opinion Poll, January 23, 1941, in Cantril, *Public Opinion*, 1083.

73. For example, William Hard, "American Relations with Britain," *Annals of the American Academy of Political and Social Science* 216 (July 1941): 151.

74. Adolf Berle, diary, April 30, 1941, Box 212, AB.

75. "America First Will Dissolve; Urges War Aid," *Chicago Tribune*, December 12, 1941; and Wayne Cole, *America First: The Battle against Intervention, 1940–1941* (Madison, WI: University of Wisconsin Press, 1953) 195.

76. Albert Guérard to James Shotwell, January 20, 1942, Box 231, JS; and James Shotwell to Albert Guérard, January 27, 1942, Box 231, JS.

77. Roger S. Greene to Clyde Eagleton, October 23, 1941, Box 5, QW.

78. Rapporteur Summary, Conference on North Atlantic Relations, Session 5, September 6, 1941, Box 11, EME. The conference, held September 4–9, 1941, was a nongovernmental expression of American-British partnership; it brought U.S. academics, officials, and foundation leaders together with such British and Canadian counterparts as postwar planner Charles Webster and international lawyer Hersh Lauterpacht. For proceedings, see *Documents: Conference on North Atlantic Relations* (Princeton, NJ: American Committee for International Studies, 1941).

79. Political Group, Memorandum of Discussions, No. P-A18, December 9, 1941, CFRWPS.

80. James Shotwell, "After the War," *International Conciliation* 21, no. 376 (January 1942): 34.

81. Sweetser, Political Group, "Approaches to Postwar International Organization," Memorandum, No. P-B30.

82. 87 Cong. Rec. 8594 (November 7, 1941).

83. "America First Will Dissolve; Urges War Aid"; Cole, *America First,* 193–96; and Justus Doenecke, *Storm on the Horizon: The Challenge to American Intervention, 1939–1941* (Lanham, MD: Rowman and Littlefield, 2000), 320–22.

84. Isaiah Bowman to Hamilton Fish Armstrong, December 15, 1941, Box 74, HFA.

85. "Advisory Committee on Post-war Foreign Policy: Preliminaries," n.d., Box 54, HN.

86. Advisory Committee, Chronological Minutes 1, Meeting of February 12, 1942, Box 54, HN.

87. Hearden, *Architects of Globalism,* 156. Welles's regular meetings with Roosevelt are documented in the folder titled Talks with FDR, 1942–1944, Box 54, HN.

88. Sumner Welles, Address at Memorial Services at the Tomb of President Wilson in the Washington Cathedral, November 11, 1941, Box 195, SW.

89. Subcommittee on International Organization, Chronological Minutes 4, Meeting of August 14, 1942, Box 85, HN.

90. Subcommittee on Political Problems, Chronological Minutes 2, Meeting of March 14, 1942, Box 55, HN.

91. Leo Pasvolsky to Cordell Hull, "Proposal for the Organization of Work for the Formulation of Post-war Foreign Policies," September 12, 1941, Box 54, HN.

92. The planning committee contained a range of officials across government departments, including, from the State Department, Dean Acheson, Adolf Berle, Herbert Feis, Harley Notter, and Leo Pasvolsky; from Roosevelt's staff, Benjamin Cohen and David Niles; and from Vice President Henry Wallace's Board of Economic Warfare, Milo Perkins. See Christopher O'Sullivan, *Sumner Welles, Postwar Planning, and the Quest for a New World Order, 1937–1943* (New York: Columbia University Press, 2002), 64–70.

93. Subcommittee on Political Problems, Chronological Minutes 3, Meeting of March 21, 1942, Box 55, HN.

94. Subcommittee on Political Problems, Chronological Minutes 2.

95. Advisory Committee, Chronological Minutes 1.

96. Subcommittee on Political Problems, Chronological Minutes 4, Meeting of March 28, 1942, Box 55, HN.

97. Subcommittee on Political Problems, Chronological Minutes 9, Meeting of May 2, 1942, Box 55, HN.

98. Subcommittee on International Organization, Document 2, James Shotwell, "Preliminary Draft on International Organization," July 31, 1942, Box 86, HN.

99. Subcommittee on Political Problems, Chronological Minutes 1, Meeting of March 7, 1942, Box 55, HN, emphasis in the original.

100. Subcommittee on Political Problems, Chronological Minutes 3.

101. Subcommittee on Political Problems, Chronological Minutes 4.

102. Subcommittee on International Organization, Chronological Minutes 2, Meeting of July 31, 1942, Box 85, HN.

103. Subcommittee on International Organization, Chronological Minutes 2; and Subcommittee on International Organization, Chronological Minutes 4.

104. Subcommittee on International Organization, Chronological Minutes 2; and Subcommittee on International Organization, Chronological Minutes 3, August 7, 1942, Box 85, HN.

105. Subcommittee on International Organization, Chronological Minutes 5, August 21, 1942, Box 85, HN.

106. On U.S. planning with respect to colonial empire, see Hearden, *Architects of Globalism,* 93–146; William Roger Louis, *Imperialism at Bay: The United States and the Decolonization of the British Empire, 1941–1945* (New York: Oxford University Press, 1978), pt. 2; O'Sullivan, *Sumner Welles,* chs. 4–5; and Neil Smith, *American Empire: Roosevelt's Geographer and the Prelude to Globalization* (Berkeley: University of California Press, 2003), ch. 13.

107. Subcommittee on Territorial Problems, Document 214-c, "Tentative Views of the Territorial Subcommittee (March 7, 1942—March 5, 1943)," March 10, 1943, Box 54, HN. See also the first plan drawn up for international trusteeship: Subcommittee on Political Problems, Document 118, "An International Trusteeship for Non-Self-Governing Peoples," October 22, 1942, Box 56, HN.

108. "Talks with FDR," January 2, 1943, Box 54, HN.

109. Leo Pasvolsky, "Notes on a Meeting at the White House," February 3, 1944, Box 5, LP, quoted in Hearden, *Architects of Globalism,* 167.

110. Subcommittee on Political Problems, Chronological Minutes 5, Meeting of April 4, 1942, Box 55, HN.

111. Sumner Welles, *Seven Decisions That Shaped History* (New York: Harper, 1951), 133.

112. In May, for instance, CFR president Norman H. Davis spoke with Roosevelt and reported to other members of the Subcommittee on Security Problems that the president's mind was "already pretty well made up": the United States, Great Britain, Russia, and China must control the postwar settlement alone. Subcommittee on Security Problems, Chronological Minutes 4, Meeting of May 20, 1942, Box 76, HN. See also Robert Dallek, *Franklin D. Roosevelt and American Foreign Policy, 1932–1945,* 2nd ed. (New York: Oxford University Press, 1995), 342, 389–90.

113. FDR-Molotov Conference, May 29, 1942, *FRUS: Diplomatic Papers, 1942,* vol. 3, *Europe,* 568–69.

114. O'Sullivan, *Sumner Welles,* 72–73; and Benjamin Welles, *Sumner Welles: FDR's Global Strategist: A Biography* (New York: St. Martin's, 1997), 334.

115. Subcommittee on International Organization, Document 123-e, "Draft Constitution of the International Organization," March 26, 1943, Box 88, HN.

116. Hoopes and Brinkley, *FDR and the Creation of the U.N.,* 52–54.

117. Franklin D. Roosevelt, quoted in Warren F. Kimball, "The Sheriffs: FDR's Postwar World," in *FDR's World: War, Peace, and Legacies,* ed. David B. Woolner, Warren F. Kimball, and David Reynolds (New York: Palgrave Macmillan, 2008), 100.

118. Churchill entertained a variety of ideas and had proposed to endorse "effective international organization" in the Atlantic Charter, but in 1942 and 1943 he landed on

a regionalist solution featuring a Council of Europe with an international police force. E. J. Hughes, "Winston Churchill and the Formation of the United Nations Organization," *Journal of Contemporary History* 9, no. 4 (October 1974): 177–94.

119. Dallek, *Franklin D. Roosevelt and American Foreign Policy,* 519–22.

120. Kimball, "The Sheriffs," 100.

121. Raymond Leslie Buell to C. L. Stillman, March 31, 1942, Box 24, RLB.

122. Milo Perkins to Harry Hopkins, December 1, 1942, Box 329, HH.

5. THE DEBATE THAT WASN'T, 1942–1945

1. Toynbee made the trip in his capacity as a semiofficial British postwar planner with the Foreign Research and Press Service, based in Balliol College, Oxford. He was research director of Chatham House from 1925 to 1955. Summarizing Toynbee's career is Christopher Brewin, "Arnold Toynbee, Chatham House, and Research in a Global Context," in *Thinkers of the Twenty Years' Crisis: Interwar Idealism Revisited,* ed. David Long and Peter Wilson (New York: Oxford University Press, 1991), ch. 11. See also Ian Hall, "Time of Troubles: Arnold J. Toynbee's Twentieth Century," *International Affairs* 90, no. 1 (2014): 23–36; and William H. McNeill, *Arnold J. Toynbee: A Life* (New York: Oxford University Press, 1989).

2. Arnold J. Toynbee, "Visit to the United States, 23rd August to 20th October, 1942," Box 92, AJT.

3. Toynbee, "Visit to the United States."

4. Henry Wallace, *The Price of Free World Victory* (New York: L. B. Fischer, 1942). For pronouncements on colonialism by Wallace and others in 1942, and British reactions, see Lloyd Gardner, "FDR and the Colonial Question," in *FDR's World: War, Peace, and Legacies,* ed. David B. Woolner, Warren F. Kimball, and David Reynolds (New York: Palgrave Macmillan, 2008), 123–27; and James P. Hubbard, *The United States and the End of British Colonial Rule in Africa, 1941–1968* (Jefferson, NC: McFarland, 2011), 11–14, 30. On Anglo-American negotiations over Lend-Lease compensation, see Patrick Hearden, *Architects of Globalism: Building a New World Order during World War II* (Fayetteville, AR: University of Arkansas Press, 2002), 28–32, 42–46, 64–91, 247–49, 314–15; and Warren F. Kimball, *The Juggler: Franklin Roosevelt as Wartime Statesman* (Princeton, NJ: Princeton University Press, 1991), ch. 3. The classic work is Richard N. Gardner, *Sterling-Dollar Diplomacy: Anglo-American Collaboration in the Reconstruction of Multilateral Trade* (Oxford: Clarendon Press, 1956).

5. Toynbee, "Visit to the United States."

6. Robert Divine, *Second Chance: The Triumph of Internationalism in America during World War II* (New York: Atheneum, 1967). "Second chance" became a trope starting in 1941 as part of the teleological argument that the United States had passed up the opportunity for global supremacy in World War I, as though many Americans at the time advocated supremacy but were thwarted by other Americans. See Charlotte Burnett Mahon, ed., *Our Second Chance* (New York: Woodrow Wilson Foundation, 1944); Henry Wallace, "America's Second Chance," April 8, 1941, in *Prefaces to Peace* (New York: Simon and Schuster / Doubleday / Doran / Reynal and Hitchcock / Columbia University Press, 1943), 363–64; and John Boardman Whitton, ed., *The Second Chance: America and the Peace* (Princeton, NJ: Princeton University Press, 1944).

7. Elizabeth Borgwardt, *A New Deal for the World: America's Vision for Human Rights* (Cambridge, MA: Harvard University Press, 2005), 160.

8. Dorothy B. Robins, *Experiment in Democracy: The Story of U.S. Citizen Organizations in Forging the Charter of the United Nations* (New York: Parkside, 1971).

9. For Taft's speech announcing his vote in favor of ratifying the U.N. Charter, see 91 Cong. Rec. 8151–58 (July 28, 1945).

10. See Joseph Baratta, *The Politics of World Federation* (Westport, CT: Praeger, 2004), esp. 54–61; and Jon Yoder, "The United World Federalists: Liberals for Law and Order," in *Peace Movements in America,* ed. Charles Chatfield (New York: Schocken, 1973), 95–115.

11. Examining the early Cold War, John Fousek documents a globalist outlook in public discourse, namely in the Truman administration, the mass print media, organized labor, and the African American community. Only in the African American press does he find significant disagreement over America's global role. John Fousek, *To Lead the Free World: American Nationalism and the Cultural Roots of the Cold War* (Chapel Hill, NC: University of North Carolina Press, 2000). On black internationalism in World War II, see Penny von Eschen, *Race against Empire: Black Americans and Anticolonialism, 1937–1957* (Ithaca, NY: Cornell University Press, 1997); Gerald Horne, *Facing the Rising Sun: African Americans, Japan, and the Rise of Afro-Asian Solidarity* (New York: New York University Press, 2018); James Meriwether, *Proudly We Can Be Africans: Black Americans and Africa, 1935–1961* (Chapel Hill, NC: University of North Carolina Press, 2002), ch. 2; Brenda Gayle Plummer, *Rising Wind: Black Americans and U.S. Foreign Affairs, 1935–1960* (Chapel Hill, NC: University of North Carolina Press, 1996), 83–166; and Nico Slate, *Colored Cosmopolitanism: The Shared Struggle for Freedom in the United States and India* (Cambridge, MA: Harvard University Press, 2012), esp. 125–60.

12. Harry S. Truman, "Radio Report to the American People on the Potsdam Conference," August 9, 1945, Harry S. Truman Library and Museum, https://www.trumanlibrary .gov/library/public-papers/97/radio-report-american-people-potsdam-conference.

13. "A Plan of Action for Woodrow Wilson Foundation: Fisdale [*sic*] Report on Program and Policy," 1942, Box 21, WWF.

14. "A Plan of Action."

15. On Freudianism in twentieth-century American popular culture, see Lawrence Samuel, *Shrink: A Cultural History of Psychoanalysis in America* (Lincoln, NE: University of Nebraska Press, 2013).

16. "A Plan of Action."

17. Charlotte Burnett Mahon, "Annual Report of the Foundation, 1943–1944," April 1944, Box 1, WWF; Charlotte Burnett Mahon, ed., *Our Second Chance* (New York: Woodrow Wilson Foundation, 1944); Minutes of the Meeting of the Executive Committee, June 13, 1944, Box 1, WWF; and Memorandum on the Dumbarton Oaks Proposals, December 4, 1944, Box 5, WWF. On the film *Wilson,* see Thomas J. Knock, "'History with Lightning': The Forgotten Film *Wilson,*" *American Quarterly* 28, no. 5 (Winter 1976): 523–43.

18. Louise Wright, "Comments on Recommendations of the Committee on Policy and Awards," April 17, 1942, Box 1, WWF.

19. Andrew Johnstone, "Shaping our Post-war Foreign Policy: The Carnegie Endowment for International Peace and the Promotion of the United Nations Organisation during World War II," *Global Society* 28, no. 1 (2014): 28–30.

20. Inderjeet Parmar, *Think Tanks and Power in Foreign Policy: A Comparative Study of the Role and Influence of the Council on Foreign Relations and the Royal Institute of International Affairs, 1939–1945* (New York: Palgrave Macmillan, 2004), 54–55.

21. Andrew Johnstone, "Americans Disunited: Americans United for World Organization and the Triumph of Internationalism," *Journal of American Studies* 44, no. 1 (February 2010): 7.

22. Charles W. Yost to Leo Pasvolsky, April 14, 1942, quoted in Inderjeet Parmar, "The Issue of State Power: The Council on Foreign Relations as a Case Study," *Journal of American Studies* 29, no. 1 (April 1995): 92.

23. Andrew Johnstone, "Creating a 'Democratic Foreign Policy': The State Department's Division of Public Liaison and Public Opinion, 1944–1953," *Diplomatic History* 35, no. 3 (June 2011): 486–91.

24. Justin Hart, *Empire of Ideas: The Origins of Public Diplomacy and the Transformation of U.S. Foreign Policy* (New York: Oxford University Press, 2013), 65–66; and Townsend Hoopes and Douglas Brinkley, *FDR and the Creation of the U.N.* (New Haven, CT: Yale University Press, 1997), 168.

25. Robins, *Experiment in Democracy,* 114–29. See also James Shotwell, "San Francisco Just STARTED It!" *Rotarian,* November 1945, 8–10, Box 276, JS.

26. Johnstone, "Creating a 'Democratic Foreign Policy,'" 483–503.

27. Not only did international organization garner 73 percent approval, but those respondents approved of an international police force to "keep peace throughout the world." Division of Special Research, "Summary of Opinion and Ideas on International Post-war Problems," No. 1, July 15, 1942, Box 190, SW. For polling data, see American Institute of Public Opinion Poll, July 29, 1941, in Hadley Cantril, *Public Opinion, 1935–1946* (Princeton, NJ: Princeton University Press, 1951), 373.

28. Borgwardt, *A New Deal for the World,* 156.

29. Charles Beard to Edwin Borchard, May 6, 1945, Box 1, EB.

30. Arthur H. Vandenberg Jr., ed., *The Private Papers of Senator Vandenberg* (Boston: Houghton Mifflin, 1952), 1.

31. John A. Thompson, *A Sense of Power: The Roots of America's Global Role* (Ithaca, NY: Cornell University Press, 2015), ch. 6.

32. Vandenberg, *The Private Papers of Senator Vandenberg,* 95.

33. James Shotwell, "Charter of the Golden Gate," *Survey Graphic,* July 1945, 313, Box 276, JS.

34. Charles Beard to Edwin Borchard, March 11, 1945, Box 1, EB.

35. "The Great Beginning," *New York Herald Tribune,* June 27, 1945.

36. Taft declared, "Our people must commit themselves to use military force under certain conditions where aggression has been found by an international body to exist." "U.S. Must Keep Its Sovereignty After War: Taft," *Chicago Sunday Tribune,* June 20, 1943.

During the war, however, Taft most consistently promoted universal compacts obligating the judicial and arbitral settlement of international disputes. He also opposed the Bretton Woods agreement. His major speeches were Robert A. Taft, "Peace or Politics?" *American Bar Association Journal* 29, no. 11 (November 1943): 639–41, 647–9; and 91 Cong. Rec. 8151–58 (July 28, 1945). See also Clarence E. Wunderlin, *Robert A. Taft: Ideas, Tradition, and Party in U.S. Foreign Policy* (Lanham, MD: Rowman and Littlefield, 2005), 78–87.

37. Raymond Leslie Buell to Henry R. Luce, C. Manfred Gottfried, T. S. Matthews, John Osborne, Bill Olson, Albert L. Furth, and John K. Jessup, March 1, 1944, Box 23, RLB.

38. "And Now the Senate," *Washington Post,* July 1, 1945.

39. Andrew Johnstone, *Dilemmas of Internationalism: The American Association for the United Nations and U.S. Foreign Policy, 1941–1948* (Burlington, VT: Ashgate, 2009), 24–27.

40. The president of the League of Women Voters wrote, "The slogan 'Stop Isolationism Now' is descriptive of the League's present activities. Inevitably there is to continue here a series of tests between international and isolationist sentiments of one kind and [sic] another and sometimes not easily recognized." Marguerite Wells to Louise Wright, May 19, 1943, Box 82, HFA.

41. See Hart, *Empire of Ideas,* esp. 116–20.

42. Steven Casey, *Cautious Crusade: Franklin D. Roosevelt, American Public Opinion, and the War against Nazi Germany* (New York: Oxford University Press, 2001), 17.

43. Subcommittee on Political Problems, Chronological Minutes 9, Meeting of May 2, 1942, Box 55, HN.

44. "A Plan of Action," emphasis in the original.

45. Across the entirety of the war, from 1939 to 1945, the peak years for the use of "isolationism" were 1942 and 1943. In the next two years, the term's frequency remained at or above pre-1942 levels. For example, "isolationism" averaged appearances in 60 articles per year from 1942 to 1945 in the *Atlanta Constitution,* compared with an annual average of 37 from 1940 to 1941. In the *Boston Globe,* the average was 56.5 from 1942 to 1945, after a 45.5 average from 1940 to 1941. Articles referencing "isolationism" jumped in the *Chicago Tribune,* from 12.5 in 1940 and 1941 to 42.75 in the next four years. Likewise, in the *New York Times,* the averages rose from 140 in 1940 and 1941 to 230.75 from 1942 to 1945. In the *New York Herald Tribune,* they increased from 132 to 212.25. *Washington Post* articles mentioning "isolationism" rose from 57.5 to 92.5. Statistics according to searches of the ProQuest Historical Newspapers database conducted on December 4, 2017.

  Similarly, academic journals saw "isolationism" increase in usage after 1941. The peak years tended to come in 1944 or 1945, perhaps because books on the postwar settlement of both world wars were discussed and reviewed then. In the *American Historical Review* and *American Journal of International Law,* the peak year was 1944, when "isolationism" appeared in six and five items, respectively. It was 1945 in the *Annals of the American Academy of Political and Social Science,* which featured 11 items containing "isolationism." Statistics according to searches of JSTOR conducted on December 4, 2017.

46. Franklin D. Roosevelt, "State of the Union Address," January 6, 1945, American Presidency Project, https://www.presidency.ucsb.edu/documents/state-the-union -address-1; Walter Lippmann, "Idealism without Imagination," *New York Herald Tribune,* December 30, 1944; Anne O'Hare McCormick, "Abroad: A World That Waits to Be Reshaped," *New York Times,* January 31, 1945; and "Senator Ball Urges World Collaboration: Win Peace Now," *Christian Science Monitor,* April 29, 1943.

47. Digest of Discussion, "The United States and the United Nations in War and Peace," Study Group, First Meeting, December 4, 1942, quoted in Parmar, "The Issue of State Power," 84.

48. 91 Cong. Rec. A671 (February 16, 1945) (statement of Rep. Smith on February 12, 1945).

49. Johnstone, *Dilemmas of Internationalism,* 5–9.

50. Stephen Wertheim, "The League That Wasn't: American Designs for a Legalist-Sanctionist League of Nations and the Intellectual Origins of International Organization, 1914–1920," *Diplomatic History* 35, no. 5 (November 2011): 799, 808–10.

51. Donald Craig to Hugh Moore, November 29, 1943, quoted in Johnstone, *Dilemmas of Internationalism,* p. 78.

52. Wendell Willkie, *One World* (New York: Simon and Schuster, 1943), 146, 130.

53. See Samuel Zipp, *The Idealist: Wendell Willkie's Wartime Quest to Build One World* (Cambridge, MA: Belknap Press of Harvard University Press, 2020).

54. Philip C. Nash to James Shotwell, June 24, 1943, Box 242, JS. See also Philip C. Nash to Quincy Wright, December 21, 1942, Box 5, QW; and Philip C. Nash to James Shotwell, December 17, 1942, Box 5, QW.

55. CSOP developed a blueprint in 1943 but considered it too detailed to show the public. Commission to Study the Organization of Peace, "Fourth Report," *International Conciliation* 22 (January 1944): 3–110; and Johnstone, *Dilemmas of Internationalism,* 78.

56. Henry R. Luce to Managing Editors, Time Inc. Post-War Committee, August 17, 1943, Box 23, RLB.

57. The meeting was organized by the CFR postwar planners. Steering Committee, "Special Conference on the Dumbarton Oaks Proposals," Princeton, New Jersey, Digest of Discussion, No. SC-C2, October 20–22, 1944, Box 75, HFA.

58. "Special Conference on the Dumbarton Oaks Proposals," Third Session, October 21, 1944, Box 75, HFA.

59. "Special Conference on the Dumbarton Oaks Proposals," Final Session, October 22, 1944, Box 75, HFA.

60. Quoted in Thompson, *A Sense of Power,* 223.

61. Hans Morgenthau, "The Machiavellian Utopia," *Ethics* 55, no. 2 (January 1945): 145, 147. For a reading of Morgenthau as an ethical realist, see William Scheuerman, *Hans Morgenthau: Realism and Beyond* (Malden, MA: Polity, 2009).

62. Walter Lippmann, *U.S. Foreign Policy: Shield of the Republic* (Boston: Little, Brown, 1943), 164–65; and Walter Lippmann, *U.S. War Aims* (Boston: Little, Brown, 1944).

63. Walter Lippmann, "The Dumbarton Agreement," *New York Herald Tribune,* October 12, 1944.

64. David M. Jordan, *FDR, Dewey, and the Election of 1944* (Bloomington, IN: Indiana University Press, 2011), 219–20.

65. Robert Divine, *Second Chance: The Triumph of Internationalism in America during World War II* (New York: Atheneum, 1967), 248–50.

66. Divine, *Second Chance,* 251–52; Harold Josephson, *James T. Shotwell and the Rise of Internationalism in America* (Rutherford, NJ: Fairleigh Dickinson University Press, 1974), 241, 249; and Andrew Preston, *Sword of the Spirit, Shield of Faith: Religion in American War and Diplomacy* (New York: Alfred A. Knopf, 2012), ch. 21.

67. See Samuel Moyn, *The Last Utopia: Human Rights in History* (Cambridge, MA: Harvard University Press, 2010), 55–62.

68. The most detailed treatment of wartime international policing ideas is Roger Beaumont, *Right Backed by Might: The International Air Force Concept* (Westport, CT: Greenwood, 2001). For a range of contemporaneous views on an international police force, see Julia Johnsen, ed., *International Police Force* (New York: H. W. Wilson, 1944).

69. See Margaret Olson to Members of the Sub-Committee on a Constitution for the United Nations, "Constitution for the United Nations of the World," November 27, 1943, Box 242, JS; Armaments Group, "Various Types of Problems Arising in the Operation of International Policing Arrangements," Memorandum, No. A-B83, March 29, 1943, CFRWPS; and Armaments Group, "Relations between an International Political Organization and an International Police Force," Memorandum, No. A-B92, June 21, 1943, CFRWPS.

70. This quota system was named the Military Staff Committee. Beaumont, *Right Backed by Might,* 123–28; and Robert Hildebrand, *Dumbarton Oaks: The Origins of the United Nations and the Search for Postwar Security* (Chapel Hill, NC: University of North Carolina Press, 1990), 144–56.

71. James Shotwell to Charles Dollard, June 30, 1942, Box 226, JS.

72. Johnstone, *Dilemmas of Internationalism,* 97–111.

73. Yoder, "The United World Federalists," 100.

74. *The International Law of the Future: Postulates, Principles, and Proposals* (Washington, DC: Carnegie Endowment for International Peace, 1944).

75. Manley O. Hudson, "The International Law of the Future," *Proceedings of the American Society of International Law at Its Annual Meeting* 38 (April 28–29, 1944), 17–18; and Herbert Hoover and Hugh Gibson, *The Problems of Lasting Peace* (Garden City, NY: Doubleday, Doran and Company, 1942), 244.

76. Gerhart Niemeyer, "World Order and the Great Powers," in Whitton, ed., *The Second Chance,* 37, 64.

77. Ely Culbertson, *Summary of the World Federation Plan: An Outline of a Practical and Detailed Plan for World Settlement* (Garden City, NY: Garden City Publishing, 1943); and Ely Culbertson, *Total Peace: What Makes Wars and How to Organize Peace* (Garden City, NY: Doubleday, Doran and Company, 1943).

78. Roosevelt, "State of the Union Address."

79. Bosley Crowther, "'Wilson,' an Impressive Screen Biography, in Which Alex Knox Is the Star, Has Its World Premiere at the Roxy," *New York Times,* August 2, 1944.

80. Ruhl J. Bartlett, *The League to Enforce Peace* (Chapel Hill, NC: University of North Carolina Press, 1944), 209.

81. Thomas A. Bailey, *Woodrow Wilson and the Great Betrayal* (New York: Macmillan, 1945), vi; and Thomas A. Bailey, *Woodrow Wilson and the Lost Peace* (New York: Macmillan, 1944).

82. Other works on Wilson or the League of Nations, presenting America's failure to join the League as a tragedy, include Roger Burlingame and Alden Stevens, *Victory without Peace* (New York: Harcourt, Brace, 1944); Alan Cranston, *The Killing of the Peace* (New York: Viking, 1945); Ruth Cranston, *The Story of Woodrow Wilson* (New York: Simon and Schuster, 1945); Gerald Johnson, *Woodrow Wilson: The Unforgettable Figure Who Has Returned to Haunt Us* (New York: Harper and Brothers, 1944); David Loth, *The Story of Woodrow Wilson* (New York: Woodrow Wilson Foundation, 1944); and Karl Schriftgiesser, *The Gentleman from Massachusetts: Henry Cabot Lodge* (Boston: Little, Brown, 1944).

83. Sumner Welles, "The American Opportunity," Address at Lafayette College, PA, June 24, 1944, Box 196, SW.

84. Harry S. Truman, "Address before a Joint Session of Congress on Universal Military Training, as Broadcast over the Columbia Broadcasting System, 12:30 P.M. EST," October 23, 1945, Harry S. Truman Library and Museum, https://www.trumanlibrary.gov/soundrecording-records/sr64-17-president-trumans-address-joint-session-congress-universal-military.

85. Fousek, *To Lead the Free World*, 70.

86. John Balfour to Ernest Bevin, August 9, 1945, quoted in Stephen Brooke, *Reform and Reconstruction: Britain after the War, 1945–51* (Manchester, U.K.: Manchester University Press, 1995), 67.

87. Winston Churchill, Address to the House of Commons, August 16, 1945, in *Blood, Toil, Tears and Sweat: The Speeches of Winston Churchill*, ed. David Cannadine (Boston: Houghton Mifflin, 1989), 282.

88. A member of the Yale Institute for International Studies, William T. R. Fox, was among the first to use the term. William T. R. Fox, *The Super-Powers: The United States, the Britain, and the Soviet Union—Their Responsibility for Peace* (New York: Harcourt, Brace, 1944).

89. Referring to a bipolar Cold War are, for example, John Lewis Gaddis, "The Long Peace: Elements of Stability in the Postwar International System," *International Security* 10, no. 4 (Spring 1986): 99–142; Richard N. Haass, "The Age of Nonpolarity: What Will Follow U.S. Dominance," *Foreign Affairs* 87, no. 3 (May/June 2008): 44–56; John J. Mearsheimer, "Back to the Future," *International Security* 15, no. 1 (Summer 1990): 5–56; and Glenn H. Snyder and Paul Diesing, *Conflict Among Nations: Bargaining, Decision Making, and System Structure in International Crises* (Princeton, NJ: Princeton University Press, 1977), 418–19, 472.

90. W. M. Scammell, *The International Economy Since 1945*, 2nd ed. (New York: Macmillan, 1984), 21.

91. Welles, "The American Opportunity."

92. See Gareth Porter, *Perils of Dominance: Imbalance of Power and the Road to War in Vietnam* (Berkeley: University of California Press, 2005), ch. 1.

93. Memorandum of Conversation by Charles Bohlen, April 20, 1945, in *FRUS: Diplomatic Papers, 1945,* vol. 5, *Europe,* 232–33.

94. See Gardner, *Sterling-Dollar Diplomacy,* 188–253; Kimball, *The Juggler,* 185–93; Robert Skidelsky, *John Maynard Keynes: Fighting for Freedom, 1937–1946* (New York: Viking, 2000), 403–58; and Benn Steil, *The Battle of Bretton Woods: John Maynard Keynes, Harry Dexter White, and the Making of a New World Order* (Princeton, NJ: Princeton University Press, 2013), esp. 309.

95. "Power vs. Conscience," *Life,* June 5, 1944, 30.

96. *The Charter of the United Nations: Hearings before the Senate Committee on Foreign Relations,* 79th Cong., 1st Sess (July 12, 1945), 520.

97. Eduard Mark, "American Policy toward Eastern Europe and the Origins of the Cold War, 1941–1946: An Alternative Interpretation," *Journal of American History* 68, no. 2 (September 1981): 313–36.

98. Harry S. Truman, "Special Message to the Congress Recommending the Establishment of a Department of National Defense," December 19, 1945, Harry S. Truman Library and Museum, https://www.trumanlibrary.gov/library/public-papers/218/special-message-congress-recommending-establishment-department-national.

99. 90 Cong. Rec. 8003 (July 14, 1944).

100. Walter Lippmann, "Well Done," *New York Herald Tribune,* June 26, 1945.

101. Franklin D. Roosevelt, "Radio Address at a Dinner of the Foreign Policy Association, New York, N.Y.," October 21, 1944, American Presidency Project, https://www.presidency.ucsb.edu/documents/radio-address-dinner-the-foreign-policy-association-new-york-n-y.

102. John W. Davis, W. W. Grant, Philip C. Jessup, George Rublee, James T. Shotwell, and Quincy Wright, "Our Enforcement of Peace Devolves upon the President," *New York Times,* November 5, 1944.

103. Roosevelt, "Radio Address at a Dinner of the Foreign Policy Association."

104. Robert Sherwood, quoted in Elizabeth Borgwardt, "'When You State a Moral Principle, You Are Stuck With It': The 1941 Atlantic Charter as a Human Rights Instrument," *Virginia Journal of International Law* 46, no. 3 (Spring 2006): 528.

105. "Special Conference on the Dumbarton Oaks Proposals," Final Session, October 22, 1944, Box 75, HFA. The political scientist Marc Trachtenberg concludes that U.S. architects of the U.N. "certainly did not think that the use of force without Security Council sanction and for purposes other than defense against actual armed attack would be legally impermissible no matter how divided the great powers were—no matter how poorly, that is, the Security Council regime functioned." Marc Trachtenberg, "The Iraq Crisis and the Future of the Western Alliance," in *The Atlantic Alliance under Stress: US-European Relations after Iraq,* ed. David M. Andrews (Cambridge: Cambridge University Press, 2005), 218–19.

106. Minutes of the Thirty-Second Meeting of the United States Delegation to the San Francisco Conference, May 7, 1945, in *FRUS: Diplomatic Papers, 1945,* vol. 1, *General: The United Nations,* 637.

107. John Foster Dulles, memorandum, May 8, 1945, quoted in Ronald W. Pruessen, *John Foster Dulles: The Road to Power* (New York: Free Press, 1982), 246.

108. Minutes of the Thirty-Third Meeting of the United States Delegation to the San Francisco Conference, May 8, 1945, in *FRUS: Diplomatic Papers, 1945,* vol. 1, *General: The United Nations,* 648.

109. Minutes of the Thirty-Second Meeting of the United States Delegation, 637.

110. *The Charter of the United Nations: Hearings before the Senate Committee on Foreign Relations,* 520.

111. James Shotwell, *The Great Decision* (New York: The Macmillan Company, 1944), 95, emphasis added.

112. Willkie, *One World,* 146, emphasis added.

113. Roosevelt, "Radio Address at a Dinner of the Foreign Policy Association."

114. "America First," *New York Times,* June 29, 1945.

115. William Grimes, "Donal McLaughlin, Whose Lapel Pin Sketch Became U.N. Emblem, Dies at 102," *New York Times,* October 4, 2009; and Stephen Schlesinger, *Act of Creation: The Founding of the United Nations* (Boulder, CO: Westview, 2003), 112–13.

116. On Pearl Harbor revisionism, see Harry Elmer Barnes, ed., *Perpetual War for Perpetual Peace: A Critical Examination of the Foreign Policy of Franklin Delano Roosevelt and Its Aftermath* (Caldwell, ID: Caxton, 1953); and John Toland, "Review: The Triumph of Revisionism: The Pearl Harbor Controversy, 1941–1982," *Public Historian* 5, no. 2 (Spring 1983): 87–103.

117. Anti-isolationists often attributed U.S. abstention from the League of Nations to the popular will. For example, former undersecretary of state Sumner Welles said of the League that "the greatest obstacle in the way of its success was the failure of the *people* of the United States to take part in it." Sumner Welles, Address on the Twenty-Fifth Anniversary of the League, January 10, 1945, quoted in Arthur Sweetser, "The United States, the United Nations, and the League of Nations," *International Conciliation* 24 (February 1946): 58, emphasis added.

118. Franklin D. Roosevelt, "State of the Union Address," January 7, 1943, American Presidency Project, https://www.presidency.ucsb.edu/documents/state-the-union-address-0.

119. Raymond Leslie Buell to George Ball, January 20, 1945, Box 1, RLB.

120. Benjamin Coates, *Legalist Empire: International Law, Civilization, and U.S. Foreign Relations in the Early Twentieth Century* (New York: Oxford University Press, 2016), chs. 1–3. See also Richard Megargee, "Realism in American Foreign Policy: The Diplomacy of John Bassett Moore" (PhD diss., Northwestern University, 1963).

121. John Bassett Moore to Edwin Borchard, October 30, 1943, Box 10, EB.

CONCLUSION

1. "The 2000 Campaign; 2nd Presidential Debate between Gov. Bush and Vice President Gore," *New York Times,* October 12, 2000.

2. George W. Bush, "Text of Remarks Prepared for Delivery by Texas Gov. George W. Bush at Ronald Reagan Presidential Library, Simi Valley, Calif. on November 19, 1999," *Washington Post,* November 19, 1999.

3. Ivo Daalder and James M. Lindsay, "Bush's Foreign Policy Revolution," in *The George W. Bush Presidency: An Early Assessment,* ed. Fred Greenstein (Baltimore: John Hopkins University Press, 2003), 100–37; Philip H. Gordon, "The End of the Bush Revolution," *Foreign Affairs* 85, no. 4 (July–August 2006): 75–83; and John Rielly, "The Bush Administration's Foreign Policy Legacy," *Politique Américaine* 12, no. 3 (2008): 73–86.

4. Bush, "Text of Remarks Prepared for Delivery."

5. Parker Thomas Moon, "The League Survives Its Obsequies," *New Republic,* January 22, 1930, 245.

6. Ernest R. May, *Strange Victory: Hitler's Conquest of France* (New York: Hill and Wang, 2000).

7. John Glaser and Christopher Preble, "High Anxiety: How Washington's Exaggerated Sense of Danger Harms Us All," Cato Institute, December 10, 2019, https://www.cato .org/publications/publications/high-anxiety-how-washingtons-exaggerated-sense -danger-harms-us-all; Robert Jervis, "Was the Cold War a Security Dilemma?," *Journal of Cold War Studies* 3, no. 1 (Winter 2001): 36–60; and Chaim Kaufmann, "Threat Inflation and the Failure of the Marketplace of Ideas: The Selling of the Iraq War," *International Security* 29, no. 1 (Summer 2004): 5–48.

8. Dwight D. Eisenhower, "Military-Industrial Complex Speech," January 17, 1961, Yale Law School Avalon Project, https://avalon.law.yale.edu/20th_century/eisenhower001 .asp; William Hartung, *Prophets of War: Lockheed Martin and the Making of the Military-Industrial Complex* (New York: Nation Books, 2010); Paul A. C. Koistinen, *State of War: The Political Economy of American Warfare, 1945–2011* (Lawrence, KS: University Press of Kansas, 2012); and Rebecca U. Thorpe, *The American Warfare State: The Domestic Politics of Military Spending* (Chicago: University of Chicago Press, 2014).

9. Franklin D. Roosevelt, "State of the Union Message to Congress," January 11, 1944, American Presidency Project, https://www.presidency.ucsb.edu/documents/state-the -union-message-congress.

10. Harry S. Truman, "Address in St. Louis at the Site of the Jefferson National Expansion Memorial," June 10, 1950, American Presidency Project, https://www.presidency.ucsb .edu/documents/address-st-louis-the-site-the-jefferson-national-expansion-memorial.

11. Dwight D. Eisenhower, "Address to the Republican National Conference," June 7, 1957, American Presidency Project, https://www.presidency.ucsb.edu/documents /address-the-republican-national-conference.

12. President Donald Trump could break the mold, but his predecessors all spoke pejoratively of "isolationism": John F. Kennedy, "Arrival Remarks, Bonn, Germany," June 23, 1963, John F. Kennedy Presidential Library and Museum, https://www .jfklibrary.org/asset-viewer/archives/JFKPOF/045/JFKPOF-045-011; Lyndon B. Johnson, "Remarks at a Dinner of the Veterans of Foreign Wars," March 12, 1968, American Presidency Project, https://www.presidency.ucsb.edu/documents/remarks -dinner-the-veterans-foreign-wars; Richard Nixon, "Remarks to the 89th Annual International Meeting of the Knights of Columbus in New York City," August 17, 1971, American Presidency Project, https://www.presidency.ucsb.edu/documents /remarks-the-89th-annual-international-meeting-the-knights-columbus-new-york-city;

Gerald R. Ford, "Remarks and a Question-and-Answer Session with Members of the Pittsburgh Economic Club in Pittsburgh, Pennsylvania," October 26, 1976, American Presidency Project, https://www.presidency.ucsb.edu/documents/remarks-and-question-and-answer-session-with-members-the-pittsburgh-economic-club; Jimmy Carter, "United States Defense Policy Remarks to Members of the Business Council," December 12, 1979, American Presidency Project, https://www.presidency.ucsb.edu/documents/united-states-defense-policy-remarks-members-the-business-council; Ronald Reagan, "Remarks on Signing the George C. Marshall Month Proclamation," June 1, 1987, American Presidency Project, https://www.presidency.ucsb.edu/documents/remarks-signing-the-george-c-marshall-month-proclamation; George H. W. Bush, "Address Before a Joint Session of the Congress on the State of the Union," January 28, 1992, American Presidency Project, https://www.presidency.ucsb.edu/documents/address-before-joint-session-the-congress-the-state-the-union-0; William J. Clinton, "Remarks to the Nixon Center for Peace and Freedom Policy Conference," March 1, 1995, American Presidency Project, https://www.presidency.ucsb.edu/documents/remarks-the-nixon-center-for-peace-and-freedom-policy-conference; George W. Bush, "Farewell Address to the Nation," January 15, 2009, American Presidency Project, https://www.presidency.ucsb.edu/documents/farewell-address-the-nation-2; and Barack Obama, "Commencement Address at the United States Air Force Academy in Colorado Springs, Colorado," June 2, 2016, American Presidency Project, https://www.presidency.ucsb.edu/documents/commencement-address-the-united-states-air-force-academy-colorado-springs-colorado-1.

13. Michael Hunt, "Isolationism: Behind the Myth, a Usable Past," *UNC Press Blog*, June 29, 2011, http://uncpressblog.com/2011/06/29/michael-h-hunt-isolationism-behind-the-myth-a-usable-past.

14. Inis Claude, "The Heritage of Quincy Wright," *Journal of Conflict Resolution* 14, no. 4 (December 1970): 461; and Emily Hill Griggs, "A Realist before 'Realism': Quincy Wright and the Study of International Politics between Two World Wars," *Journal of Strategic Studies* 24, no. 1 (March 2001): 75–76.

15. Quincy Wright, "Accomplishments and Expectations of World Organization," *Yale Law Journal* 55, no. 5 (August 1946): 883, 885–86.

16. Quincy Wright, "Making the United Nations Work," *Review of Politics* 8, no. 4 (October 1946): 528.

17. Wright, "Accomplishments and Expectations," 887.

18. On the world constitution formulated by a Chicago group from 1945 to 1947, see Or Rosenboim, *The Emergence of Globalism: Visions of World Order in Britain and the United States, 1939–1950* (Princeton, NJ: Princeton University Press, 2017), ch. 6.

19. Quincy Wright to Charles Bacon, April 1, 1947, Box 14, QW.

20. See William Scheuerman, *Hans Morgenthau: Realism and Beyond* (Malden, MA: Polity, 2009), esp. ch. 5.

21. Quincy Wright to Walter Lippmann, November 28, 1966, Reel 100, WL.

SOURCES

ARCHIVAL COLLECTIONS

Archives Division, London School of Economics
  Charles K. Webster Papers
Council on Foreign Relations Library, New York
  Studies of American Interests in the War and the Peace, bound volumes
Franklin D. Roosevelt Presidential Library and Museum, Hyde Park, NY
  Adolf Berle Papers
  Harry Hopkins Papers
  Map Room File
  President's Personal File
  President's Secretary's File
  Whitney Shepardson Papers
  Henry A. Wallace Papers
  Sumner Welles Papers
  John Winant Papers
League of Nations Archives, Geneva
  Registry Files, 1933–1940
Manuscript Division, Library of Congress, Washington, DC
  Raymond Leslie Buell Papers
  Norman H. Davis Papers
  Philip Jessup Papers
  Henry R. Luce Papers
  Elihu Root Papers
  Arthur Sweetser Papers
National Archives and Records Administration, College Park, MD
  Harley Notter Files, Record Group 59
  OSS Files, Record Group 226
  Leo Pasvolsky Files, Record Group 59
Rare Book and Manuscript Library, Columbia University, New York
  Carnegie Endowment for International Peace Papers
  Walter Lippmann "Today and Tomorrow" Columns, 1931–1950
  James Shotwell Papers

Seeley G. Mudd Manuscript Library, Princeton University, Princeton, NJ
  Hamilton Fish Armstrong Papers
  Committee to Defend America by Aiding the Allies Papers
  Council on Foreign Relations Papers
  Allen W. Dulles Papers
  John Foster Dulles Papers
  Edward Mead Earle Papers
  Fight for Freedom Papers
  George F. Kennan Papers
  Woodrow Wilson Foundation Papers
Shelby White and Leon Levy Archives Center, Institute for Advanced Study, Princeton, NJ
  Frank Aydelotte Faculty File
  Edward Mead Earle Faculty File
  Institute for Advanced Study General File
Special Collections Research Center, University of Chicago
  Quincy Wright Papers
Sterling Memorial Library, Yale University, New Haven, CT
  Dean Acheson Papers
  Edwin Borchard Papers
  Walter Lippmann Papers
  Henry L. Stimson Papers
  Arnold Wolfers Papers
  Yale Institute for International Studies Papers
Weston Library, Bodleian Libraries, University of Oxford
  Arnold J. Toynbee Papers
  Alfred Zimmern Papers

GOVERNMENT PUBLICATIONS

The Charter of the United Nations: Hearings before the Senate Committee on Foreign Relations. 79th Cong., 1st Sess. July 9–13, 1945.
Congressional Record. Washington, DC: Government Publishing Office, 1935–1945.
Crockatt, Richard D. G., ed. *British Documents on Foreign Affairs: Reports and Papers from the Foreign Office Confidential Print.* Series C, *North America,* Part 3, *1940–1945.* Bethesda, MD: University Publications of America, 1999.
Department of State Bulletin. Washington, DC: Government Publishing Office, 1939–1945.
Ford, Gerald R. *Public Papers of the Presidents of the United States: Gerald R. Ford, 1976-1977.* Washington, DC: Government Printing Office, 1979.
Foreign Relations of the United States. Washington, DC: Department of State, 1937–1945.
The International American Conference: Reports of Committees and Discussions Thereon. Vol. 1. Washington, DC: Government Publishing Office, 1890.
Notter, Harley A. *Postwar Foreign Policy Preparation, 1939–1945.* Washington, DC: U.S. Department of State, 1949.

DOCUMENT COLLECTIONS

American Presidency Project, University of California–Santa Barbara. https://www.presidency.ucsb.edu.

Avalon Project, Yale Law School. https://avalon.law.yale.edu/.

Burton, David H., gen. ed. *The Collected Works of William Howard Taft.* 8 vols. Athens, OH: Ohio University Press, 2003.

Cannadine, David, ed. *Blood, Toil, Tears and Sweat: The Speeches of Winston Churchill.* Boston: Houghton Mifflin, 1989.

Documents: Conference on North Atlantic Relations. Princeton, NJ: American Committee for International Studies, 1941.

Link, Arthur S., ed. *The Papers of Woodrow Wilson.* 69 vols. Princeton, NJ: Princeton University Press, 1966–1994.

Morison, Elting E., ed. *The Letters of Theodore Roosevelt.* 8 vols. Cambridge, MA: Harvard University Press, 1951–1954.

Presidential Speeches, University of Virginia Miller Center. http://millercenter.org/president /speeches.

Rosenman, Samuel I., ed. *The Public Papers and Addresses of Franklin D. Roosevelt.* Vols. 1–5. New York: Random House, 1938.

———. *The Public Papers and Addresses of Franklin D. Roosevelt.* Vols. 6–9. New York: Macmillan, 1941.

———. *The Public Papers and Addresses of Franklin D. Roosevelt.* Vols. 10–13. New York: Harper and Brothers, 1950.

Vandenberg, Arthur H., Jr., ed. *The Private Papers of Senator Vandenberg.* Boston: Houghton Mifflin, 1952.

Wunderlin, Clarence E., ed. *The Papers of Robert A. Taft.* 4 vols. Kent, OH: Kent State University Press, 1997–2006.

OTHER PUBLISHED PRIMARY SOURCES

Armstrong, Hamilton Fish. "Armistice at Munich." *Foreign Affairs* 17, no. 2 (January 1939): 197–290.

Bailey, Thomas A. *Woodrow Wilson and the Great Betrayal.* New York: Macmillan, 1945.

———. *Woodrow Wilson and the Lost Peace.* New York: Macmillan, 1944.

Bainbridge, John. "Profiles: Business behind the Lines–I; Major George Fielding Eliot." *New Yorker,* September 5, 1942, 20–28.

———. "Profiles: Business behind the Lines–II; Major George Fielding Eliot." *New Yorker,* September 12, 1942, 22–29.

Baldwin, Hanson. *United We Stand! Defense of the Western Hemisphere.* New York: Whittlesey House, 1941.

Barnes, Harry Elmer, ed. *Perpetual War for Perpetual Peace: A Critical Examination of the Foreign Policy of Franklin Delano Roosevelt and Its Aftermath.* Caldwell, ID: Caxton, 1953.

———. Review of *A Study of War* by Quincy Wright. *Harvard Law Review* 56, no. 5 (March 1943): 847–49.

Bartlett, Ruhl J. *The League to Enforce Peace.* Chapel Hill, NC: University of North Carolina Press, 1944.

Beard, Charles A. *A Foreign Policy for America.* New York: Alfred A. Knopf, 1940.

Becker, Carl L. *How New Will the Better World Be? A Discussion of Post-war Reconstruction.* New York: Alfred A. Knopf, 1944.

Bibliography on Postwar Planning. Washington, DC: Construction and Civic Development Department, Chamber of Commerce of the United States of America, 1942.

Bonn, Moritz. "The New World Order." *Annals of the American Academy of Political and Social Science* 216 (July 1941): 163–177.

Borah, William E. "American Foreign Policy in a Nationalistic World." *Foreign Affairs* 12, no. 2 (January 1934): i–xiv.

Borchard, Edwin. "The Impracticability of 'Enforcing' Peace." *Yale Law Journal* 55, no. 5 (August 1946): 966–73.

———. "The Legal Evolution of Peace," *American Law Review* 45, no. 5 (September–October 1911): 708–17.

Borchard, Edwin, and William Potter Lage. *Neutrality for the United States*. New Haven, CT: Yale University Press, 1937.

Brodie, Fawn M. *Peace Aims and Post-war Reconstruction: An Annotated Bibliography (Preliminary)*. Princeton, NJ: American Committee for International Studies, 1941.

Buell, Raymond Leslie. *American Neutrality and Collective Security*. Geneva: Geneva Research Center, 1935.

———. "The Future of American Imperialism." *Yale Review* 15 (October 1925): 13–29.

———. *Isolated America*. New York: Alfred A. Knopf, 1940.

———. *The Native Problem in Africa*. New York: Macmillan, 1928.

Burlingame, Roger, and Alden Stevens. *Victory without Peace*. New York: Harcourt, Brace, 1944.

Burritt, Elihu. *People-Diplomacy, or The Mission of Friendly International Addresses between England and France*. London: W. and F. G. Cash, 1852.

Butler, Nicholas Murray. *Across the Busy Years: Recollections and Reflections*. New York: Charles Scribner's Sons, 1939.

———. *The International Mind: An Argument for the Judicial Settlement of International Disputes*. New York: Charles Scribner's Sons, 1912.

Chase, Stuart. *The New Western Front*. New York: Harcourt, Brace, 1939.

Commission to Study the Organization of Peace. "Fourth Report." *International Conciliation* 22 (January 1944): 3–110.

Cranston, Alan. *The Killing of the Peace*. New York: Viking, 1945.

Cranston, Ruth. *The Story of Woodrow Wilson: Twenty-eighth President of the United States, Pioneer of World Democracy*. New York: Simon and Schuster, 1945.

Crawford, Bruce. "A People's Peace." *Virginia Quarterly Review* 18, no. 3 (Summer 1942): 454–61.

Culbertson, Ely. *Summary of the World Federation Plan: An Outline of a Practical and Detailed Plan for World Settlement*. Garden City, NY: Garden City Publishing, 1943.

———. *Total Peace: What Makes Wars and How to Organize Peace*. Garden City, NY: Doubleday, Doran and Company, 1943.

Curti, Merle. *The American Peace Crusade, 1815–1860*. Durham, NC: Duke University Press, 1929.

Davis, George T. *A Navy Second to None: The Development of Modern American Naval Policy*. New York: Harcourt, 1940.

Dean, Vera Micheles. "Can Democracy Win the Peace?" *Survey Graphic*, June 1941.

———. *The Struggle for World Order*. New York: Foreign Policy Association, 1941.

———. "Toward a New World Order." *Foreign Policy Report*, May 15, 1941.

"The Doctrine or the League," *North American Review* 210, no. 765 (August 1919): 145–54.

Dunn, Frederick Sherwood. *Peaceful Change: A Study of International Procedures*. New York: Council on Foreign Relations, 1937.

Earle, Edward Mead. *Against This Torrent*. Princeton, NJ: Princeton University Press, 1941.

———. "American Military Policy and National Security." *Political Science Quarterly* 53, no. 1 (March 1938): 1–13.

———. "The Future of Foreign Policy." *New Republic,* November 1939.

———. "National Defense and Political Science." *Political Science Quarterly* 55, no. 4 (December 1940): 481–95.

———. "Political and Military Strategy for the United States." *Proceedings of the Academy of Political Science* 19, no. 2 (January 1941): 2–9.

———. "Power Politics and American World Policy." *Political Science Quarterly* 58, no. 1 (March 1943): 94–106.

Faunce, W. H. P. *Christian Principles Essential to a New World Order.* New York: Association Press, 1919.

Fox, William T. R. *The Super-Powers: The United States, Britain, and the Soviet Union—Their Responsibility for Peace.* New York: Harcourt, Brace, 1944.

Frank, Jerome. *Save America First: How to Make Our Democracy Work.* New York: Harper, 1939.

Galloway, George B. *A Survey of Institutional Research on American Postwar Problems.* New York: Twentieth Century Fund, 1941.

Gott, Virginia L. "The National Socialist Theory of International Law." *American Journal of International Law* 32, no. 4 (October 1938): 704–18.

Griswold, A. Whitney. *The Far Eastern Policy of the United States.* New York: Harcourt, 1938.

———. "The Influence of History upon Sea Power: A Comment on American Naval Policy." *Journal of the American Military Institute* 4, no. 1 (Spring 1940): 1–7.

Gryzanovski, E. "The Means of Lessening the Chances of War." *Advocate of Peace* 5, no. 9 (September 1874): 68–69.

———. "On the International Workingmen's Association: Its Origin, Doctrines, and Ethics." *The North American Review* 114, no. 235 (April 1872): 309–76.

Guides for Post-war Planning. Washington, DC: National Planning Association, 1941.

Hamilton, Alexander. "The Utility of the Union in Respect to Commercial Relations and a Navy," Federalist Paper No. 11, 1788. In *The Federalist Papers,* ed. Lawrence Goldman, 55–60. New York: Oxford University Press, 2008.

Hard, William. "American Relations with Britain." *Annals of the American Academy of Political and Social Science* 216 (July 1941): 150–55.

Herz, John H. "The National Socialist Doctrine of International Law and the Problems of International Organization." *Political Science Quarterly* 54, no. 4 (December 1939): 536–54.

Hoover, Herbert, and Hugh Gibson. *The Problems of Lasting Peace.* Garden City, NY: Doubleday, Doran and Company, 1942.

Howard, Graeme K. *America and a New World Order.* New York: Charles Scribner's Sons, 1940.

Hudson, Manley O. "The International Law of the Future." *Proceedings of the American Society of International Law at Its Annual Meeting* 38 (April 28–29, 1944): 271–81.

The International Law of the Future: Postulates, Principles, and Proposals. Washington, DC: Carnegie Endowment for International Peace, 1944.

Jefferson, Thomas. *The Inaugural Addresses of President Thomas Jefferson, 1801 and 1805.* Edited by Noble E. Cunningham Jr. Columbia, MO: University of Missouri Press, 2001.

Jessup, Philip C. *The United States and the Stabilization of Peace: A Study of Collective Security.* New York: Council on Foreign Relations, 1935.

Johnsen, Julia E., ed. *International Police Force.* New York: H. W. Wilson, 1944.

Johnson, Gerald W. *Woodrow Wilson: The Unforgettable Figure Who Has Returned to Haunt Us.* New York: Harper and Brothers, 1944.

Johnson, Walter. *The Battle against Isolation.* Chicago: University of Chicago Press, 1944.

Kennedy, Foster. "The Psychology of Isolationism." *Virginia Medical Monthly* 69 (April 1942): 176–79.

Kennedy, John F. *Why England Slept.* New York: W. Funk, 1940.

Knox, Frank. "World Peace Must Be Enforced: We Should Prevent the Rise of New Hitlers." Address to the American Bar Association, Indianapolis, October 1, 1941. *Vital Speeches of the Day* 8, no. 1 (November 15, 1941): 18–21.

Ladd, William. *An Essay on a Congress of Nations for the Adjustment of International Disputes without Resort to Arms.* Boston: Whipple and Damrell, 1840.

Lerner, Daniel. *The Passing of Traditional Society: Modernizing the Middle East.* Glencoe, IL: Free Press, 1958.

Lerner, Max. "American Leadership in a Harsh Age." *Annals of the American Academy of Political and Social Science* 216 (July 1941): 117–24.

Lieber, Francis. *Fragments of Political Science on Nationalism and Inter-Nationalism.* New York: Scribner and Company, 1868.

Lindbergh, Anne Morrow. *The Wave of the Future: A Confession of Faith.* New York: Harcourt Brace, 1940.

Lippmann, Walter. "America and the World." *Life,* June 3, 1940.

———. "The American Destiny." *Life,* June 5, 1939.

———. "The Atlantic and America." *Life,* April 7, 1941, 91.

———. "The Economic Consequences of a German Victory." *Life,* July 22, 1940.

———. "Education vs. Western Civilization." *American Scholar* 10, no. 2 (Spring 1941): 184–193.

———. "Seapower: Weapon of Freedom." *Life,* October 28, 1940.

———. *U.S. Foreign Policy: Shield of the Republic.* Boston: Little, Brown, 1943.

———. *U.S. War Aims.* Boston: Little, Brown, 1944.

Loth, David. *The Story of Woodrow Wilson.* New York: Woodrow Wilson Foundation, 1944.

Luce, Henry R. "The American Century." *Life,* February 17, 1941.

Mahon, Charlotte Burnett, ed. *Our Second Chance.* New York: Woodrow Wilson Foundation, 1944.

Mallery, Otto Tod. "Economic Union and Enduring Peace." *Annals of the American Academy of Political and Social Science* 216 (July 1941): 125–34.

McCance, Letha F. *Post-war Planning: A Bibliography.* Washington, DC: National Resources Planning Board, 1942.

Megargee, Richard. "Realism in American Foreign Policy: The Diplomacy of John Bassett Moore." PhD diss., Northwestern University, 1963.

Miller, Douglas. *You Can't Do Business with Hitler.* Boston: Little, Brown, 1941.

Miller, Francis Pickens. "The Atlantic Area." *Foreign Affairs* 19, no. 4 (July 1941): 727–28.

———. *Man from the Valley: Memoirs of a 20th Century Virginian.* Chapel Hill, NC: University of North Carolina Press, 1971.

Moore, John Bassett. *The Monroe Doctrine: Its Origin and Meaning.* New York: Evening Post Publishing, 1895.

Morgenthau, Hans J. "The Machiavellian Utopia." *Ethics* 55, no. 2 (January 1945): 145–47.

Mowrer, Edgar Ansel. *The World or the Western Hemisphere.* Charlottesville, VA: Institute of Public Affairs, 1941.

Official Report of the Proceedings of the Seventeenth Republican National Convention. New York: The Tenny Press, 1920.

Potter, Pitman B. *Collective Security and Peaceful Change: The Relations of Order and Progress in International Society.* Chicago: University of Chicago Press, 1937.

———. "The Nature of American Foreign Policy." *American Journal of International Law* 21, no. 1 (January 1927): 53–78.

Prefaces to Peace. New York: Simon and Schuster / Doubleday / Doran / Reynal and Hitchcock / Columbia University Press, 1943.

Preuss, Lawrence. "National Socialist Doctrines of International Law." *American Political Science Review* 29, no. 4 (August 1935): 594–609.

Proceedings of the National Farm Institute. Des Moines, IA: National Farm Institute, 1941.

Research and Postwar Planning: Bibliography. Vol. 1. New York: Section for Information on Studies in Postwar Reconstruction, Inter-Allied Information Center, 1942.

Rippy, J. Fred. Review of *American Foreign Policy, Formulation and Practice: Selected Readings* by Wilson Leon Godshall. *American Historical Review* 43, no. 4 (July 1938): 883–84.

Robins, Dorothy B. *Experiment in Democracy: The Story of U.S. Citizen Organizations in Forging the Charter of the United Nations.* New York: Parkside, 1971.

Robinson, Corinne Roosevelt. *My Brother, Theodore Roosevelt.* New York: Charles Scribner's Sons, 1921.

Rogers, Robert Wells. *The Basis of a World Order.* Boston: Gorham, 1918.

Roosevelt, Theodore. *Roosevelt in the Kansas City Star: War-Time Editorials.* Boston: Houghton Mifflin, 1921.

Schriftgiesser, Karl. *The Gentleman from Massachusetts: Henry Cabot Lodge.* Boston: Little, Brown 1944.

Schwarzenberger, Georg. *William Ladd: An Examination of an American Proposal for an International Equity Tribunal.* London: New Commonwealth Institute, 1935.

"Seminar on Isolation, Name and Thing." *Huntington Library Quarterly* 8, no. 1 (November 1944): 7–33.

Sherwood, Robert. "Plan for Union." *Life,* October 7, 1940.

Shotwell, James T. "After the War." *International Conciliation* 21, no. 376 (January 1942): 31–35.

———. *The Great Decision.* New York: Macmillan, 1944.

———. *On the Rim of the Abyss.* New York: Macmillan, 1936.

Simpson, Smith. "The Commission to Study the Organization of Peace." *American Political Science Review* 35, no. 2 (April 1941): 317–24.

Spencer, Henry R. "International Politics and History." *American Political Science Review* 17, no. 3 (August 1923): 392–403.

Spykman, Nicholas J. *America's Strategy in World Politics: The United States and the Balance of Power.* New Brunswick, NJ: Transaction, 2007.

Staley, Eugene. "The Myth of the Continents." *Foreign Affairs* 19, no. 3 (April 1941): 481–94.

Stimson, Henry L. "The Pact of Paris: Three Years of Development." *Foreign Affairs* 11, no. 1, special supplement (October 1932): i–ix.

Streit, Clarence K. *Union Now with Britain.* New York: Harper, 1941.

Sweetser, Arthur. "The United States, the United Nations, and the League of Nations." *International Conciliation* 24 (February 1946): 51–59.

Taft, Robert A. "Peace or Politics?" *American Bar Association Journal* 29, no. 11 (November 1943): 639–41, 647–49.

Taracouzio, Timothy A. *The Soviet Union and International Law: A Study Based on the Legislation, Treaties and Foreign Relations of the Union of Socialist Soviet Republics.* New York: Macmillan, 1935.

Thomas, Norman. "How to Fight for Democracy." *Annals of the American Academy of Political and Social Science* 216 (July 1941): 58–64.

Upgren, Arthur. "A Trade Policy for National Defense." *Foreign Affairs* 19, no. 2 (January 1941): 282–96.

Vinacke, Harold M. "What Shall America Defend?" *Yale Review* 30, no. 3 (March 1941): 499–520.

Wallace, Henry A. *The Price of Free World Victory.* New York: L. B. Fischer, 1942.

"A War for Sea Power." *Christian Century,* April 16, 1941, 520–21.

Washington, George. *An Address to the People of the United States.* New Castle, DE: Samuel and John Adams, 1796.

Watson, Thomas J. "After the War—What?" *International Conciliation* 20 (September 1940): 328–34.

Weinberg, Albert K. "The Historical Meaning of the American Doctrine of Isolation." *American Political Science Review* 34, no. 3 (June 1, 1940): 539–47.

Welles, Sumner. *Seven Decisions That Shaped History.* New York: Harper, 1951.

Whitton, John B., Gordon A. Craig, and Gerhart Niemeyer. *The Second Chance: America and the Peace.* Princeton, NJ: Princeton University Press, 1944.

Willkie, Wendell L. *One World.* New York: Simon and Schuster, 1943.

Wittke, Carl. Review of *The Dominions and Diplomacy: The Canadian Contribution* by A. Gordon Dewey. *American Historical Review* 35, no. 3 (April 1930): 619–21.

World Organization: A Balance Sheet of the First Great Experiment. Washington, DC: American Council on Public Affairs, 1942.

Wright, Quincy. "Accomplishments and Expectations of World Organization." *Yale Law Journal* 55, no. 5 (August 1946): 870–88.

———. "The Lend-Lease Bill and International Law." *American Journal of International Law* 35, no. 2 (April 1941): 305–14.

———. "Making the United Nations Work." *Review of Politics* 8, no. 4 (October 1946): 528–32.

———, ed. *Public Opinion and World-Politics.* Chicago: University of Chicago Press, 1933.

———. *A Study of War.* Chicago: University of Chicago Press, 1942.

———. "The Transfer of Destroyers to Great Britain." *American Journal of International Law* 34, no. 4 (October 1940): 680–89.

Yearbook, 1938. Washington, DC: Carnegie Endowment for International Peace, 1938.

Zimmern, Alfred. "Nationalism and Internationalism." *Foreign Affairs* 1, no. 4 (June 1923): 115–26.

ACKNOWLEDGMENTS

In writing this book, I have been fortunate to accumulate more debts than I can repay. The least I can do is acknowledge them. The research for this book began at Columbia University, where the cohort of 2008 made it through the Great Recession with intellects and lives formed and reformed. My thanks to the many people in and around campus who provided vision, know-how, and cheer, starting with the members of my committee. Matthew Connelly, my supervisor, brought me to Columbia and provided tireless support throughout my studies and in every dimension of mentorship. He made me see international and global history as a distinct field, not reducible to the history of the United States. Duncan Bell shared insights equal in brilliance and generosity and made me feel welcome during the years I subsequently spent at the University of Cambridge. Mark Mazower's influence appears everywhere in these pages, or those worth reading. We pieced together the history of internationalism at a crucial moment, and I am grateful for his intellectual companionship. Although Anders Stephanson might find this manuscript a tad antiteleological, I will grant that he showed me where I wanted to go all along. "What would Anders say" remains my best device for writing and thinking. Before she left us, I got to benefit from Marilyn Young's boundless encouragement, careful edits, and unparalleled company at La Lanterna. I miss her deeply. I also want to thank Robert David Johnson, Erez Manela, Ernest R. May, and Daniel Sargent: they made me a historian in college and continue to inspire my interest in U.S. foreign relations.

A community of scholars from several disciplines read and commented on chapters of this book or related papers. With apologies to anyone I have forgotten, I thank Daniel Bessner, Alan Brinkley, Megan Donaldson, Ted Fertik, Anne L. Foster, Gary Gerstle, Arunabh Ghosh, Michaela Hoenicke-Moore, Andrew Johnstone, Joris Larik, Philippa Levine, Rebecca Lissner, Andrew Liu, Thomas Meaney, Mario Del Pero, Andrew Preston, Justin Reynolds, Amy Sayward, and Bob Vitalis. I inflicted more than my fair share of drafts on Volker Berghahn, Daniel Immerwahr, Ira Katznelson, Samuel Moyn, and John A. Thompson, and they responded with penetrating insights that helped me reconceive parts of the book. Special thanks to Trent MacNamara, Oliver Murphey, and Simon Stevens, members of a writers' group convened by Matthew Connelly; we read, edited, and commiserated together.

First at Columbia and then at Princeton and Cambridge, I have gained important perspectives from conversations with Jeremy Adelman, Charles Armstrong, Emily Baughan, Elizabeth Blackmar, Elizabeth Borgwardt, Elisheva Carlebach, Benjamin Coates, Elizabeth Cobbs Hoffman, Victoria de Grazia, Christopher Dietrich, Susan Ferber, Luke Fletcher, Eric Foner, Aimee Genell, Michael Geyer, Tony Greco, Nicolas Guilhot, Andrew Hurrell, G. John

Ikenberry, Ryan Irwin, Wallace Katz, Jeremy K. Kessler, Stephen Kotkin, Paul Kramer, Charlie Laderman, Sam Lebovic, Joe Maiolo, Jamie Martin, William McAllister, Christopher McKnight Nichols, David Milne, Dirk Moses, Sherzod Muminov, Alanna O'Malley, Chris Parkes, Inderjeet Parmar, Susan Pedersen, Katharina Rietzler, J. Simon Rofe, Noah Rosenblum, Mira Siegelberg, Joyce Seltzer, Timothy Shenk, Joshua R. Shifrinson, James Sparrow, Adam Tooze, and Patrick Weil. A sincere thanks for all the time and stimulating ideas you provided me.

This book has improved mightily due to talks and conferences where I was able to hone my arguments and workshop chapters. Thank you to the participants at events hosted by the John Quincy Adams Society; the American Historical Association and its Pacific Coast Branch; St Antony's College, University of Oxford; Birkbeck, University of London; the Center for the Cold War and the United States, New York University; the Center for the Study of Statesmanship, Catholic University; the Centre for International Studies and Diplomacy, SOAS; City, University of London; the European University Institute; the Interdisciplinary Center for Innovative Theory and Empirics, Columbia University; the International Studies Association; King's College, University of Cambridge, and the university's seminars on American history and political thought and intellectual history; King's College London; the London School of Economics; the National History Center's International Seminar on Decolonization; the Princeton Program in American Studies; the Society for Historians of American Foreign Relations; the Society for U.S. Intellectual History; and the University of East Anglia. A portion of Chapter 4 was first published in "Instrumental Internationalism: The American Origins of the United Nations, 1940–3," *Journal of Contemporary History* 54, no. 2 (2019): 265–83.

Financial and organizational support from foundations, universities, and the U.S. government enabled the activities of the protagonists of this book. Such support did the same for its author. I am grateful for fellowships and grants awarded by the History Department of Columbia University, the Jacob K. Javits Fellowship of the U.S. Department of Education, the John Anson Kittredge Educational Fund, the Andrew W. Mellon Foundation, and the Doris G. Quinn Foundation. At the postdoctoral stage, I was fortunate to have the support of King's College and the Lauterpacht Centre for International Law at the University of Cambridge and of the University Center for Human Values and the Woodrow Wilson School of Public and International Affairs at Princeton University.

Completing each stage of the book came with unexpected pleasures of working with new people. I am grateful to a long list of archivists, especially Virginia Lewick at the Franklin D. Roosevelt Presidential Library and Museum for assisting my research and keeping the documents intact. My thanks to Bill Keegan and Kristen Noble Keegan for rendering the march to global supremacy through beautifully constructed maps. Gunar Olsen provided invaluable research assistance in the closing months; I am very grateful for his help. Not least, Andrew Kinney shepherded a few dense chapters into an actual, gosh-darn-it book. Without his forward movement, I would still be adding endnotes to Chapter 1. Thank you to him and his team at Harvard University Press.

In the past two years, my career took an unexpected and energizing turn beyond the academy. I want to thank the colleagues with whom I cofounded the Quincy Institute for Responsible Statecraft—Andrew Bacevich, Eli Clifton, Suzanne DiMaggio, and Trita Parsi—for supporting the completion of a book on the birth of U.S. global supremacy and for creating an organization that may witness its end. Thanks also to the incredible staff, fellows, and donors of the Quincy Institute. I also particularly appreciate the assistance given to me when I needed it by Robert Jervis at the Saltzman Institute of War and Peace Studies and Line Lillevik and Anders Stephanson in the History Department, both at Columbia University.

For a labor of love, writing a book has a way of accentuating the wrong half of the equation. Friends and family helped me to endure the labor and rediscover the love. Chats, drinks, emails, and Skype sessions with Seth Anziska, David Jackson-Hanen, Ana Isabel Keilson, and Natasha Wheatley sustained my spirit and shaped me well beyond this project. The same goes for Thomas Meaney, Justin Reynolds, and Simon Stevens, in whom I had the best of collaborators from the start of the project. My parents, Alex and Linda, were there for me at every turn, sharing in my happiness and smoothing out the dips. I have been working on this book for as long as I have known Kristen Loveland. It was a fortuitous meeting in Morningside Heights. Kristen was and remains my closest and most insightful reader and my foundation of support, who got me to finish what I started. I think we have managed to accentuate the love.

INDEX